The Five Questions

The Five Questions

An Academic Handbook in Youth Ministry Research

Jos de Kock
Bård Norheim

foreword by Malan Nel

PICKWICK *Publications* · Eugene, Oregon

THE FIVE QUESTIONS
An Academic Handbook in Youth Ministry Research

Copyright © 2022 Jos de Kock and Bård Norheim. All rights reserved. Except for brief quotations in critical publications or reviews, no part of this book may be reproduced in any manner without prior written permission from the publisher. Write: Permissions, Wipf and Stock Publishers, 199 W. 8th Ave., Suite 3, Eugene, OR 97401.

Pickwick Publications
An Imprint of Wipf and Stock Publishers
199 W. 8th Ave., Suite 3
Eugene, OR 97401

www.wipfandstock.com

PAPERBACK ISBN: 978-1-5326-4667-6
HARDCOVER ISBN: 978-1-5326-4668-3
EBOOK ISBN: 978-1-5326-4669-0

Cataloguing-in-Publication data:

Names: de Kock, Jos, author. | Norheim, Bård Eirik Hallesby, author. | Nel, Malan, foreword.

Title: The five questions : an academic handbook in youth ministry research / Jos de Kock and Bård Norheim : foreword by Malan Nel.

Description: Eugene, OR : Pickwick Publications, 2022 | Includes bibliographical references and index.

Identifiers: ISBN 978-1-5326-4667-6 (paperback) | ISBN 978-1-5326-4668-3 (hardcover) | ISBN 978-1-5326-4669-0 (ebook)

Subjects: LCSH: Church work with youth. | Church work with youth. | Church work with teenagers. | Teenagers—Religious life. | Church group work with youth. | Church group work with teenagers.

Classification: BV4447 .D42 2022 (print) | BV4447 .D42 (ebook)

In writing chapter 16 we have partly used and partly reworked or extended existing texts from the inaugural address of Jos de Kock in 2019: *Wait a minute in stressful times. A practical theological account of learning in encounter* (Leuven: Jos de Kock, ETF Leuven).

Scriptures taken from the Holy Bible, New International Version®, NIV®. Copyright © 1973, 1978, 1984, 2011 by Biblica, Inc.™ Used by permission of Zondervan. All rights reserved worldwide. www.zondervan.com The "NIV" and "New International Version" are trademarks registered in the United States Patent and Trademark Office by Biblica, Inc.™

This book is dedicated to
the International Association for the Study of Youth Ministry
(IASYM)

"The number of children and young people who are actually part of a congregation, as well as the current youth-specific needs of children, adolescents and young adults critically necessitates an own discipline. To some extent the subject will be a 'youth conscience' for the other disciplines within the field of Practical Theology - but it is more. It includes a field of study that is simply not covered by any other theological discipline."

MALAN NEL

In: "Youth Ministry as Practical Theology: Making a Case for Youth Ministry as an Academic Discipline." *Journal of Youth and Theology* 2 (2003), 78.

Contents

Foreword | ix

Preface | xi

    Introduction | 1

PART 1: WHO ARE THE YOUTH IN YOUTH MINISTRY?

Who Are the Youth in Youth Ministry?
Introduction to Part 1 | 17

    1. Youth, Culture, and Youth Culture | 19

    2. Being Young as a Stage of Life | 35

    3. Religious Identity, Faith Development, and Spirituality | 46

    4. Individual and Communal Aspects of Faith Development among Youth | 60

PART 2: WHERE IS GOD IN YOUTH MINISTRY?

Where Is God in Youth Ministry?
Introduction to Part 2 | 79

    5. God's Presence in Youth Ministry | 81

    6. Researching God's Presence in Youth Ministry | 106

Part 3: What Is the Purpose of Youth Ministry?

What Is the Purpose of Youth Ministry?
Introduction to Part 3 | 123

    7. Typologies of Goals | 125

    8. Theologically Loaded Goals | 144

Part 4: Who Is the Youth Minister in Youth Ministry?

Who Is the Youth Minister in Youth Ministry?
Introduction to Part 4 | 161

    9. The Youth Minister as a Leader in Times of Change | 163

    10. The Youth Minister as *Jesus*? | 173

    11. The Youth Minister as *Teacher* | 183

    12. The Youth Minister as *Pastor* | 198

    13. The Youth Minister as *Prophet* | 207

    14. The Role of the Youth Minister in *Community* | 216

Part 5: How to Research Practices in Youth Ministry?

How to Research Practices in Youth Ministry?
Introduction to Part 5 | 227

    15. Research Methodologies | 229

    16. A Practical Theological Research Framework | 242

    17. Designing a Youth Ministry Research Project | 252

Bibliography | 263

Index | 279

Foreword

THIS book is an excellent contribution to our continuing opportunity to serve God, youth, Youth Ministry and the world! It adds value to international research on a ministry to, in my own context, more than 50 percent of the population under twenty-five. God's world we live in, is indeed in many contexts fairly young.

I am honoured to endorse this research by two excellent scholars and colleagues in the field. To have journeyed with the two authors in different contexts has enriched my life in so many ways. Our main common research community is the International Association for the Study of Youth Ministry (IASYM). I commend you for dedicating this book to IASYM. To have been involved in the founding of this Association remains one of the highlights of my academic and research journey.

According to the authors, "This handbook aims to be both a textbook and a reference book. The intended audiences include all those who wish to obtain an overview of the discipline of youth ministry and its key subthemes." As such it is a welcome addition to the research and contributions of the many authors referred to in this book. "The Five Questions" are so much more than the title of this new book. The questions are on our minds all the time. The book is, to my mind, an excellent co-journeying with many of us who have dealt with the same questions in our personal research.

The entire book is worth exploring. I mean by this more than just reading it. To highlight just two major issues in Youth Ministry: Why are we doing it? Why, being motive and purpose. We do it for God's sake (part 2 of the book). I once tried to motivate this in a Trinitarian way. I remain deeply convinced that when we know why we do what we do in Youth Ministry, creative youth and youth leaders will continue to find new ways for how we do it in a changing context and culture!

And why as purpose (part 3 of the book)? The authors used the concept of Whole-making (chapter 7). Are we not in more than one way humbly facilitating becoming of who we already are in Christ? And we do so journeying with main role players in the faith community (like family—however constituted, etc.).

The book will hopefully become a jewel in the library—whether electronically on the screen of a youth leader or on the shelves of many universities and colleges. Once again: I applaud the two authors. I consider myself blessed to be associated with them and this volume.

Malan Nel
University of Pretoria, South Africa.

Preface

Where do the best ideas emerge? Not infrequently in situations where people come together, have a great time, and where there is plenty room for creativity. We have often found ourselves in such a state of creativity during the bi-annual conferences of the International Association for the Study of Youth Ministry (IASYM). These meetings of the international community of youth ministry scholars have been the breeding ground for the development of this handbook that is in your hands or on your screen now.

The two of us have met regularly at IASYM meetings. At the same time, we have both been involved in serving the association in different roles. For five years, Jos was chief editor of *Journal of Youth and Theology* (JYT), an international academic peer-reviewed journal, originally published by IASYM, now published by Brill Publishers. And for many years, Bård served on the executive board of IASYM, also serving as president of the association. During these years, we both developed a specialism as practical theologians in youth ministry research.

On one of these occasions, at the international conference in London in January 2015, we came up with the idea of writing an academic handbook on youth ministry research. The aim was to bring together the principal research themes and research outcomes in the field of youth ministry. Our motivation was rooted in one particular observation: we found a great deal of in-depth academic reflection and research on youth ministry, both at conferences and in journal publications, but limited resources and attention were being given to a comprehensive ordering of the "red threads" in youth ministry research. Between 2015 and 2022 lie seven years of processing our original idea towards a published handbook that is now available for everyone who is interested in systematic reflection on youth ministry and youth ministry research.

It is important to emphasize that the handbook is *a* handbook on youth ministry and youth ministry research and not the only (imaginable) handbook on youth ministry research. Youth ministry research has always been keen to pay attention to *context*. Although the aim of this academic handbook is to give an overview of international youth ministry research, it is not written from an a-contextual meta-position. It is written by two scholars who have been actively involved in IASYM, who are based at European Universities/Higher Institutions, are two white males in their forties with Protestant backgrounds—and the list of contextual features could go on. The point is: although the handbook covers significant research ground, it does not make any claims to being fully extensive. The handbook offers a selective, but purposeful and intentional, assessment of youth ministry research over the past four decades, with particular focus on the past two decades.

We have focused mainly on research articles in English that have been published in a few key journals and books in the academic field of youth ministry. More information on criteria for selecting these sources is presented in the introductory chapter. These selections both limit and situate the study of this academic handbook. At the same time, we believe that focusing youth ministry research through the lens of five key questions will help the reader to engage with a wider variety of youth ministry research, in dialogue with the research presented and reviewed here. We also hope that our evaluation of youth ministry research may lay open some of the lacuna in academic youth ministry and motivate further research in the field.

Where the best ideas are helped by creativity, writing a handbook is helped by order. By addressing five key questions, we try to lead the reader through the rich repository of wisdom that originates in youth ministry research during the past decades. Whether you are a graduate student in theology or another discipline, a university professor or a PhD student, a professional youth minister or youth ministry trainer: we hope this handbook will help you to get an overview of the scholarly discipline of youth ministry and provide you with a body of knowledge that informs and guides your thinking and acting.

Where do the best ideas emerge? Sometimes while reading a book. We wish that many good ideas for further research in the field of youth ministry will originate from reading this handbook.

Jos de Kock and Bård Norheim

Introduction

THIS academic handbook provides for a state-of-the-discipline overview of youth ministry research. Although the handbook is rooted in a rigorous literature review, it is not a mere review of the literature. The handbook tries to answer five key questions with the help of the youth ministry research literature. Its purpose is to enable readers to learn about the outcomes of youth ministry research and important concepts in the field, within an organizing framework of five key questions that facilitates integration. In this handbook, a broad range of outcomes of youth ministry studies and scholarly works on youth ministry are brought together to meet this goal. The five questions are:

1. Who are the youth in youth ministry?
2. Where is God in youth ministry?
3. What is the purpose of youth ministry?
4. Who is the youth minister in youth ministry?
5. How to research practices in youth ministry?

The term "youth ministry" in this handbook refers to practices in which professionals and volunteers, inspired by Christian faith, work with children and young people with the aim of discovering, learning and practicing the gospel. The handbook will present in-depth conversations among scholars interested in the practices of youth ministry. These scholars are often involved in the "young" academic discipline of youth ministry research. At the same time, practical theology and religious education, among others, are two academic disciplines in which scholarly publications on youth ministry can also typically and regularly be found. The purpose of this handbook is to bring all this scholarly work into debate with the broader academic field of reflection on youth, theology, and formation, and offer a portal through which readers can construct evidence-based and scholarly informed interpretations, visions, and practices with regard to youth ministry.

In this introduction, we will first give a brief overview of youth ministry's historical context, and subsequently a (historical) overview of the main theme of youth ministry research: What are the origins of this particular academic discipline and how has it developed in past decades? Next, we will describe how the content of the handbook has been constructed. We will conclude with an overview of the rest of the handbook and its intended readership.

The Historical Context of Youth Ministry

In his article on youth ministry's historical context, Mark Cannister points to the Great Awakening movements of the mid-eighteenth century as a starting point for organized youth ministry in the North American context.[1] He also claims that the development of youth ministry has constantly struggled with the tension between *education* and *evangelism*. On the one hand, the purpose of youth ministry has been to nurture the faith of the teenagers of the church, on the other hand youth ministry has focused on reaching irreligious adolescents with the gospel of Jesus Christ.

With the development of parachurch movements such as YMCA and the international Sunday School movement during the beginning and middle of the nineteenth century, youth ministry was taken a step further. A similar development took place in the European context: The parachurch organizations became key agents in the developing of a new strategy towards youth: As the industrial revolution left young people with more spare time, the established churches were eager to connect with young people on this new arena. The industrial revolution also brought more young people into the rapidly growing cities and the social problems this brought about underscored the need for churches and Christian youth movements to "reach out" to the new generations of young people. But the establishment of a professional youth and student ministry also has to be interpreted as an attempt to build a "fence" in

---

1. Cannister, "Youth Ministry's Historical Context," 94–110.

relation to the developing atheistic or agnostic science brought about by the turn to positivism in the nineteenth century.

Professional youth ministry was therefore formed as a tool for reaching out to young people in the tides of a shifting, urbanizing Western culture. The churches of the Western hemisphere saw it as a problem that they were not able to reach out to these new expressions of youth culture using their previous methods. Although professional youth ministry has a strong North American profile, the context or rather the "need" that fuels the development of professional youth ministry is much more radical in the European context. Sociologist Grace Davie has argued that when it comes to secularization, Europe is in many ways an exceptional case. In the context of the evolving religious market, young and old Europeans seem to be "believing without belonging." One of the particular challenges for the church in Europe, which contrary to the church in the US is unfamiliar with the dynamic of a religious market, is the extent to which the church in Europe is capable of making use of the evolving religious market.[2]

Youth ministry can therefore be seen as one way of making use of the new emerging religious market in Europe, and in the rest of the world. In his book *Growing up Evangelical*, Pete Ward underlines that the evangelical parachurch movements saw it as their "grand strategy" to reach out to the young generation in order to "secure" the future of the church: "Between the wars," according to Bebbington, evangelicals

---

2. Davie, *Europe*, 147–48.: "At the start of the twentieth century, a whole set of interrelated shifts are occurring in the religious life in Europe. First the historic churches—despite their continuing presence—are systematically losing their capacity to discipline the religious thinking of large sections of the population, especially amongst the young. That is abundantly clear. The latter respond, however, in complex ways—they are just as ready to experiment with new forms of belief as they are to reject the notion of belief altogether, a tendency that is (or appears to be) inversely related to the capacities of the churches to exert control. At the same time, the range of choice is becoming wider as innovative forms of religion come into Europe from outside, largely as the result of the movement of people. Populations that have arrived in Europe primarily for economic reasons bring with them different ways of being religious, some Christian and some not. And quite apart from the incoming movements, European people travel the world, experiencing amongst other things considerable religious diversity. In this sense a genuine religious market is emerging in most parts of the continent. The crucial question lies, however, not in the existence of the market in itself but in the capacities of Europeans to make use of this, the major point of contrast with the United States."

Davie advocates on the basis of this that "secularisation is essentially a European phenomenon." Davie, *Europe*, 161.

hit upon a "grand strategy" which was designed to secure the future for them.³ He quoted Bishop Taylor Smith's comment: "Concentrate on the young people, they will bring you in the greatest dividends."⁴

After World War II professional youth ministry sharpened this focus on reaching out to the emerging youth culture to secure the future, or the religious market shares, of the church, through the establishment of evangelistic parachurch agencies such as Young Life and Youth for Christ. During the coming decades they developed a number of strategies, ranging from youth rallies and youth clubs to teen-to-teen evangelism.

Through the developing of a commercially based youth culture, youth ministry coupled with the expressions of the arising consumer culture. The task of youth ministry was to supply the church with "youth culture"-sensitive "reach-out" methods which fitted the new and changing expressions of the post war youth culture. Through this strategy, the youth ministry of the parachurch movements aimed at building bridges between the established churches and youth culture, by taking on the cultural expressions of contemporary youth culture and applying them for purposes of evangelism. This turn within evangelical parachurch-based youth ministry was also due to the critique by the WCC in the 1960s of separate youth groups.⁵ Modern professional youth ministry in the Western wrapping has been occupied with reaching out to a youth culture seemingly estranged from the established churches.⁶

In 1968, Youth Specialities was founded by Mike Yaconelli as the first independent provider of youth ministry resources in North America. Later, through internet sales, Youth Specialities expanded heavily into the European market. At the end of the twentieth century, almost every denomination had established youth ministry resource initiatives. At the same time, Youth Specialities had started "producing" more academic resources on youth ministry. In many ways, Mike Yaconelli and Youth Specialities also became theologically formative in much of the development within professional youth ministry. In his book, *The CORE Realities of Youth Ministry: Nine Biblical Principles that Mark Healthy Youth Ministries* (2003), he sums up his theological convictions concerning youth ministry. He describes youth ministry as a "sanctuary," and the

3. Ward, *Growing Up Evangelical*, 45.

4. Bebbington, *Evangelicalism in Modern Britain*, 224.

5. For a recent reflection on the theology of parachurch youth organizations, see Schoon Tanis, *Making Jesus Attractive*.

6. Cf. Norheim, "The Global Youth Culture."

basic tenet of youth ministry as "that above all it's a place where students are safe. Our job is not to make non-Christians clean up their language; our job is to treat non-Christians with grace and respect, loving them where they are."[7]

Youth Ministry Research: a Brief (Historical) Overview

Referring to Shepherd (2014), Borgman (1997), and Ward (1995),[8] De Kock and Norheim in 2018 defined the term "youth ministry" as referring to "practices in which professionals and volunteers, inspired by the Christian faith, work with children and young people to discover, learn, and practice the gospel. Adults establish meaningful relationships with and among children and young people and may participate in different roles, like the missionary, the social worker or the pastor. Faith practices of children and young people refer to such situations as gatherings, habits, actions, rituals, networks, and communities, in which children or young people are engaged and form their faith, either individually or collectively. Faith practices can be found both within and outside of the church."[9] In this handbook, we follow this definition, which means that we reflect on practices of youth ministry within the Christian tradition. For the interested reader, in 2003, Len Kageler published a short reflection on what can be learned from comparing Christian youth ministry with youth ministry perspectives in Islam and traditional Asian religions.[10]

Youth Ministry as an Academic Discipline: Theology or Practical Theology?

Where and when can we locate the beginning of the systematic and academic study of youth ministry practices? We think the foundation of the International Association for the Study of Youth Ministry (IASYM) in 1995 was an important moment in this regard. IASYM is set at "furthering the study, research and teaching of youth ministry internationally."[11]

    7. Yaconelli, *The CORE Realities of Youth Ministry*, 94.
    8. Shepherd, "Being a Christian," 1–12; Borgman, *When Kumbaya Is Not Enough*; Ward, "Christian Relational Care," 13–40.
    9. De Kock and Norheim, "Youth Ministry Research," 70.
    10. Kageler, "Youth and Youth Ministry."
    11. IASYM," About IASYM."

Following the founding of the international association for youth ministry researchers and teachers, the *Journal of Youth and Theology* (JYT) published its first issue in 2002. In the second issue of JYT, in 2003, Malan Nel made a case for youth ministry as an academic discipline.[12] He argued that youth ministry should be understood as a sub-discipline within practical theology. Until that time, youth ministry had often been conceived as part of Christian education or as merely "a practical form of assistance to desperate churches and organisations," Nel found.[13] Nel envisioned practical theology as the mother science of youth ministry. In this regard, the academic sub-discipline of youth ministry should, by empirical investigation, focus on communicative actions serving the gospel, "in order to direct and to improve the intentional actions directed at the youth, in collaboration with the youth and by the youth in our modern society."[14]

Although, Malan Nel also made a plea for theological reflection in a broad sense,[15] it is interesting to note that in this publication Nel situated youth ministry as a sub-discipline within the discipline of practical theology. Indeed, we will see throughout this handbook that many contributions to youth ministry research are framed as practical theological accounts. At the same time, youth ministry has been studied from a much broader perspective. To illustrate this, we can look at the scope of the *Journal of Youth and Theology* as defined on the webpage of the publisher Brill: "The journal aims at furthering the academic study and research of youth and youth ministry, and the formal teaching and training of youth ministry. The academic efforts are rooted in the Christian theological tradition and ecumenical. The scope of the journal is to serve scholarship in the broad field of children, youth, faith, church, theology and culture. Research articles in the journal mainly have theology (both practical, systematic and biblical theology) as a core discipline. At the same time, contributions are often interdisciplinary, which implies theological reflection combined with e.g. pedagogical, sociological or psychological perspectives."[16] And this we will also see illustrated in this handbook: academic accounts on practices of youth ministry coming from a broad

---

12. Nel, "Youth Ministry as Practical Theology." See also Nel, "Methodological."
13. Nel, "Youth Ministry as Practical Theology," 68–69.
14. Nel, "Youth Ministry as Practical Theology," 73.
15. See, e.g., Nel, "Why Theology?"
16. "Journal of Youth and Theology."

range of disciplines, not only within theology but also outside theology and in interdisciplinary studies. Youth ministry research, whether as theological research or as interdisciplinary research, distinguishes itself from youth research in general, the latter not incorporating a conversation with theological considerations. At the same time, youth research in different countries or continents is often of help for youth ministry scholars, as Sharlene Swartz, for example, shows in her publication on the state of youth research in South Africa and its implications for youth ministry.[17]

Whether youth ministry as an academic discipline should be focused on theology more broadly, on practical theology, or be multi- or interdisciplinary, has been debated within the circles of youth ministry scholars from the dawn of youth ministry as a research practice in its own right. At the beginning of the twenty-first century, Kenda Creasy Dean was one of the scholars who made a plea for theology as a leading discipline for youth ministry research. In an essay in 2000, she claimed: "Twentieth-century youth ministry has never had sure theological footing, but the cacophony of the information age and millennial angst underscore the church's need to ground youth ministry in theology rather than in fields such as psychology, sociology, or education."[18] In the same essay Dean argued for a theological orientation in youth ministry towards the cross of Jesus Christ, because this fundamentally meets the quest for salvation of any man, and young people in particular. Furthermore, just as had Malan Nel,[19] she observed that practical theology, until the end of the twentieth century, had been absent in youth ministry discourses and pleads for more practical theological reflection on youth and youth ministry theologically rooted in the concept of salvation in Jesus Christ. In a later publication in 2003 in the *Journal of Youth and Theology*, Dean explained that for this (practical) theological reflection on youth ministry, scholars need to see youth ministry as ministry instead of merely an aspect of Christian Education.[20] Furthermore, she points at global postmodernity being a main context factor for this (practical) theological reflection on youth ministry.[21]

---

17. Swartz, "The State of Youth Research in South Africa."
18. Dean, "Proclaiming Salvation," 526.
19. Nel, "Youth Ministry as Practical Theology."
20. Dean, "The New Rhetoric of Youth Ministry."
21. See chapter 1 for a discussion of postmodernity.

The central theme of salvation in Jesus Christ in Kenda Creasy Dean's argument is a good illustration of the role of (biblical or systematic) theological concepts in the academic discipline of youth ministry research. Throughout the handbook we will see many other examples of key theological concepts functioning in both the practice and the understanding of youth ministry. At the same time, youth ministry is not only conceived as a practice in which theological concepts are applied, but, the other way around, also conceived as a practice from which (new) theological concepts and understanding originate. This is the core plea of Bert Roebben in his 2005 article: "Light of Day: Scaffolding a Theology of Youth Ministry." According to Roebben, for youth ministry research to have the potential for constructing theology, it needs to be involved in the lives of young people: "initially, by noticing and respecting their voices, secondly through crafting space within our theorising for young people's insight to shape theological understanding and thirdly by embracing the lives of young people as a site for connection with God and the construction of theology."[22]

Further (Practical) Theological and Ecumenical Development

Later, in 2012, the same Bert Roebben reviewed the international developments in the emerging field of youth ministry research from the beginning of the twenty-first century.[23] Roebben detected four different contexts in which youth ministry research was situated: (a) large-scale data sets in the Western world on youth and religion, religiosity, and spirituality; (b) ecclesiological and ministry studies; (c) youth ministry and young adult ministry studies, foremost related to the context of the school campus; (d) the body of research on children's and youth spirituality, and theologizing with children and youth. Next, Roebben showed four thematic or recurrent dimensions existent in these contexts of youth ministry research: globalization, vulnerability, politics, and interreligious encounter. Many of these dimensions will be discussed later in this handbook, for example, in part 1, in which a core theme is what is meant by "youth" and what might be the role of youth culture and societal developments in the development of young people.

---

22. Roebben, "Light of Day," 23.
23. Roebben, "International Developments."

Bert Roebben concluded his article by presenting a couple of challenges for future practical theological research on youth ministry. Although Roebben reviewed contexts of youth ministry research that varied in terms of disciplinary backgrounds, we find, again, a proposal to study youth ministry from the angle of practical theology, a proposal that mirrors the choice of Malan Nel in 2003, as discussed earlier.[24] Two main challenges Roebben addresses in this regard are: practical theological research on youth ministry needs (a) the development of new research designs that also promote longitudinal and interdisciplinary approaches and (b) the development of a strong relationship with systematic theology in engaging a globalizing society in trying to understand in the light of the gospel what is going on in and among young people. Roebben's plea corresponds with the vision of Kenda Creasy Dean as expressed in 2011, saying "youth ministry brings a distinctive lens to the practical theological conversation, emerging from theological reflection on practices of discipleship formation and issues of Christian identity in young people."[25]

At the same time, even in the very early years of youth ministry as an academic discipline, explicit biblical and systematic accounts on youth ministry were brought into the debate. This has to do with what Roebben called the development of a strong relationship with systematic theology. Examples of these forms of theological accounts are those of Andrew Root on the centrality of a theology of the cross in youth ministry,[26] and David White on the centrality of the Christ image in youth ministry.[27] In 2011, Bard Norheim even argued that different understandings of youth ministry, including the underscoring of such biblical-theological concepts as "the cross" or "Christ image," stem from different confessional backgrounds of faith communities and/or research communities. In the same article, Norheim challenged youth ministry research in two ways: (a) hermeneutically: youth ministry research should articulate "more broadly and openly how confessional traditions and confessional contexts influence youth ministry research";[28] and (b) ecumenically: by displaying differences in terms of confessionality, youth ministry research could possibly contribute to enhancing the unity of the church.

---

24. Nel, "Youth Ministry as Practical Theology."
25. Dean, "Reflections on the Future of Youth Ministry," 91.
26. Root, "God's Hiddenness, Absence, and Doubt."
27. White, "The Fire and Light."
28. Norheim, "Confessionality," 62.

Recent Developments

In recent years, at least in the western world, youth ministry research has been more than ever conducted in a context of post-Christendom. Among the main developments in youth ministry in this regard, according to Jos de Kock (2017), liquid communities for young people are replacing static or fixed faith communities alongside a growing focus on missionary practices in churches' youth ministry.[29] Youth ministry research is often directed towards proposals for youth ministry models that meet the conditions of a post-Christian context.[30] In the current handbook, we will discuss several strategies and models of youth ministry as reflected upon in youth ministry research.

Another salient development in the academic research on youth ministry in recent times is the explicit reflection on research methodology. This reflection is a result of increasing experience with empirical research and consequent publications that follow a practical theological framework, a framework that has been often proposed by different scholars, as we have seen. Two main themes in this reflection can be distinguished: (a) the role of the empirical in youth ministry research, and (b) the role of normativity in youth ministry research. When it comes to the role of the empirical, in 2018 Jos de Kock and Bård Norheim elaborated on how empirical observations can be a starting point for theological reflection on the faith practices of children and young people.[31] They proposed a threefold set of research skills for the youth ministry researcher: observation as reception, listening as reception, and the ability to "learn language." In part 5 of the handbook, we will elaborate further on the issue of research methodology and the role of empirical research in the field of youth ministry.

The second theme, the role of normativity in youth ministry research, is directly in line with what Bård Norheim called the hermeneutical challenge for youth ministry research, namely to articulate the confessional context influencing the particular research project.[32] In 2018, Jos de Kock, Ronelle Sonnenberg, and Erik Renkema broadened this challenge by moving the focus from simply church-like confessionality to

---

29. De Kock, "Challenges to Apprenticeship Learning."
30. See, e.g., Myers, "Youth Ministry after Christendom."
31. De Kock and Norheim, "Youth Ministry Research."
32. Norheim, "Confessionality."

normativity in the broad sense of the word.³³ They proposed that youth ministry researchers should reflect explicitly on four layers of normativity in research projects: the layer of the youth ministry practice under study, the layer of normativity of professional theories in these practices, the layer of normativity of academic theories used in the study, and the meta-theoretical layer of the research project. In 2019, Jos de Kock proposed a practical theological perspective for studying youth ministry practices combining both the concern of empirical investigation and the concern of normativity in youth ministry research projects.³⁴

The Construction of the Content of the Handbook

The editors of this handbook are deeply involved in the International Association for the Study of Youth Ministry (IASYM): De Kock as one of the former chief editors of the *Journal of Youth and Theology* (JYT), an international academic peer-reviewed journal, originally published by the IASYM, now published by Brill, and Norheim as the former president of the IASYM (2014–22). IASYM as a research guild forms an important context for the developing of the academic youth ministry research over the last two decades. The IASYM started publishing JYT in 2002. The publications of youth ministry scholars that found their way into this journal have therefore been an important resource for writing this handbook.

In addition to JYT, two other peer-reviewed academic journals were important resources for what is presented in this handbook: the journal *Religious Education* (RE), a publication of the Religious Education Association, and the *International Journal of Practical Theology* (IJPT). In RE, regular articles on youth ministry have been published, typically with an eye on the formational and learning aspect of youth ministry practices. As we have observed above, the discipline of practical theology has become an important haven for theological research of youth ministry practices and reflection on them. For this reason IJPT has also been an important resource.

We chose to root the handbook in published articles in peer-reviewed academic journals. This is not to say that any publication, whether a book

33. De Kock et al., "Normativity in Empirical Youth Ministry Research."
34. De Kock, *Wait a Minute in Stressful Times.*

publication or a non-reviewed journal article is not relevant or would not be worthwhile. The principal reason is that to make this volume a state-of-the-art handbook, we found it necessary to base its content on publications of research outcomes that had passed a minimal form of critical review by a broad network of scholars around the world. To limit ourselves for pragmatic reasons and to strive for actuality for reasons of principle, we chose to consider all the issues of the three journals mentioned that were published between 2001 and 2020, thus covering twenty years of youth ministry. One of the side effects of this strategy is that we lean heavily on work that has been published in English and occasionally in German. We are aware of this limitation, and this is not to say that publications in other languages would not be relevant or worthwhile.

In addition, we searched for additional relevant publications on the basis of the bibliographies from the articles in the three journals, including books that appeared to be key publications in the academic conversations in the journals and relevant journal articles from other journals or issues earlier than 2001. The publications selected as sources for this handbook, about two hundred articles and more than one hundred books, were then discussed using a framework of five key questions that are explained in the following subsection.

Composition of the Handbook: Five Key Questions

The handbook is composed around five key questions. Part 1 of the handbook focuses on the question: Who are the youth in youth ministry? Chapters in this part discuss how youth is understood in youth ministry research, the phenomenon of youth culture and youth as a stage of life, identity development, and faith development theories, and what empirically has been investigated with regard to religious beliefs and practices of young people.

Part 2 of the handbook asks the question: Where is God in youth ministry? This part of the handbook contains a couple of chapters reflecting on how recent youth ministry research contributions conceptualize the presence of God in youth ministry practices and in relations and encounters in youth ministry. With a profound theological assessment of youth ministry research, these chapters bring together biblical, systematic, and practical theological accounts of youth ministry (research). The second part of the handbook focuses on the human, the divine and the quest for God and discusses a variety of perspectives on God's revelation in relation to man's actions.

Part 3 of the handbook poses the question: What is the purpose of youth ministry? This part focusses on goal setting in youth ministry practices by presenting different typologies of goals, discussing both general developmental goals and theologically loaded goals in particular, and in addition some empirical studies in which goals in youth ministry practices are investigated.

Part 4 of the handbook focuses on the question: Who is the youth minister? The chapters in this part discuss the role of the youth minister and the implications of other academic disciplines like pedagogy, sociology, and psychology in interpreting the role of leadership in youth ministry. Furthermore, this part sheds light on the particular characteristics of the youth minister.

Part 5 of the handbook deals with the question: How do you research practices in youth ministry? These chapters are about research methodology: different methodological approaches in youth ministry research are presented and a particular practical theological research framework is proposed. This part concludes with a chapter providing directions for designing a youth ministry research project. The research framework we propose (chapter 17) is a practical theological framework with a focus on empirical research. We are aware of other perspectives and fully agree with David White (2017)[35] that there are other relevant approaches to youth ministry research, such as biblical theological or systematic accounts. However, we propose this particular practical theological framework for research projects in youth ministry, and in Part 5 we will elaborate in more detail on the reasons for promoting this proposal.

The attentive reader will probably have missed an important question: Why? There are many possible "whys" that could emerge from the theme of a book like this: Why do youth ministry in the first place, and why do research on youth ministry? We are aware of the absence of the "Why?" question. At least, it is absent from the list of the five key questions shaping the outline of this book. At the same time, the "why?" question is present as an underlying interest in all the five questions. Working with the five questions will hopefully also make the reader better equipped to answer the fundamental "why" question: Why youth ministry?

---

35. White, "The Fire and Light."

Furthermore, in the final chapter of the handbook (chapter 17, "Designing a Youth Ministry Research Project") we present the why question as the first step in taking on the research journey. Every research project has a reason. Why does the researcher start the project? Where does the idea originate? The answer to the "why?" question can be embedded in practical experiences, in theoretical considerations, or in both. The reason for setting up a research project can be embedded in what we see as lacking in previous and current youth ministry research: blank spots in the academic research, intriguing questions triggered by theory or empirical data. We hope the different parts of this handbook help the reader to discover reasons for further research in interesting areas of youth ministry.

Intended Readership

This handbook aims to be both a textbook and a reference book. The intended audiences include all those who wish to obtain an overview of the discipline of youth ministry and its key subthemes. Members of this audience include graduate students in theology or any other discipline who are specializing in youth ministry, university professors, PhD students in youth ministry, and professional youth ministers and youth ministry trainers searching for a body of knowledge to inform, guide and/or justify their practices. As a textbook, this international handbook on youth ministry research is focusing on students at master and PhD-level as a principal group of readers: it is intended to be a practice oriented, but research-based handbook. It can be used in youth ministry courses in universities and colleges. It is definitely supplementary for practical theology courses and Christian pedagogical courses and bachelor introductory courses in universities and colleges.

Part 1

WHO ARE THE YOUTH IN YOUTH MINISTRY?

Who Are the Youth in Youth Ministry?
Introduction to Part 1

THE first part of the handbook focuses on the question: Who are the youth in youth ministry? We start this part of the handbook by addressing the theme of culture and youth culture in chapter 1. We chose this theme as a starting point because describing youth within the framework and terminology of youth culture is a dominant perspective in youth ministry research. In chapter 1, we assess how research on youth ministry practices conceptualizes youth, culture, and youth culture itself, with special attention to the interpretative frameworks of postmodernism and individualism.

Chapter 2 focuses on adolescence and more broadly on "being young" as a stage of life and the characteristics that can be associated with this stage. The chapter takes a generational perspective in answering the question of "who are the youth?" In doing so, it also discusses biblical and theological perspectives. The chapter introduces the faith development theory of James Fowler which is further discussed in more detail in chapter 3. Religious identity and faith development are the central themes in chapter 3. What is meant by development in faith? How does the concept of religious identity relate to the concept of faith and how is spiritual growth different from faith development? Chapter 3 reviews studies on a variety of research themes: identity, identity development, religious identity, faith development, and spiritual development. Psychological, theological, and sociological accounts on these issues will be discussed.

The faith of youth can be approached by looking at both the individual dimension and the communal dimension. Chapter 4 describes youth in relationship to faith, bringing together literature that shed light on one or both of these two dimensions. We will see not only that social context influences individual faith development, but that the reverse is also true: individual faith or faith practices influence the community of faith. Chapter 4 discusses subjective theologies among children and youth, the role of the youth group for faith development, and the specific practice of youth worship.

Throughout the chapters in part 1 we find at least two overarching themes. The first one is the theme of spirituality and how youth can be characterized by particular characteristics of spirituality, and asks what consequences these characteristics have for their identity formation. This latter topic, identity formation, is the second theme we see coming to the fore more than once in the content of this part of the handbook. Who are the youth in youth ministry? By looking at spirituality and identity formation as core themes, together with a variety of related concepts, this part of the handbook tries to answer this first key question.

1

Youth, Culture, and Youth Culture

"We all know churches and pastors (bishops and church leaders) ignoring culture. Church, for them, is a church thing, its own separate culture and institution. In such places we often find a sterile gospel and a church fighting for retention of members. We are also aware of churches and youth ministries accepting uncritically a large measure of cultural substance—usually on the basis of attracting outsiders. Here the personalities and styles of the pastor, leaders, worship leader, and musicians with clever use of media can become overly important. As Christians in culture, we are being called to a clear understanding of our culture and the counterclaims of the gospel of Jesus Christ. We are called to courageous Christ-following."[1]

The quote above is from Dean Borgman who with these words concludes a chapter with the heading "Relating to Christ in Culture." Culture and youth culture is the main theme of the current chapter. This part of our handbook is principally focused on the question: "Who are the youth in youth ministry?" Although many different perspectives can be chosen when answering this question, the perspective of describing youth in terms of youth culture appears to be a dominant one in youth ministry research. For that simple reason we start this part of the handbook with the theme of culture and youth culture.

The quote from Dean Borgman addresses different concerns that we regularly observe in debates in church and among youth ministers. How

1. Borgman, *Foundations for Youth Ministry*, 204.

can we appropriately understand the culture we live in? And what are specific characteristics of youth culture? How does youth culture relate to culture in general? Is church, as a phenomenon, something far different from other institutions to be found in society? And, as a consequence, is church culture opposed to culture in general and youth culture in particular? Or do we need to think the other way around: does youth ministry need to embrace youth culture? Does it need to do so with an eye on every child or youngster or only with a special eye on outsiders? How can Scripture and the gospel be related to youth culture? Does Scripture contain counterclaims or counter voices in the direction of dominant voices in youth culture? In other words: is the gospel a correction of dominant voices in youth culture or do we observe characteristics in youth culture that are fully in line with core principles in Scripture?

Against the background of these often-expressed concerns, we will evaluate how research on youth ministry conceptualizes the meaning of youth, culture, and youth culture. This chapter will summarize the main arguments found in youth ministry research with regard to the topic of youth culture. In section 1.1, the concepts of culture and youth culture are introduced. Next, the main characteristics of youth culture are presented, with special attention to the interpretative framework of postmodernism (section 1.2). Section 1.3 will describe challenging aspects in culture and youth culture for identity formation of the youngest generation. Next, youth culture is discussed in terms of spirituality characteristics found among young people, with special attention to music and worship preferences (section 1.4). Finally, section 1.5 will present studies that critically engage with main concepts in youth culture studies, with a special eye on the interpretative framework of individualism. The chapter ends with some concluding remarks in section 1.6.

1.1 Culture and Youth Culture

In youth ministry research, the focus is on youth, their faith practices, or the activities and programs that youth ministers are offering them. Explicitly or implicitly, in youth ministry studies there are particular views on youth. Who are the "youth?" What characteristics do they have? How is youth understood in terms of a life stage in between early childhood and young adulthood? Almost every study bears an implicit answer to these questions. In this chapter we review studies in which a more explicit reflection on youth is provided or where an understanding of youth even is the central theme. Because the question of who is the youth in youth ministry often is linked to a discussion of characteristics of the surrounding culture and more in particular characteristics of youth culture, this chapter chooses its focus in a broad sense: a discussion of youth, culture, and youth culture.

In the current handbook, a broad understanding of youth is chosen: all those who can be classified as children, youth, and teenagers; even young adults are sometimes the focus of what is labeled youth ministry research. Thus, in this handbook youth refers to the "youngest generation" of societies in general and faith communities in particular. Characteristics of this youngest generation reflect what is often called "the surrounding culture."

Culture can be described as the manifestation of values, practices, beliefs (including religious beliefs), norms, and habits within a group of people, a community or society, often sharing the same geographical location and language. On one hand, culture organizes or forms the daily life and development of people in general and young people in particular (socialization processes); on the other hand, culture is formed or transformed by the daily life, the choices and development processes of people, especially those of the youngest generation. It is difficult to speak about "the" culture of a community, country, or society because many host different sub-cultures and are multicultural, composed of groups of participants rooted in different geographical, ethnic, or linguistic backgrounds.

Youth culture can be seen as a particular example of a subculture. For example, Dean Borgman explains: "When youth or an ethnic minority, for instance, sense their identities are not being respected nor their needs attended to, they begin naturally to construct a language, sense of ironic humor, behaviors, music, and so forth that constitute a special or subculture and binds them together."[2] As a subculture, youth culture can function within a broader culture of a society or country, within a culture of a particular community or even as a global phenomenon within the context of the global village. Youth culture can be described as the whole manifestation of values, practices, beliefs (including religious beliefs), norms, and habits within the youngest generation of a community, society, or country. As a subculture, youth culture has its particular dynamics that are different from—or contrasts with—other subcultures

---

2. Borgman, *Foundations for Youth Ministry*, 170.

in the broad context of a society, or the "dominant culture" of a society or community in general. Authors differ in their evaluation of how different youth culture is from culture in general: Is there a major fault line between them? Is youth culture to be interpreted as a counter-culture? Or is there just a slight difference between the broad culture and youth culture where the youngest generation is only a little bit more progressive than older generations? In this chapter we will see the different ways in which culture and youth culture are described, interpreted, and evaluated in youth ministry research.

1.2 Characteristics of Youth Culture

Comparative Perspective on Youth Culture

As said, we cannot speak of culture and youth culture as a universal global phenomenon. The description and interpretation of culture and youth culture are dependent on time and place. Just as an example, contemporary youth culture in Western Europe needs a different interpretative framework from youth culture in North America in the 1960s. This hermeneutical challenge applies not just diachronically, but even synchronically: In a 2004 article on the development of faith in Africa, Saneto Maiko argued: "Having an African academic perspective on youth culture, I find the culture of teens in the West different from that of African youth and tend to conclude that this is due to a greater spectrum of cultural background and orientation given to them by the already adult established culture."[3] Therefore, when presenting and comparing writings about culture and youth culture we should be aware of the geographical and time perspectives of authors and be precise in our comments.

Some youth ministry publications on the topic of youth culture make comparisons between different continents. In 2011, Russell Haitch described a particular characteristic of youth culture at that time, namely the desire for freedom and does so by comparing the desire for freedom among youth on three continents: America, Europe, and Africa.[4] Haitch conceives freedom as a core value that can be found among youth across the globe. How this core value turns out in America, Europe, and Africa is explained along the lines of a couple of "isms" that attach themselves

---

3. Maiko, "A Psycho-Theological Synopsis," 29.
4. Haitch, "Free as a Bird."

to freedom as a core value: "individualism, the freedom to be myself; postmodernism, the freedom to be different; consumerism, the freedom to buy myself; proteanism, the freedom to change myself; and fundamentalism, the freedom to surrender myself."[5] These different "isms," and the underlying value of freedom and the desire of to develop oneself towards more freedom, are highlighted in quite a number of studies that will be discussed later in this chapter. Postmodernism appears to be a key interpretative framework for youth ministry scholars evaluating current societies and developments among youth. At the same time, "isms" as interpretative frameworks are critiqued by youth ministry scholars, for example, individualism in the study of De Kock, Roeland, and Vos (see 1.4).[6]

To characterize youth culture, authors around the globe use a variety of concepts. In 2001, arguing from a German perspective, Gerd Buschmann framed the youth culture of the 1990s as techno-culture.[7] This refers to the popular music of that time and he argues that this culture can also be described in religious terms as secular religion in a postmodern society. "[T]echno-culture represents the idea of holiness in a post-modern society based on adventure."[8] Interestingly for youth ministers and youth ministry scholars, by doing so, Buschmann identifies youth culture in itself as a religious phenomenon or at least as a phenomenon which can be understood in religious terms. In techno-culture, Buschmann sees dance, rhythm, ecstasy, ritual, and shamanism as substantial and functional notions of religion.

Where Buschmann opts for describing youth culture as techno-culture, in 2004 Ellen Alexander, speaking from the perspective of India, discussed the nature of youth culture in terms of "tattooed collage."[9] Based on literature research, observation, and a qualitative field research that included interviews with college students in the city of Bangalore, the author sums up important characteristics of youth culture under the title of *"Tattooed Collage"—A Perspective of Youth Culture*. According to Alexander, the term "Tattooed Collage" captures two of the most significant characteristics of youth culture: "A fascination with the body—so we see

---

5. Haitch, "Free as a Bird," 5.
6. De Kock et al., "Beyond Individualisation."
7. Buschmann, "Jugendkultur 'Techno.'"
8. Buschmann, "Jugendkultur 'Techno,'" 204.
9. Alexander, "Tattooed Collage."

them tattooed, gelled, dressed the way they do and an amazing interest in fitness dance, drama, choreography anything that involves the body. And it is also a culture that seeks to mix and match, pick and choose—a fusion—collage rather than distinct, linear or clearly defined—it is not a 'melting pot'—more a fruit salad."[10] These two characteristics, being fascinated with the body and having a "pick and choose" attitude, have consequences for, or are linked up with, youth practices in different life spheres such as ethics and morals, music, and media but also the religious area when it comes to e.g. conceptions of God and the development of own spirituality. Obviously, all such hermeneutical framings of youth culture can be challenged in terms of comprehensiveness, as they are contextual and situated. At the same time, a non-contextual, meta-situated description of youth culture is even more questionable.

Postmodernism/Postmodernity

We have already pointed out how postmodernism or postmodernity appears to be a key interpretative framework for youth ministry scholars evaluating current societies and developments among youth. A study by Stefan Gärtner on sex educational concepts in pastoral care of youth is a good example.[11] The German Catholic pastoral care of youth was the background of Gärtner's study in 2003 in which perspectives for sex educational concepts in pastoral care of youth were provided. In his article, Gärtner addresses general social conditions that form children's and adolescent's sexuality in postmodern society. One of these conditions is society being pluralized and individualized, where all citizens, both youth and adults are challenged to make own choices in the midst of multiple (formerly) existing traditional models. Against this background Gärtner argues that "sex education has already achieved quite a lot if it succeeds in enabling young people to take their own responsible decisions, instead of leaving them exposed to the pressure to conform to the peer group and/or the images of sexuality presented in the mass media."[12] Two other social conditions Gärtner shows are the detachment of sexual activity from marriage and the earlier sexual maturity of young people.

---

10. Alexander, "Tattooed Collage," 40.
11. Gärtner, "Education through and to Love."
12. Gärtner, "Education through and to Love," 98.

For Gärtner, the postmodern condition of society is an important aspect of youth culture. But what is postmodernity or postmodernism? Postmodernism and its relationship to young people discovering Jesus Christ is the main theme in an article of Richard James from 2004.[13] Referring to Jürgen Moltmann,[14] James argues postmodernity can be seen as a "debate about reality," in terms of both language, meta-narratives, and the construction of self. And following Graham Cray, James distinguishes between three facets of postmodernism: "the loss of faith in big ideals (grand stories), truth that is constructed rather than discovered, the awareness of the shallowness of consumerism.[15]

The first two facets of postmodernism are observed in the study of Van Wijnen and Barnard published in 2014.[16] Observations by Van Wijnen and Barnard in a qualitative research of five small groups of adolescents (aged fifteen to twenty-one years) related to local protestant congregations in The Netherlands show youth ministry practices are not always in line with the way adolescents think, feel, and behave in daily life.[17] The authors show young people "are searching for groups that are 'just' groups"[18] and not groups where there is an explicit intention from adults to convert them to an ideology or set of rules. Furthermore, in relation to faith, young people appear to use language based on experiences and narratives in their daily lives more than language based on abstract, rational, cognitive faith concepts.

The third facet as mentioned by James, consumerism, is addressed, for example, by Joyce Ann Mercer in her book *Welcoming Children: A Practical Theology of Childhood*. She explains that consumerism as characteristic of the habitus or wider society in which congregations are embedded impacts the way that children are envisioned and encountered. "The problem, then, is not merely the cultural construction of a distorted idea of children as consumers, against which a better, Christian understanding of childhood can constitute a correction. The problem is that consumerism as a habitus forms persons into patterns of action, attitudes, dispositions, and habits of interpretation that inform how they engage the

---

13. James, "Discovering Jesus as a Postmodern Young Person."
14. Moltmann, *The Way of Jesus Christ*.
15. Cray, *Postmodern Culture and Youth Discipleship*, 17.
16. Van Wijnen and Barnard, "From Organized Faith to Lived Faith."
17. Van Wijnen and Barnard, "From Organized Faith to Lived Faith."
18. Van Wijnen and Barnard, "From Organized Faith to Lived Faith," 17.

various elements of Christian faith, including beliefs and practices with children. Constructing a more adequate vision of childhood or retrieving a better theological view of children from within Christian tradition is not at all incidental to the work of transforming theology and church life to welcome children."[19] Dean Borgman defines consumerism as "raising material consumption to the highest good"[20] and argues, as Mercer does, that it considerably impacts the identity development of young people.

Thus, postmodernity as an interpretative framework in youth ministry studies has to do with the observation of societies being pluralized, individualized, and steered by consumerism, where young people construct truth and where grand stories lose ground for discovering who you are to an identity concept that is defined experientially and narratively. The theme of identity formation is central in youth ministry publications on youth culture and will be the topic of the next section.

For a further reading on postmodernism and youth culture we recommend *Welcoming Children: A Practical Theology of Childhood* from Joyce Ann Mercer, particularly chapter 3, "A Problem of Ambivalence: Children as Consumers in America." This chapter deals with the themes of consumerism and postmodernity and how these are related to the lives of children and their educators. Furthermore, we suggest Dean Borgman's *Foundations for Youth Ministry: Theological Engagement with Teen Life and Culture*, particularly part 3, "Practical Theology Engaging Culture." This part of Borman's book contains a number of chapters covering a theological reflection on youth culture in relation to, among other themes, consumerism. And we recommend the article, "Beyond Individualisation: Neo-Evangelical Lessons for Religious Socialisation," from De Kock et al. In this article the authors plead for the readjustment of the dominant sociological narrative of individualization by accompanying it with the awareness that the socially embeddedness of religiosity of youth has been reconfigured or transformed from traditional communities into new forms of sociality.

---

19. Van Wijnen and Barnard, "From Organized Faith to Lived Faith," 32.
20. Borgman, *Foundations for Youth Ministry*, 232.

1.3 Youth Culture and Challenges for Identity Formation

In 1997, Bert Roebben provided a cultural-psychological analysis of the contemporary identity formation of youth in Western Europe.[21] This analysis is informed by West European cultural psychology and youth research. Roebben detects what he calls "three problematic aspects of identity formation of contemporary youth"[22] that he understands not only as social and moral issues but also as a religious issue.

The first aspect is the commercialization of the environment of young people. Young people have all kinds of opportunities when it comes to making choices in life, in using their leisure time or building a career, but also in adopting religious ideas. The environment of young people is commercialized by the huge number of inputs and impetuses that are on offer when it comes to making these choices and setting up one's individual life project. As a result, young people become fatigued, partly because they are also held responsible for the choices they make. "They also feel insecure about what is really worthwhile in a chaotic society."[23] In 2019, De Kock, from a Dutch perspective, typified this as a stressful time for young people, "confronted with a great amount of expectations from their environment (school, parents, etc.), pressure to achieve, and the complicatedness of finding out who they are at a time when the concept of identity is more and more 'liquid' as a result of a highly fragmented world with an enormous amount of subgroups and temporary choices."[24]

The second aspect is the mediatization of the youth period. This aspect is about the trend for young people to spend less time on interactions in real life in favor of spending more time on interactions in virtual reality by means of electronic media and watching television, in an own age atmosphere that separates them from adults. One of the risks of this trend, according to Roebben, is a decrease in moral sensibility among young people. The development of this moral sensibility among young people needs critical encounters with others, virtually and with other age groups; the trend towards mediatization during youthful years challenges

---

21. Roebben, "Shaping a Playground for Transcendence."
22. Roebben, "Shaping a Playground for Transcendence," 332.
23. Roebben, "Shaping a Playground for Transcendence," 334; Gärtner, "Education through and to Love."
24. De Kock, *Wait a Minute in Stressful Times*, 6.

society in general and educators in particular to provide sufficient contexts in which these encounters can take place.

The third aspect is the risk of what Roebben calls the "Fall into Insignificance": "In a world of flexibility, competition, and conformity through media and consumerism, the fundamental moral experience of vulnerable contingency, sensible commitment, radical incompleteness, and therefore hope for the future is at risk of being extinguished."[25] Roebben analyzes youth as having the experience of not being heard and not being understood in their search for meaning. Young people lack community and are afraid of being meaningless for their environment, for society, for the future. This observation is shared by Dean Borgman who sees existential emptiness as the ultimate effect of consumerism in the lives and context of young people.[26] Roebben explains: "The mental 'playground' of young people—the field of opportunities in which they learn to grow into the person they are uniquely destined to become—has shrunk dramatically."[27]

What Roebben in 1997 called the mediatization of the period of youth has developed in the years that followed. Where Roebben observed on the one hand "real life" and on the other hand a "virtual reality," twenty years later, Tobias Faix observes that the boundaries between the virtual and the real world are coalescing and can no longer be separated.[28] Nowadays, according to Faix, youth culture is stamped by two important simultaneous global developments: globalization and digitalization. As a result, young people have so called "hybrid identities," meaning "that the two realities, the virtual in the area of social media and the real in the adolescents everyday life, converge so closely that they blend together."[29] The internet, social media and all kinds of online networks and communities are important places where young people construct and reconstruct their identities, and, according to Faix, the significance of these places for young people also transforms the way they search for spirituality and spiritual growth. What is true for youth culture in general is also true for youth spirituality in particular: it is a hybrid field where the virtual reality and the "real" reality blend together.

25. Roebben, "Shaping a Playground for Transcendence," 337.
26. Borgman, *Foundations for Youth Ministry*.
27. Roebben, "Shaping a Playground for Transcendence," 332.
28. Faix, "Hybrid Identity."
29. Faix, "Hybrid Identity," 70.

Chapter 3 will provide for a more detailed discussion of identity development and religious development among youth. For a further reading on youth, religion, and globalization we recommend *Youth, Religion, and Globalization: New Research in Practical Theology*, edited by Richard Osmer and Kenda Creasy Dean. This edited book contains a number of chapters on the theme of youth, religion, and globalization and covers different geographical regions, e.g., Germany, Ghana, Japan, and Paraguay.

1.4 Youth Culture and Spirituality

To understand youth, youth ministry scholars try to understand culture and youth culture in particular. Besides postmodernity as a central interpretative framework (section 1.2), we saw globalization and digitalization as important developments youth ministry scholars take into account (section 1.3). In this section, we consider studies focusing on how these developments are mirrored in the characteristics of spirituality and, in relation to this, in the particular music and worship preferences among young people.

Spirituality Characteristics

From the perspective of the Australian context in particular, Engebretson describes characteristics of the spirituality of the young.[30] With spirituality, the author means the "apprehension of a sacred dimension in life, and the implications that this has for the way one lives."[31] Her description of the characteristics of spirituality was provided in a publication in 2003 and was directed towards the 16–25 age group, on the basis of a selective survey of literature and research concerning young people. The spirituality characteristics among Australian young people that Engebrentson describes can be summarized as follows:

Youth have a private, individualized spirituality, searching for meaningful personal experiences. This is linked to a tendency toward privatization of belief and an increase of eclecticism in a (religiously) plural society, a characteristic of post-modernity in which the individual developmental task is to construe your own "self" and "meaning" on the basis of myriad interpretations. At the same time, young people have a

---

30. Engebretson, "Young People, Culture, and Spirituality."
31. Engebretson, "Young People, Culture, and Spirituality," 6.

need for belonging and intimacy and are searching for community by building relationships with peers and with other significant people in their environment. Young people seek social justice and portray an attitude of tolerance, opposing discrimination of any kind.

Although this can be viewed as a general "all time" characteristic of the developmental stage of youth, it is important to see the following characteristic of spirituality in the light of the aforementioned time specific characteristics: based on their day to day experiences, young people are actively reexamining the thinking about the sacred and about images of God: "to either readopt these in more thoughtful ways, to abandon them all together or to reconstruct them."[32]

Chapter 2 will discuss the topic of youth spirituality in more detail, whereas chapter 3 will elaborate on the theme of spiritual formation.

Music and Worship (Songs)

One other area in youth ministry research where characteristics of youth and youth culture become visible is the area of music and worship (songs). This area, in a way, is closely related to the area of the spirituality characteristics of young people as just discussed. For example, musical preferences are the subject of study in Christopher Rodkey's research on how the musical preferences of youth influence conceptions of the transcendence and imminence of the Divine.[33] The author states: "Music, whether Christian or secular, is perhaps the primary source for teens for their theology; and music is a foundational staple for many youth ministries as a means of identifying that ministry's or community's ideology or beliefs; and, as such, sacred music is, and historically always has been, among the most useful practices of faith for teens outside of formal public worship."[34] We will come back to this study in chapter 5, part 2. Two more important examples of this kind of research are studies by David Bailey on theological shorthand in worship songs, which we will present in part 4, and the research by Steve Emery-Wright.[35]

---

32. Engebretson, "Young People, Culture, and Spirituality," 18.
33. Rodkey, "The Practice of Music in Youth Ministry."
34. Rodkey, "The Practice of Music in Youth Ministry," 47.
35. Bailey, "Living amongst the Fragments"; Emery-Wright, "A Qualitative Study Construction."

In 2003, Steve Emery-Wright published results from a qualitative research project involving case studies at three local Methodist churches in the United Kingdom.[36] The study was about finding out how young people (fourteen–sixteen years) understood worship. One of the findings of the study was that there is a "possible relationship between a young person's ability to identify a significant worship experience and their continuing attendance at church."[37] The notion of experience or youth experience is central in this suggestion and the author explains the meaning of this notion as follows. The term "youth experience" refers to the importance of the presence of peers in worship, and this can be theologically interpreted as the importance of *koinonia* as being both connected with God and connected with other community members. Youth experience can also be understood as referring to symbols and concerns from youth culture which are utilized or incorporated in worship, underlining that God can also be present in youth culture as a separate realm from adult life.

Chapter 4 will elaborate on the phenomenon of youth worship.

1.5 Critical Engagement with Youth Culture Concepts

In youth ministry research, from time to time there is a critical engagement with the main concepts and interpretative frameworks with regard to youth culture that are used in studies. Steve Emery-Wright, for example, shows how concepts such as culture, popular culture, youth culture, and church culture are described differently and valued differently within the (academic) discourse on young people and worship practices.[38] One of the concepts that often recurs in writings on youth culture is individualism (referring to one's freedom to be oneself). Theories that form a basis for the interpretation of individualism are called individualization theories, and are frequently applied in the domain of religion and religious developments in general, and in relation to youth in particular.

In 2011, De Kock, Roeland, and Vos put it this way: "Many accounts of religion among young people are frequently inspired by taken-for-granted grand theories, such as the theory of individualisation. According to many experts in this area, the display of contemporary religion among

---

36. Emery-Wright, "A Qualitative Study Construction."
37. Emery-Wright, "A Qualitative Study Construction," 76.
38. Emery-Wright, *Now That Was Worship*.

young people would be highly individualised, allegedly contrasting with the socially embedded religions of the past."[39] The authors, coming from a Dutch background, discuss the tendency in literature to propose models of (religious) socialization that take individualized culture into account.

Next, they critically examine the assumptions behind the idea of individualization that leads to an evaluation in terms of one-sidedness. The literature on individualization processes in relation to religion often only focuses on young people's search for a personally relevant religiosity. However, the authors also observe in practices of neo-evangelicalism in Western Europe "a desire of many young people to accommodate their search for a personal religious identity in the—what is experienced as—warm and exciting forms of sociality and communal religious life, which have emerged in the post-Sixties era."[40] Examples of forms of sociality can be found in all kinds of religious events and online communities. Therefore, based on this observation and analysis of practices of neo-evangelicalism among young people in Western Europe, the authors plead for the readjustment of the dominant sociological narrative of individualization by accompanying it with awareness that the socially embeddedness of religiosity of youth has been reconfigured or transformed from traditional communities into new forms of sociality.

Where in 2011, De Kock, Roeland, and Vos critically evaluated the assumptions behind the individualization tendency as presented in literature, in 2014, Scott evaluated the whole "portrait" of young adults that comes to the fore in the research literature on religious education and youth ministry: "young adults are (1) spiritual, not religious, (2) anti-institutional, anti-church, and (3) apathetic, if not dismissive, of tradition."[41] The author pleads for an educational response and for this portrait to be corrected. Scott evaluates the concept of being spiritual as too vague or fuzzy, meaning just about anything other than being religious. At the same time, she pleads for a renewed interest in religion that can function as a restraint on the spiritual quest of young people. Young people being anti-institutional and anti-church should be interpreted as an evaluation of the health of the institutional church and but not of the institution of the church as such. Scott states that a private, non-institutional religion does not exist and that "enduring religions

---

39. De Kock et al. "Beyond Individualisation," 329–30.
40. De Kock et al. "Beyond Individualisation," 332.
41. Scott, "Inviting Young Adults," 471.

have both institutional and communal elements."[42] And when it comes to being apathetic about tradition, Scott states that one cannot deny that we live within traditions. A tradition can degenerate into traditionalism, which can be evaluated negatively by young people. The solution, then, is not to deny or step out of tradition but instead involve young people in transforming tradition in its rich diversity.

Besides critical engagement with concepts, youth ministry research also provides critical evaluation of tendencies in (youth) culture, as, for example, Bert Roebben's argument on problematic aspects of identity formation in Western Europe (see 1.3).[43] There are authors who are in search of guidelines to interpret contemporary youth culture in the light of the gospel, such as Don Richter in a chapter "Growing Up Postmodern: Theological Uses of Culture" in a book authored by Kenda Creasy Dean, Chap Clark, and Dave Rahn entitled "Starting Right: Thinking Theologically about Youth Ministry."[44] And there are authors who evaluate culture, youth culture, and its underpinning characteristics like postmodernism as threatening the healthy development of young people. A good example is Kenda Creasy Dean who, in 2000 in *Theology Today*, stated: "The unmitigated relativism of postmodernity coupled with the constant and overwhelming necessity of moment-by-moment choice, compromises identity formation's requirement that the adolescent invest in a central, governing life-view (what Erikson called an 'ideology')."[45] To understand and critically engage with these kinds of evaluations, we need a clear understanding of youth as a stage of life and of the processes of identity and religious development and formation during childhood and youth stage. These are the main themes of chapters 2 and 3 where the influential identity development theory of Erikson will also be discussed.

1.6 Conclusion

This chapter assessed different perspectives on youth culture that are prominent in a broad variety of youth ministry research. In this research literature, youth culture is conceived as a subculture that functions within a broader culture of a particular society or in the context of the

---

42. Scott, "Inviting Young Adults," 479.
43. Roebben, "Shaping a Playground for Transcendence."
44. Dean et al., *Starting Right*, 73–93.
45. Dean, "Proclaiming Salvation," 534.

global village. Youth culture refers to the particular manifestation of values, practices, beliefs, also religious beliefs, norms, and habits among the youngest generation of a society. Authors differ in how they see the exact relationship between youth culture and culture, and the same is true of how they believe youth culture should be evaluated in relation to church life and the faith formation of youth. In general, postmodernism or postmodernity is a recurrent concept with which youth culture is understood nowadays among youth ministry scholars. Different authors show how characteristics of postmodernism challenge the identity and formation of young people and how this translates into the spirituality characteristics of youth.

Who are the youth in youth ministry? In this chapter, we saw that the perspective of describing youth in terms of youth culture is a dominant one in youth ministry research. And this is not without reason. Youth culture as a manifestation of the core values, practices, and beliefs of youth teaches youth ministers a lot about how to appropriately understand their main "purpose group." At the same time, youth ministers, inspired by the Christian faith, work with children and young people with the aim of discovering, learning and practicing the gospel. This discovering, learning and practicing is embedded in a particular culture and a particular youth culture. Thus, youth culture not only stamps youth but also stamps youth ministry practices. Therefore, youth ministers, and churches and pastors alike, should not and cannot ignore youth culture.

2

Being Young as a Stage of Life

"Adolescence is changing—and quickly. Puberty is starting earlier and resolving the questions of identity and autonomy later and later. This means that the concept of *youth* can no longer be limited to the two programmatic foci of North American youth ministry, junior and senior high. From fifth grade to the mid-20s, young men and women are finding themselves in a state of flux, continually on the lookout for anyone who would bless, affirm, and help them to finally lad as a unique responsible person."[1]

It is difficult to "fix" adolescence in terms of age, but is it true that the phase of puberty has expanded in the course of the past decades, as is suggested by Chap Clark in the quote above? This chapter will not provide a definitive answer to that question; instead, it deals more broadly with "being young" as a stage of life and what characteristics can be associated with this stage. What does it mean to say youth is in a state of flux? The quote from Clark also suggests an end goal for developing oneself in this state of flux: becoming a unique responsible person. This reflects an often-articulated vision of young people not being responsible or at least not fully capable of being responsible, in contrast to adults who are, or are supposed to be, responsible persons. Is this true, and what more can be said about being young as a stage of life?

This chapter reviews views on youth, childhood, and adolescence as a stage of life from a generational perspective, based on youth ministry

1. Dean et al., *Starting Right*, 71.

research. We therefore start with a brief discussion of the issue of generations and the social construction of "being young" in youth ministry (section 2.1). What follows is a discussion of youth as a stage of life from a biblical and theological perspective (2.2). Next, a theme is discussed that is often addressed in youth ministry research when it comes to typifying youth as a particular stage of life. The theme is spirituality (2.3). The chapter ends with some concluding remarks in section 2.4.

2.1 On Generations and the Social Construction of "Being Young"

In 2008, German scholar Ulrich Schwab addressed the transmission of faith across generations as a recurring theme in literature on youth ministry and religious education.[2] In particular, he reviewed the post-1945 history of inter-generational relationships within the church in Germany. Schwab approached the transmission of faith as "dialogue between generational perspectives and practices."[3] This means that youth cannot and should not only be analyzed as an isolated phenomenon or stage of life but also as a phenomenon and stage to be understood as relating to other generations and stages in life.

Following Mannheim,[4] Schwab conceives a generation as a phenomenon explaining "frequent similarities in world view among a specific peer group."[5] From this perspective, Schwab sees the generation that is children and adolescents not primarily as a group of young people who should themselves pass on the traditions handed down by a former generation. Instead, he understands a generation of young people as "creatures in their own rights"[6] whose development of faith follows its own logic. Schwab pleads that the church needs to relate to young people, both members and non-members. This means being in dialogue with young people. In so doing, the church is a church *im semper reformanda*.

Young people as "creatures in their own rights" do have particular characteristics that have to do with their particular developmental stage. For many youth ministry scholars and youth ministry practitioners,

---

2. Schwab, ". . . try and find the thread . . ."
3. Schwab, ". . . try and find the thread . . . ," 10.
4. Mannheim, "Das Problem der Generationen," 23–48.
5. Schwab, ". . . try and find the thread . . . ," 14.
6. Schwab, ". . . try and find the thread . . . ," 21.

when thinking about youth as a stage of life, the identity theory of Erik Erikson[7] and the psychological theory of stages of faith presented by James Fowler[8] will come to the fore. Following Erikson's theory, adolescence (the developmental phase of twelve to eighteen years) is characterized by the challenge to find identity and to develop loyalty. Using Erikson's conceptual identity framework, and based on empirical research, Fowler points at faith development during adolescence starting from a personal view of life that is closely linked to the community to which one belongs and moving towards a type of faith that is based on individual responsibility accompanied by the ability to critically view one's own and others' thinking.

But can we speak about adolescence as a specific stage of life as these developmental theories of Erikson and Fowler suggest? Is adolescence more probably a period that has been "invented" or socially constructed in modern times? The latter question is the central topic of David White's discussion of the 2015 publication *In Search of Adolescence: A New Look at an Old Idea* by Crystal Kirgiss.[9] Kirgiss rejects this dominant narrative in the discipline of youth ministry, whereas White argues the phenomenon of adolescence is quite new since the period between the mid-nineteenth and early twentieth centuries, although there are ancient antecedents of the concept of adolescence. White states: adolescence is "a prolonged status in which youth have less than full power for longer than any other age cohort in the history of the world."[10] Whereas Kirgiss' thesis is that adolescence is a universal phenomenon which has not been only recently invented, White states that adolescence is a recent "social institution," with youth having distinct social roles and expectations to meet while at the same time searching for identity and purpose in life.

In addition, White presents two particular evaluations of the phenomenon of adolescence: (1) "the struggle of young people to find a sense of identity in the modern institution of adolescence creates high levels of stress reflected in suicide rates, emotional problems, and delinquency."[11] (2): "In theological terms, we might say that the contemporary institution of adolescence by restraining the curiosity, creativity, experimentalism,

---

7. Erikson, *Identity, Youth, and Crisis*.
8. Fowler, *Stages of Faith*.
9. White, "Adolescence"; Kirgiss, *In Search of Adolescence*.
10. White, "Adolescence," 118.
11. White, "Adolescence," 122.

and public agency of youth inhibits their inherent gifts—the goodness and glory by which youth reflect God in the world."[12] These evaluations mirror the analysis of identity formation of current youth by Bert Roebben as discussed in chapter 1.[13] Against the same background of adolescence understood as a socially constructed phenomenon raised out of twentieth century industrial/economic processes, professional/academic processes and popular culture developments, David Penn provides for a theological evaluation comparable with David White's and argues that congregations should make better use of the particular capabilities of young people and integrate them into the congregational community much more.[14] In particular, Penn pleads for congregations to support young people in developing individual virtues (positive youth development) by way of communal practices.

2.2 Youth from a Biblical and Theological Perspective

What can be said about being young from a theological perspective? In 2006, Ron Becker *challenged* the dominance of practical theology in the academic study of youth ministry and made a plea for more comprehensive attention to biblical theology.[15] In his article, Becker drew on study of the Old Testament offering two exegeses, one on the anonymous Israelite girl in 2 Kings 5 and one on the person of Joseph. Becker chooses to focus on stories of individual youths in biblical narratives rather than generations or cohorts because the latter too often results in depersonalization of the category of youth, conceiving it as a "not yet" stage. Formulated more positively: "Reading the stories and appearances of youths is an exciting adventure with its own exegetical and hermeneutical dynamics. It criticizes any approach that neglects the potential that God put in each person."[16]

The latter is one of the important insights Becker's exegetical work provides: God puts potential in every young person, in the times of the Old Testament writers and in current era; in particular, young people provide a prophetic voice. Another example of scholars focusing on exegesis

12. White, "Adolescence," 123.
13. Roebben, "Shaping a Playground for Transcendence."
14. Penn, "Against the Generation Gap."
15. Becker, "Beyond a Godless Understanding of Youth."
16. Becker, "Beyond a Godless Understanding of Youth," 25.

of Scriptural figures and its relevance for youth ministry and youth ministry research is offered by Jennifer Lewis, who, in 2019, discussed the person of Miriam in the Scripture passage of Exodus 1–2.[17] Lewis shows how Miriam may be a model for female youth, being courageous and taking leadership. She turns the focus away from Moses towards the person of Miriam: Without her leadership, Moses would not have survived. And the way in which Miriam intervenes is linked up with the nature of her child-status: watching, waiting, collaborating, quick-thinking and learning. Lewis put Miriam to the fore as a role model of agency and leadership for today's female youth in church communities.

Contributions like those of Becker and Lewis illustrate a search for what is called a "theology of youth." According to Christian Noval, a theology of youth aims at gaining a theological understanding of youth.[18] Noval states: "A theological vision of youth is important whether we reflect on youth from a systematic theological point of view or we are engaged with Youth Ministry through Practical Theology."[19] Instead of rooting a theology of youth in a theological anthropology classically based on the creation account in Genesis, Noval proposes one rooted in Old Testament wisdom literature and, in particular, Job's narrative of his creation in Job 10. The creation account in Genesis reads: "So God created mankind in his own image, in the image of god he created them; male and female he created them" (Gen 1:27 NIV). The problem of taking this creation account as a basis for a theology of youth, according to Noval, is that the image of God is explained as both the origin and destiny of one's life; as being perfect, only leaving room for devaluation because of the Fall. In this way, a theology of youth leaves no room for a potential of positive development in the lives of young people.

Against this background, Noval argues that Wisdom literature proves more appropriate in this regard, and illustrates this argument with the so called "double creation accounts" in Job 10. The first creation account is about Job "being created by God through the natural process of being brought forth 'out of the womb'. . . . More than just being a moment, God's relating to us creatively is a process. It isn't just the first moment of our existence but a lifelong relationship between the creator and the

---

17. Lewis, "Girl Power Gone Right in Exodus 1–2."
18. Noval, "Youth and Creation"; Noval, "Wired for Holiness."
19. Noval, "Youth and Creation," 36.

individual."²⁰ The second creation account is about Job "being given a living body directly by God and not through a natural process as in the first account.... In being born Job is his living body, but in being given a living body, there is distinction between Job and his living body. In this distinction lies both the limited nature of the human being, its freedom and its possibility to act wisely according to how God relates through the act of creation."²¹

On the basis of this exegetical work on the creation accounts of Job, Noval draws five implications for a theology of youth: (1) What makes someone human is his/her living body; (2) one is created in the concreteness of the context in which one lives; (3) there is a call to live wisely in relationship with the creator; (4) "Since children and youth more than others expresses growth and development, they might have a special role in our understanding of God's continuous relating to us as our creator";²² (5) the worth of children and youth should be seen as they are in their actuality, not in their potentiality.

Theologies of children and youth, for which Noval presents some ingredients, are provided by several authors. In 2005, Nathan Frambach, argued that children and young people are active agents of faith, and are therefore not only participants in faith communities but are also leaders and theological educators.²³ In 2016, Frantisek Štěch presented a theological vision of youth in his article "Who are Youth in Theological Perspective?" In it, Štěch seeks a specific Christian approach to understanding what youth is about and claims this must be a theological approach. To summarize his argument, a lengthy quote is presented now:

"From a theological perspective, youth is not a strictly age-related group, but rather a viewpoint, the special way human beings relate to God.... [O]ur childhood and youth stays within us for the whole of our life. In spite of this, youth is still the 'kairos,' a very opportune time, distinct from others. Youth is distinctive due to its characteristics (e.g. longing for love and acceptance, searching for meaning, openness, excitement, activity, creativity, hope, pursuing development, expecting the future to come, etc.), but yet, these are inseparable from the totality of being human."²⁴

20. Noval, "Youth and Creation," 42.
21. Noval, "Youth and Creation," 43.
22. Noval, "Youth and Creation," 44.
23. Frambach, "Seen & Heard."
24. Štěch, "Who Are Youth in Theological Perspective?," 129.

According to Štěch, it is not a consequence of this that no development is necessary for young people. Theologically, salvation through Jesus Christ requires a development of any human being, and of young people also. Development is not a goal in itself but has salvation as its ultimate goal. Štěch pleads for a youth theology where a theological understanding of youth is a prerequisite for any theological engagement with young people and theological engagement with young people is a prerequisite for theological understanding of youth.

Where theology of youth is the main background for Štěch's article, theology of children or child theology is the main focus in Karl Ernst Nipkow's account on "Theologie des Kindes und Kindertheologie in Zeitschrift für Theologie und Kirche." In this article, Nipkow argues a theology of the child is needed for the so-called movement of "Kindertheologie" (Children's theology). In particular, this theology of the child has a New Testament perspective, and a systematic theological perspective. The New Testament perspective draws from a variety of Scripture passages, e.g., passages on the concept of "children of God" (in the letters of Paul), and the story of the blessing of the children (gospel of Mark). The systematic theological perspective has to do with the self-reflection of children on faith, producing theology as they do so. The theology of the child is complementary to the children's theology movement: "Diese fordert die Theologie heraus, sich der komplexen Welt der Kinder in der vollen Pluralität unserer Zeit auszusetzen und mit Kindern zu lernen."[25]

Where Nipkow reflects on children "producing" theology, in 2014 Friedrich Schweitzer addressed the theme of "adolescents as theologians."[26] Schweitzer theoretically and practically distinguishes between three dimensions when conceiving young people as theologians: (1) theology of adolescents, (2) theology with adolescents, and (3) theology for adolescents. The first dimension reflects the idea of adolescents being theologians, having their own theologies. The second dimension reflects the idea of helping adolescents further in developing one's own views, theologies, convictions, etc. by being in relationship and conversation with them, putting their own questions on the agenda as a starting point. The third dimension, according to Schweitzer, is meant to enrich and extend the theology of adolescents and theology with adolescents. Theology for adolescents is about providing insights theology has to

---

25. Nipkow, "Theologie des Kindes und Kindertheologie," 442.
26. Schweitzer, "Adolescents as Theologians."

offer. This is not necessary in the first instance because of the institutional expectations of churches but because of the expectations of adolescents themselves. Furthermore, Schweitzer stresses the need to distinguish between "adolescents as theologians and theological views concerning adolescence as a phase in the human lifecycle . . . . [B]oth perspectives refer to different things and both of them are needed."[27]

Besides theological views on youth, and youth as theologians, there is another theological perspective one may take on young people in relation to faith: it is what Bert Roebben in 2005 called a "theology of youth ministry."[28] Here, the plea of Roebben is for the (youth) minister to take the theology of adolescents seriously by engaging in their daily lives; and in doing so, becoming involved in theologizing with adolescents and giving them access to a rich array of theological sources (theology for adolescents). This theology of youth ministry is about engaging in and embracing of the daily lives of young people in which God might be found and theology construed.

For a further reading on children and youth in youth ministry practices from a theological perspective we suggest the book edited by Dean, Clark, and Rahn, *Starting Right: Thinking Theologically about Youth Ministry*, and in particular chapter 2, authored by Chap Clark, "The Changing Face of Adolescence: A Theological View of Human Development." This chapter addresses theoretical and empirical perspectives on adolescence from social science literature and how youth ministry can make philosophical (and theologically informed) decisions on the basis of this information. We also recommend *The Theological Turn in Youth Ministry* by Root and Dean who connect practicing youth ministry with conducting theology in the first place; but in doing so they also provide theological lenses through which to look at youth in the course of these practices. In addition, František Štěch's article "Who Are Youth in Theological Perspective?" is recommended. The title speaks for itself!

2.3 On Spirituality

In addition to philosophical, biblical and theological accounts on youth, youth ministry research is also regularly informed by (empirical) accounts on youth spirituality. One of the issues often (empirically)

---

27. Schweitzer, "Adolescents as Theologians," 196.
28. Roebben, "Light of Day."

addressed in youth ministry research when it comes to typifying youth as a particular stage of life is the theme of their spirituality. In chapter 1, the work of Kathleen Engebretson on young people, culture, and spirituality was discussed.[29] Engebretson describes spirituality as "apprehension of a sacred dimension in life, and the implications that this has for the way one lives."[30] From the particular perspective of the Australian context, Engebretson describes characteristics of the spirituality of the young as observed in 2013. Her description of spirituality characteristics among Australian youth in the age group of sixteen to twenty-five can be summarized as follows.

Youth have a private, individualized spirituality, in which they search for meaningful personal experiences. This is linked up with the tendency to privatization of belief and an increase of eclecticism in a (religiously) plural society that is characteristic of post-modernity in which the task of individual developmental is to construe one's own "self" and "meaning" on the basis of myriad interpretations. At the same time, young people have a need for belonging and intimacy and are searching for community by building relationships with peers and with other significant people in their environment. Young people seek social justice and portraying an attitude of tolerance, opposing discrimination of any kind. Furthermore, young people are actively re-examining the thinking about the sacred and about images of God: "to either readopt these in more thoughtful ways, to abandon them all together or to reconstruct them."[31]

With regard to spiritual development, Tobias Faix observes that the internet, social media, and all kinds of online networks and communities are important places where young people construct and reconstruct their identities. As a consequence, the significance for young people of these places also transforms the way they search for spirituality and spiritual growth (see also chapter 1).[32] The research on youth spirituality in youth ministry research is often done against the backdrop of a decrease in (institutional) church allegiance among youth. In 2004, Paul McQuillan observed, on the basis of a survey among Australian high school students aged sixteen to eighteen, that the level of experiential spirituality was

---

29. Engebretson, "Young People, Culture, and Spirituality."
30. Engebretson, "Young People, Culture, and Spirituality," 6.
31. Engebretson, "Young People, Culture, and Spirituality," 18.
32. Faix, "Hybrid Identity."

remarkably high, where at the same time church allegiance was low.[33] It is interesting that to avoid any negative connotations for young people in the survey with regard to religion and experiencing spirituality, the concept of Limit Experience is used: "An experience that reveals a reality of life beyond the self, beyond the here and now. It may be recognition of our own fragility and vulnerability as much as a joyous awareness of a reality beyond our normal encounter with life."[34] A couple of years later, in 2007, McQuillan reviewed a particular selection of youth ministry research with an eye to the theme of youth spirituality: two articles from Australia, two from the United States and two from the United Kingdom.[35] Here, McQuillan comes to the conclusion that in the Western world there is an "increasing tendency to mute the individual's capacity for that form of consciousness, 'relational consciousness,' that allows us to experience the spiritual, transcendent dimensions of our lives."[36]

At the same time, there are tendencies to serve or nurture the spirituality of young people in new ways. In 2012, on the basis of a small scale research (books, flyers, and website analyses), Tone Stangeland Kaufman reported an example of this: the Scandinavian movement *Korsvei* (CrossRoad Movement).[37] Kaufman observes in the CrossRoad movement practices the phenomenon of "retraditionalization": old spiritual practices are approached in new ways. The article focuses on the one-week ecumenical summer festival organized by the CrossRoad movement where people, including youth, from a great variety of Christian backgrounds come together. Kaufman asks how Christian discipleship in this practice is enacted and understood, and why the practice is considered relevant by an increasing number of young people.

The CrossRoad Movement is characterized or defined by four so called signposts: (1) Seeking Jesus Christ, (2) Building Communities, (3) Living More Simply, and (4) Pursuing Justice. Kaufman analyzes these four signposts as an interpretation of both the gospel and of current times, taking seriously "the concern of personal experience and choice, included in the concept of subjectivization,"[38] and at the same time re-

---

33. McQuillan, "Youth Spirituality."
34. McQuillan, "Youth Spirituality," 12.
35. McQuillan, "Youth Ministry in a World of Diversity."
36. McQuillan, "Youth Spirituality," 81.
37. Kaufman, "A New Old Spirituality?"
38. Kaufman, "A New Old Spirituality?," 50.

flecting core values and practices of the Christian tradition: retraditionalization. In a reflection on consequences for youth ministry, Kaufman concludes that practices such as the CrossRoad Movement festivals serve young people in their subjective spiritual quest by providing external authoritative sources in a vitalized or retraditionalized way.

For a further reading on the spiritual and religious development of youth we recommend *The Handbook of Spiritual Development in Childhood and Adolescence*, edited by Eugene Roehlkepartain. In Chapter 4 in this handbook is a particularly worthwhile contribution with regard to how the concepts of spiritual development and religious development are related to each other. The chapter is authored by David Hay, Helmut Rech, and Michael Utsch and is entitled *Spiritual Development: Intersections and Divergence with Religious Development*.

2.4 Conclusion

This chapter has addressed the theme of being young and the concept of adolescence. What characteristics can be associated with being young as a stage of life? First of all, many youth ministry scholars emphasize that young people should be understood as creatures in their own right. Although developmental theories such as those of Erikson and Fowler suggest young people are on a developmental path towards maturity, according to youth ministry scholars being young means more than being "not yet." This is underlined, for example, by biblical theological accounts including exegeses of stories of youths in biblical narratives. These result in so-called theologies of youth that are important lenses in addition to or as a complement to the lens of development theories in youth ministry.

Thus, these and other accounts as discussed in this chapter challenge the often-articulated vision of young people being not responsible or at least not fully capable of being responsible. At the same time, the different accounts confirm the idea of young people being in search of their own unique identity. Furthermore, different authors argue that congregations should make better use of the particular capabilities of young people and integrate young people into the congregational community much more. This is for the simple reason that youth are not only receivers of theology but also producers of theologies, based on a particular youth spirituality and rooted in who they are and how they are: namely, being young.

3

Religious Identity, Faith Development, and Spirituality

"I believe faith is a human universal. We are endowed at birth with nascent capacities for faith. How these capacities are activated and grow depends to a large extent on how we are welcomed into the world and what kinds of environments we grow in. Faith is interactive and social; it requires community, language, ritual and nurture. Faith is also shaped by initiatives from beyond us and other people, initiatives of spirit or grace. How these later initiatives are recognized and imaged, or unperceived and ignored, powerfully affects the shape of faith in our lives."[1]

THE quote above is found in the introductory chapter of the influential book of James Fowler: *Stages of Faith: The Psychology of Human Development and the Quest for Meaning*. In this book, Fowler presents a theory of growth in faith. In chapter 2, we have already referred to Fowler's theory in the context of youth being a specific stage of life. Section 3.3 will offer some more details on the developmental model of Fowler. But what do we mean by growth in faith, as Fowler puts it? This question is at the very heart of this chapter. And there is a good reason to pay special attention to the idea of growth in faith: in chapter 8 we will learn, namely, that faith and the development or growth of faith is an important goal that functions in youth ministry practices.

1. Fowler, *Stages of Faith*, xiii.

What can be learned from the title of this chapter is that we approach its main theme broadly: we will come to speak not only about faith development, but also about religious identity development and spiritual development. This is because the youth ministry literature varies in which concept it puts to the fore. At the same time, the different concepts in the chapter title do not mean exactly the same. What is religious identity other than faith? And how is spiritual growth different from faith development? The bold statement of James Fowler is: faith is a human universal. But what does that claim mean for the development of young people in relation to faith and faith traditions? This chapter presents studies on how youth develops, in particular in relation to faith and spirituality. In this respect, the chapter will describe studies on a variety of themes: identity, identity development, religious identity, faith development, and spiritual development. Psychological, theological, and sociological accounts of these issues will be discussed. In the next section, 3.1., we start by giving a brief explanation of how we see these different themes interconnect. Section 3.2 reviews the research which can be categorized under the heading of (religious) identity development, whereas Section 3.3 brings together studies that have been published under the heading of faith development. Following that, the main topic of section 3.4 is spiritual formation with section 3.5 providing a conclusion to the chapter.

3.1 A Brief Introduction to the Concepts

To start with, we need to clarify the concept of *identity*. Following Erik Erikson's ego identity theory (1968), one might conceive identity as an "invigorating sense of personal sameness and historical continuity."[2] According to Anne-Marije De Bruin et al., this conception of ego identity envisions identity as originating from different identities that are comprised in one identity.[3] These different identities are, for example, racial, national, or religious identities. De Bruin et al. argue that this vision is in contrast with a vision of identity where multiple identities are organized in a hierarchical manner, as Lori Peek suggests, and where one specific identity is more salient than another.[4]

---

2. Erikson, *Identity, Youth, and Crisis*, 19.
3. De Bruin-Wassinkmaat et al., "Being Young and Strictly Religious."
4. Peek, "Becoming Muslim."

In relation to the main theme of youth ministry, it is important to be aware of these two visions of how identity can be conceived. When youth ministry is about the religious development of young people, what, then, is going on exactly? Is youth ministry serving the development of a particular religious fragment of the identity of young people or is it serving the development of religious identity as a hierarchically all-encompassing part of young people's identity? Setting aside this distinction between these two visions, what do we mean by religious identity? We speak about *religious identity* when we envision identity as colored by or directed by a religious worldview of a person that gives a foundation for a person's attitudes, behaviors, beliefs, and experiences. A religious identity can be a category of how someone perceives himself or a category with which we try to understand another person's identity. "Religious" is understood broadly here, referring to both worldviews that include an idea of a transcendent reality and worldviews that include a belief in a God. Where identity development in general can be described as "an active process in which an adolescent deals with past and present identifications in order to create an identity for adulthood,"[5] *religious identity development* in particular can be defined as a process of dealing with identifications "in which individuals explore and commit to a set of religious beliefs and practices."[6]

In the literature on the religious identity development of young people, more restricted concepts are sometimes used, namely: faith and faith development. When it comes to the faith tradition of Christianity, *faith* can be envisioned as an identity colored by or directed by a Christian worldview rooted in the Christian belief in God and which directs a person's attitudes, behaviors, beliefs, and experiences. As a consequence, *Christian faith development* can be described as an active process in which young people deal with past and present identifications, among others with Christians and/or Christian communities, exploring and committing to Christian beliefs and practices. Section 3.2 will review the research which can be categorized under the heading of (religious) identity development, whereas Section 3.3 will bring together studies that has been published under the heading of faith development.

The concepts of identity, religious identity, and faith are used regularly to cover a whole set of multiple aspects: attitudes, behaviors, beliefs,

---

5. De Bruin-Wassinkmaat et al., "Being Young and Strictly Religious," 11.
6. Visser-Vogel et al., "Sources for Religious Identity Development," 91.

experiences, practices, etcetera. Sometimes in the youth ministry literature, the concept of *spirituality* is used to refer to this same set of multiple aspects. In this way, spirituality is more or less used as a synonym for (religious) identity or even faith. But sometimes, the term spirituality is reserved for the aspect of (religious) belief; sometimes it is set aside for the aspect of experience; and sometimes it is seen as a synonym for "lived faith." The term spirituality is thus used in many different ways in youth ministry literature. Section 3.2. is focused on studies that have been published under the heading of spirituality and spiritual formation.

3.2 (Religious) Identity Development

Construction of the Self

Not infrequently, the (religious) identity development of young people is considered as—sometimes even problematized as—a process of self-construction. An example of such an approach is offered in an article published in 2016 by Tobias Faix who addresses the concept of "hybrid identity."[7] The author illustrates how nowadays young people are living simultaneously in real places in everyday life and virtual places online, where global and digital developments are impacting them directly on a continuous basis. The merging of boundaries between the "real" world and the online world leads to the formation of a so-called hybrid identity: an identity which is the result of a creative process of personally negotiating who you are in a global and highly digital context. In his article, Faix discusses a variety of consequences for youth ministry practices of this new reality of hybrid identities.

In 2002, with an eye on second-generation Korean American young adults in the Korean American church, Steve Kang proposed a view on identity based on the literature of socioculturual constructionism and the multivoiced self.[8] Identity is about the construction of the "self," which is "the ongoing result of historically situated interchanges among active, cooperative and creative endeavors of human beings in relationship in and to the world."[9] For the Korean American church serving young adults, this means providing creative and imaginative methods to connect faith

---

7. Faix, "Hybrid Identity."
8. Kang, "The Socioculturally Constructed Multivoiced Self."
9. Kang, "The Socioculturally Constructed Multivoiced Self," 83.

traditions with current experiences, and, in order to live out the Christian faith, providing space for working on one's reflexive projects of the self, engaging in an analysis of how young adults have been socioculturally constructed.

In terms of the construction of the "self" and with an eye on the non-Western young people growing up in North America's dominant culture, Greer Anne Wenh-In Ng (2004) argues for the important role of culture-specific stories from learners' own heritage.[10] These stories, in addition to mere biblical stories, are crucial for a more holistic identity formation for these youngsters in immigrant Christian faith communities. Ng states that without the acquisition of these culture-specific stories, young people "run the danger of failing to arrive at the stage of their bicultural/multicultural identity."[11] In 2011, Reginald Blount also addressed the theme of identity formation in the midst of conflicting cultures.[12] Blount in particular reflects on African American youth in a context of racism and conflicting cultural forces. Based on the work of theologian Howard Thurman,[13] Blount pleads for churches to help these youth in the identity development process of "whole-making," which is "the foundational human desire to be in both interpersonal and intrapersonal community."[14]

Beliefs, Commitments, and Identity

In 2004, Shraga Fisherman published research on the relationship between spiritual identity and ego identity on the basis of a questionnaire study among 78 religiously observant adolescents (tenth graders) in Israel.[15] These boys and girls were studying in religious dormitory institutions. In this study two scales were used: (a) the Adolescents Ego Identity Scale (AEIS) developed by David Tzuriel,[16] and (b) the Religious Beliefs Questionnaire (RBQ) developed by Fisherman herself in 1996. The concept of spiritual identity in this study refers to what Fisherman calls the cornerstone of the process of religious identity development, namely the

10. Wenh-In Ng, "Beyond Bible Stories."
11. Wenh-In Ng, "Beyond Bible Stories," 128.
12. Blount, "Toward Whole-Making."
13. Thurman, *The Search for Common Ground*.
14. Blount, "Toward Whole-Making," 35.
15. Fisherman, "Ego Identity and Spiritual Identity."
16. See, e.g., Tzuriel, "The Development of Ego Identity."

religious beliefs. Fisherman concludes that throughout the study's sample there is a significant, moderate, positive correlation between belief and general ego identity; this finding shows religious belief being a vital component of the ego identities of religiously observant adolescents.

Trying to explain the process of the weakening of religious identity among young people, Richard Rymarz, in 2007, proposed speaking about a "Catholic Plateau" in the religious identity development of young people.[17] The concept of "Catholic Plateau" was introduced as part of the interpretation of interviews with six, what he calls, active Catholic adolescents of seventeen and eighteen years old. These six adolescents were interviewed three years earlier for the first time, together with fifty-two other interviewees from regional Australia. The narratives of these six adolescents show different phases of the "Catholic Plateau" typified by "reaching a level of maximum commitment relatively early and then experiencing a stabilization often followed by a gradual reduction in commitment."[18]

A review book that is often referred to in the literature when it comes to the theme of religious beliefs and commitments in childhood and adolescence and that we recommend for further reading is *Religion in Childhood and Adolescence: A Comprehensive Review of the Research* by Kenneth Hyde, a publication from 1990. This book contains an examination of empirical research studies (in the broad field of psychology of religion) in the United States and other English-speaking countries. Topics that are addressed are among others, religious beliefs, attitudes and values, religious experiences and behaviors, and religious schooling.

Growing Interest in Strictly Religious Adolescents

In 2012, Elsbeth Visser-Vogel et al. proposed a research framework to further investigate religious identity development processes among highly committed or so called "orthopraxy" religious youngsters.[19] The conceptual article is presented as a first step toward gaining qualitative insights into religious identity development among orthopraxy believers; the authors observe a research gap when it comes to this particular group. Although the article's focus is on this particular group, the theoretical

17. Rymarz, "Reaching the Plateau."
18. Rymarz, "Reaching the Plateau," 9.
19. Visser-Vogel et al., "Developing a Framework."

framework for investigating religious identity and religious identity development is helpful for investigating different groups of adolescents. The core of the proposed framework is centered around four components. First, the framework is based on the Identity Status approach as developed in James Marcia's Identity Status Interview model.[20] Second, a narrative approach is proposed, based on the work of Dan P. McAdams.[21] Third, special attention is given to exploration processes with use of the theory of Cohen-Malayev, Assor, and Kaplan (2009).[22] Fourth, partly based on the previously mentioned work of Dan P. McAdams and on the work of Schachter and Ventura (2008), a contextual approach to religious identity development is proposed.[23]

The conceptual article by Visser-Vogel et al. has been one of the articles included in the review study of Anne-Marije de Bruin-Wassinkmaat et al. published in 2019, aiming at understanding, in particular, the religious identity development of adolescents who are strictly religious.[24] This review study was presented against the background of adolescents who were strictly religious and growing up in highly religious contexts that are in contrast with the surrounding pluralist and secularized culture in many societies today. Fifteen studies were included in the literature review. One of the main findings of the review study is that there is little empirical and theoretical research into the religious identity development of adolescents who are strictly religious. At the same time, the studies that exist appear to be diffuse and ambiguous when it comes to conceptualizations and the research methods used. The article concludes with a couple of suggestions that are important stepping stones for further investigating this particular population.

Critique

Much of the literature on the (religious) identity development of young people incorporates a developmental psychological perspective, as many of the studies described above do. However, some authors offer a critique

---

20. Marcia, "Development and Validation"; Adelson, *Handbook of Adolescent Psychology*.
21. See, e.g., McAdams, "Personal Narratives and the Life Story," 241–61.
22. Cohen-Malayev et al., "Religious Exploration in a Modern World."
23. Schachter and Ventura, "Identity Agents."
24. De Bruin-Wassinkmaat et al., "Being Young and Strictly Religious."

of the developmental psychologist perspective in young people's upbringing in Christian faith communities. A good example is Brett Webb-Mitchell who, in 2001, criticized theories of developmental psychology for being influenced too much by Enlightenment ideals, and religious education in churches for being influenced too much by developmental psychologist theories.[25] The author detects five characteristics or ideals of the Enlightenment in development psychologist theories: (a) individualism, (b) opposition to authority, (c) centrality of the mind, (d) natural religion, and (e) universalism. These are the characteristics stamping the language and practice in churches in envisioning growth for young people. Webb-Mitchell argues this needs to be corrected, seeing growth more in terms of community, obedience to authority, with a vision of the interconnection of mind, body, and spirit in Christ and with an accent on both the particularity of Christianity and the particularity of contexts and individual lives.

In this regard, Webb-Mitchell proposes the use of the rhetoric of "Christian pilgrimage" as an alternative for developmental psychologies. This can be understood as replacing a developmental psychologist perspective on growth with a theological perspective on growth that is rooted in Old and New Testament accounts of pilgrimage. "Christian pilgrimage is different from developmental psychology in five ways: (1) as a community and its story, (2) in obedience to authority, (3) as mind-bodyspirt in Christ, (4) as God in Christ, and (5) as a chosen people of a particular god."[26]

3.3 Faith development

James Fowler

The concept of faith development is closely connected to the theory of James Fowler on stages of faith development.[27] Using Erikson's conceptual framework[28] and based on empirical research with people of different ages (N=359; 3.5 to 84 years of age) and different religious backgrounds (Protestant, Catholic, Jewish, Orthodox), Fowler defines

---

25. Webb-Mitchell, "Leaving Development Behind."
26. Webb-Mitchell, "Leaving Development Behind," 145.
27. Fowler, *Stages of Faith*.
28. Erikson, *Identity, Youth, and Crisis*.

six stages of faith development: (1) Intuitive-Projective Faith (foremost until six/seven years), (2) Mythic-Literal Faith (from seven years), (3) Synthetic-Conventional Faith (from eleven years), (4) Individuative-Reflective Faith (from seventeen years), (5) Conjunctive Faith (rarely before the age of thirty), (6) Universalizing Faith (rarely occurrent).[29] This stage theory on faith development has been widely used and at the same time widely criticized. Critical accounts of Fowler's faith development theory are also given in the discourse of religious education and youth ministry research. One of these accounts comes from Timothy Jones in 2004.[30]

Starting from an evangelical perspective, Jones concludes that the faith development model of Fowler cannot easily be used as a model for the development of the Christian faith. "Fowlerian stage-development may neither be equated with Christian faith-development nor amended to correspond to Christian faith-development.[31] The author postulates that the concept of faith to which Fowler refers is to be understood as the psychical context within which the Christian faith may occur and may develop. Therefore, Jones ends with the suggestion that evangelical faith-development theorists recognize the distinctive development features of, on the one hand, the concept of faith in Fowler's theory and on the other hand the concept of Christian faith, and to see how these two are related to each other.

With an eye to the application of Fowler's theory in a religious education context, in 2004 Heinz Streib critiqued the idea that more advanced styles or "stages" of faith cannot be expected or taught. "New engagement in empirical scrutiny may reveal a greater flexibility and complexity of faith development and thus confirm the enlargement of our vision of developmental growth."[32] An article by Andrew Kaethler expresses the same concern not to be too bound up by fixed characteristics in the faith development phase of adolescents.[33] Andrew Kaethler proposes combining insights from what we know about adolescent faith development and insights from philosophical hermeneutics into what he calls an "adolescent hermeneutic." With such a hermeneutic, the author wants to take the perspectives of youth seriously and to offer the

---

29. Fowler, *Stages of Faith*, 117–211.
30. Jones, "The Basis."
31. Jones, "The Basis," 355.
32. Streib, "Extending Our Vision," 433.
33. Kaethler, "Towards an Adolescent Hermeneutic."

possibility of "expanding the hermeneutic circle to include the voices, questions and interpretation of a wide range of youth."[34] Kaethler explains that the (faith) developmental task of adolescents is centered around "becoming" and, in that light, he defines four markers of an adolescent hermeneutic: it is (1) personal, (2) purposeful, (3) practical, and (4) pronto. The markers (1) and (2) are about adolescents dealing with a personal search for language to describe God and their relationship to Him and with which they can articulate a purpose in their personal life. The markers (3) and (4) point at temporality of faith development of adolescents in terms of identity and development being embodied and lived out. In this way, the author argues, faith development of each adolescent manifest itself uniquely in the context of the Christian community and tradition, including the Biblical narrative.

Empirical Research on Faith Development and Faith Formation

Shraga Fisherman, in 2016, examined the connection between raising doubts regarding religious faith and religious identity among religious (Modern Orthodox) adolescent boys in Israel in nineth, tenth, and eleventh grades (N=472).[35] The study was based on three questionnaires: The Faith Identity Questionnaire, The Religious Behavior Questionnaire, and a questionnaire developed for this particular study: Questionnaire on Past and Future Faith Doubts. This study did not follow the development of the same adolescents over the years, which means that the study cannot prove any form of faith development among young people. The author, however, concludes that there is a trend to be seen when comparing the three different age groups with each other: "the stage for intensified faith doubts is in 10th grade."[36] Fisherman, furthermore, concludes in general that the 10th grade is an important crossroads in the formation of identity.

The concept of faith development, is sometimes linked with other theoretical concepts, among which are, e.g., spiritual type theories[37] or

---

34. Kaethler, "Towards an Adolescent Hermeneutic," 34.
35. Fisherman, "Development of Religious Identity."
36. Fisherman, "Development of Religious Identity," 131.
37. See Baker, "Raised a Teenage Kataphatic."

attachment theories.[38] The last-mentioned study by Victor Counted suggests that one's experience of faith formation is actually a "care-giving experience, watered by reciprocity of proximity with a divine attachment figure."[39] In the study, in-depth interviews were conducted with fifteen Christian youths who were active members of different church denominations in South Africa, in the regions Stellenbosch and Western Cape. Counted illustrates how the phenomenon of attachment in the personal development of young people is closely connected with faith formation in their lives. Based on the analyses of the interview data, a young person's faith formation pathway might be seen as a remedy for a previous "insecure attachment experience" and as "a strategy of enhancing an already positive attachment with human relational partners."[40]

In 2005, David White published research on how youth negotiate God's call to vocation.[41] White believes that youth ministry is not merely about helping youth to form a Christian identity, but to help them develop a faith in which they know how to respond to God's call upon their whole lives. In the study, 40 in-depth interviews were conducted with primarily sixteen-year-olds in the United States, all of whom attended a summer academy at the Youth Theological Initiative at Emory University in the period 2001–4. In the analysis of the interviews, White detected four distinct profiles of youth imagining their lives in response to God's call in terms of values, views of work, roles of faith, and views of the world. The first profile is defined as "vocation as consuming" referring to youth who envision the good life as a life with wealth and status. The second profile is defined as "vocation engaging gifts" referring to youth who seek to do well in combination with finding a recognized role in the community as a result. The third profile is defined as "vocation in response to suffering" and has to do with youth willing to be concerned with the world's suffering. The fourth profile appeared to be "Vocation as finding a place in the web of life." This profile is referring to youth developing "a sense of their lives set within a complex web of systems and structures—some benevolent, others malevolent."[42] In the final part of

---

38. See Counted, "The Psychology of Youth Faith Formation."
39. Counted, "The Psychology of Youth Faith Formation," 146.
40. Counted, "The Psychology of Youth Faith Formation," 146.
41. White, "Profiles in Vocation."
42. White, "Profiles in Vocation," 21.

the research report, White mirror the results with James Fowler's view of vocation as presented in Fowler (1984).[43]

3.4 Spiritual Formation

As said, the term spirituality is used in many different ways in youth ministry literature. Sometimes, spirituality is more or less used as a synonym for (religious) identity or faith; sometimes, the term is reserved for the aspect of (religious) beliefs; sometimes it is set aside for the aspect of experience; and sometimes it is seen as synonym for "lived faith." In a 2013 publication in the Nederduitse Gereformeerde Teologiese Tydskrif (South Africa), Anita Cloete observed a growing attention within societies for spirituality and spirituality development, and in this context she pleads for the enhancement of Christian spirituality in youth ministry focusing on experiencing life as humans before God. This "could potentially counter fragmentation and foster personal integration, especially in teenagers today."[44] In the last section the current chapter, some studies that have been published under the heading of spirituality and spiritual formation are presented briefly.

In 2001, Stephen Fortosis tried to theologically underpin the stage model of spiritual formation that he had presented earlier in 1992 in the same journal *Religious Education*.[45] Rooted in a Protestant Evangelical tradition, the theory consists of three stages: (1) formative integration referring to "new" Christians or Christians who do not mature with time; (2) responsible consistency, referring to those who take responsibility for their own growth and show consistency in their Christian experience; and (3) self-transcendent wholeness, referring to few Christians who reach a stage of a "supernatural walk with God."

In 2002, James Riley Estep reflected on the implications of the developmental theory of Vygotsky for the understanding of spiritual formation.[46] Estep states that Vygotsky's understanding of development centers on the premise that the formation of one's mind or cognition is linked with the social context in which an individual lives. Although Vygotsky himself did not address the theme of spiritual formation, Estep tries to

43. Fowler, *Becoming Adult, Becoming Christian*.
44. Cloete, "Spiritual Formation as Focus of Youth Ministry," 76.
45. Fortosis, "Theological Foundations for a Stage Model."
46. Estep, "Spiritual Formation as Social."

show implications of his view on human development for spirituality and spiritual formation. These implications can be summarized in six propositions: (1) Spiritual formation begins outside the individual; (2) Spiritual formation and its ecology are holistic; (3) Spiritual formation is not a linear or unidirectional process; (4) The community of faith is an essential element for spiritual formation; (5) Spiritual formation occurs when faith is mediated between individuals; and (6) Teachers and deliberate instruction are essential for spiritual formation."[47]

One of the current influential concepts used in youth ministry practices, Godly Play, presents itself as helping nourish the spirituality of children. In part 4 of the handbook, we will more elaborately discuss the concept of Godly Play and there, among others, the conclusion of study by Brendan Hyde will be presented. He did a case study of one three-and-a-half year old showing exactly how Godly Play might nourish children's spirituality.[48] Godly Play is one of the numerous initiatives faith communities can embrace to practice faith formation and to work towards spiritual growth of young people. In 2017, Steven Emery-Wright and Ed Mackenzie published on several networks for faith formation that are needed for the spiritual growth of young people.[49] He describes not only networks in churches where young people can participate in practices like Godly Play, but also networks of families, friends, small groups, and youth gatherings.

3.5 Conclusion

In youth ministry practices and also in youth ministry research, the terms "growth" or "development" are often used in relation to the faith or spirituality of young people. But what do we mean by growth in faith or development of spirituality? To address this question and provide some answers, this chapter began by quoting James Fowler who greatly influenced the field of religious education and youth ministry with his book *Stages of Faith: The Pscyhology of Human Development and the Quest for Meaning*. But in the course of the chapter we added many other accounts from the youth ministry literature that address the issue of faith, religious identity, and spiritual development.

---

47. Estep, "Spiritual Formation as Social," 160–62.
48. Hyde, "Godly Play."
49. Emery-Wright and Mackenzie, *Networks for Faith Formation*.

We first explored the different meanings of main concepts, such as identity, religious identity, religious identity development, faith, Christian faith development, and spirituality. Next, the chapter presented several studies on how youth develops in relationship to religious identity, faith, and spirituality. We observed that the whole idea of "construction of the self" is a prominent theme in the reflection on religious identity and religious identity development. We also observed a growing interest in this development, in particular among adolescents who are strictly religious. It also became clear that speaking about religious identity development in the context of youth ministry asks for both a psychological and theological perspective. These two perspectives of developmental psychology and theology appear to come to the fore both in the literature that critically discusses the already mentioned stage model of faith development, originally presented by James Fowler and in the literature that deals with the concept of spiritual formation.

As pointed out, this chapter is an important stepping stone for the further discussion of goals that are set in youth ministry practices, and this is the main topic in part 3 of the handbook. Faith and the whole idea of faith growth or development is one of the prominent goals held by youth ministers (see chapter 8). We agree with James Fowler when he states that one's faith is partly shaped by initiatives from other people, for example from youth ministers. "How these . . . initiatives are recognized and imaged, or unperceived and ignored, powerfully affects the shape of faith in our lives." The remainder of this handbook will address these dynamics in its complexity: the dynamics between shaping youth ministry practices, the perception and reception of these practices by young people, the role of the person of the youth minister in it and how God is perceived and experienced.

4

Individual and Communal Aspects of Faith Development among Youth

"The power of the young people's meaningful worship experiences is not limited to the individual. Like a stone thrown into the middle of the pond they send out their ripples that can be felt among other worshippers and their church. . . . The young people and their passionate experiences with God are desperately needed by the whole church to keep us alive and focused on God."[1]

THE faith of youth can be approached by looking at individual dimensions of faith and by looking at the communal dimension of faith. This chapter brings together some empirical studies on faith and faith development among young people that shed light on one or both dimensions. When it comes to the communal dimension, we found in chapter 3 with Steve Emery-Wright that different networks for faith formation can be distinguished, for example churches, families, friends, small groups, and youth gatherings.[2] These different networks together form the context for what in the literature is called the (religious) socialization of a next generation. How is religious socialization related to the faith (development) of young people? If we look at the youth ministry literature we discover that although there is an individual or subjective dimension

---

1. Emery-Wright, *Now That Was Worship*, 15–16.
2. Emery-Wright and Mackenzie, *Networks for Faith Formation*.

to faith, subjective theologies of youth either have or spring from a communal context.

An interesting illustration of this point is the formation of concepts of God. Simone Roos studied the relationship between (religious) socialization and the development of God concepts. In 2006 she published the results of two studies testing hypotheses on attachment and young children's God concepts.[3] These studies were carried out among preschoolers and kindergartners in the Netherlands. The author concludes that religious socialization both in the home and in the school-context is important for the formation of children's god concepts. When it comes to the distinct impact of religious socialization on the one hand and an (early) positive relationship with a significant caregiver on the other, she concludes as follows: "It may be that for the acquisition of a potent and helping God image in young children religious socialization is more influential, whereas for the view of God as an attachment figure (a loving friend) and for the maintenance and personal meaning of certain god concepts in adolescence and adulthood an early positive relationship with at least one significant caregiver is more important."[4]

The quote from Steven Emery-Wright with which this chapter opens suggests another link between the individual and the communal dimension: it is not only the social context that influences individual faith development, it is also true the other way round: individual faith or faith practices influence the community of faith. This chapter reviews empirical studies on faith among youth from the perspective of the individual and the communal dimensions. Section 4.1 addresses the theme of subjective theologies among children and youth. Section 4.2 addresses the role of the youth group for faith development. Section 4.3 pays particular attention to practices of youth worship and how these relate to faith development. The chapter concludes in section 4.4.

4.1 Faith and Subjective Theologies

This section discusses a number of studies on faith among youth and on the subjective theologies of youth. One of the challenges in empirical research on the concept of faith is to define what it is and to find out how to detect its existence and development among youth. When it comes to

---

3. De Roos, "Young Children's God Concepts."
4. De Roos, "Young Children's God Concepts," 101.

the latter, the difficulty of finding out how faith exists in the lives of young people, the study by Mary Elizabeth Moore and Joseph Kyser, published in 2014, is of particular interest.[5]

Researching Faith among Youth

Empirical research on faith of young people is often based on their verbal expression of religion and religious convictions. Moore and Kyser, drawing from interviews, show how youth discover and use their religious voices in public and what religious motivations they have for public personas and actions.[6] In this study, thirty-five interviews with mostly US Christian youth were analyzed as part of a larger study on young people and their social contexts.

Moore and Kyser's study had two categories of results. First, results with regard to "coming out religiously." Second, results with regard to young people's "self-descriptions." When it comes to coming out religiously, the authors show three patterns among youth. The first pattern is about discovering oneself and one's own (religious) voice by experiencing difference with others. A second pattern has to do with speaking out by doing something that one does well or that has special meaning for someone. A third pattern is explained on the basis of research subject Andrew: a pattern that is seen in Andrew's story "is the seriousness with which he takes his religion (praying, studying the Bible, asking theological questions) and the seriousness with which he takes social and political issues."[7] The study also shows that giving voice to one's internal conflicts and motivations with regard to religious convictions helps youth to strengthen their sense of self. Apparently, young people adjust their voice according to whether they are speaking out within a religious context or outside of that context.

The study resulted in two findings with regard to young people's "self-descriptions." The first finding is the observation that the process of "coming out" or expressing one's own inner religious convictions is often not an impetus to speaking publicly but instead to visible action and active dreaming about future action. "they express their public personas less

---

5. Moore and Kyser, "Youth Finding and Claiming Religious Voice."
6. Moore and Kyser, "Youth Finding and Claiming Religious Voice."
7. Moore and Kyser, "Youth Finding and Claiming Religious Voice," 458.

in public words and more in public actions and plans for future action."[8] A second finding is that the link between inner religious convictions on the one hand, and outer religious expressions on the other is not always straightforward. For example, the study showed young people asking disruptive questions while at the same time being clear in themselves about their own religious passions. So there appears to be a complex relationship between inner religious voice on the one hand and public persona and action on the other.

These complex relationships between inner convictions and outer personas and actions is also at stake when researching the faith of young people. Empirical research on the faith of youth should at least try to take this complexity into account. Another study from the Norwegian context illustrates this same issue. In 2016, Jon Magne Vestøl analyzed how Christian denominations are represented in Norwegian textbooks of religious education and by young believers.[9] This study investigated all religious education textbooks used in Norwegian upper secondary schools. Furthermore, two ninety-minute group interviews were held with members of the Catholic church (five participants) and the Lutheran Church of Norway (five participants), aged seventeen and eighteen, all from a major Norwegian city. The author found out that these textbooks and the young believers present religion in quite different ways. Textbooks appear to present religion in rational and general descriptions and in relation to a global or national context. Young people present religion with emotional and relational descriptions and in relation to local and personal contexts.

For further reading on adolescents' conceptions of God, the work of Tobias Faix, *Gottesvorstellungen Bei Jugendlichen: Eine Qualitative Erhebung Aus Der Sicht Empirischer Missionswissenschaft*, is of interest. In this study, the question of the effects of one's own biography on the conceptions of God by society, church, and family is examined as well as the religious effects of the conceptions of God in the everyday life of the young people and their missionary responsiveness. Part of the study contains semi-structured interviews with eighteen adolescents. One of the results is the presentation of an empirical-theological research methodology of which youth ministry researchers can take advantage.

---

8. Moore and Kyser, "Youth Finding and Claiming Religious Voice," 463.
9. Vestøl, "Textbook Religion and Lived Religion."

Youth and Faith: Typologies

We now turn to a discussion of two more empirical studies on youth and faith, one from Germany, and one from The Netherlands. In 2014, Tobias Faix reported on a mixed methods study among adolescents commissioned by the Protestant Church of Westphalia in Germany.[10] As a first step, a theoretical framework based on a review of twenty empirical studies on youth and religiosity was made. Second, a qualitative survey was conducted (twenty individual interviews and five group interviews, in total forty-seven participants), including a collage method with which adolescents were stimulated to come up with their own words and concepts with regard to faith. A quantitative study was conducted as a third step. Based on both the theoretical framework and the qualitative study, a questionnaire of fifty questions was composed. 1085 respondents, aged fourteen to nineteen and from the district area of the Protestant Church of Westphalia, were included in the final analysis. The denominational background was as follows: 52.2% protestant, 14.7% Catholic, 8.5% free church, 1,6% Muslim, 21.4% no denomination, 1.3% others.

The analysis of the data from the qualitative study showed that according to Faix three types of youth: (a) the Religious, who show traditional faith as it can be found in various churches, (b) the Everyday Believers, for whom faith has a functional effect in everyday issues, such as family life or happiness, and (c) the Pragmatist, who experiences several contradictions in life and faith for which they have developed different copings strategies.

The analysis of the quantitative study resulted in three findings. First, adolescents' faith relates strongly to their social environment: friendships, family. Second, seven so-called faith-constructs were found among adolescents (here presented in order of appearance in the data): (1) gains meaning through social relationships, (2) belief in inter-personal values, (3) gains meaning through a sustainable lifestyle, (4) gains meaning through success and achievements, (5) belief in the supernatural, (6) Christian faith, (7) belief in happiness and fate.[11] Third, it is found that none of these faith-constructs are detached from others, showing adolescents having "a patch-work-like faith-construct"[12] overall.

---

10. Faix, "Semantics of Faith."
11. Faix, "Semantics of Faith," 48.
12. Faix, "Semantics of Faith," 48.

Also, the 2015 article of Monique van Dijk-Groeneboer presented empirical data that help to typify adolescents with regard to religion.[13] This research was conducted in The Netherlands, among Dutch pupils at Catholic secondary schools, focusing on their religion, beliefs, and values in life. This survey has been conducted every five years since 1997; the article reports on the outcomes of the 2012/2013 survey presented to 1450 pupils (a response of 95%), aged fifteen to eighteen years, in fifteen secondary schools in General Secondary Education and Pre-University Education. Respondents reported themselves as being Catholic (16%), Protestant (6%), Christian (14%), Muslim (3%), atheist (14%), and not affiliated with any church or religion (38%).[14] The study resulted in four main findings.

First, 59% did not call themselves religious where 34% claimed to be religious. At the same time, the results show that categories such as "religious," "believing," or "church-belonging" are not functional in the everyday lives of adolescents. Second, based on an analysis of open questions asking the respondents to describe in their own words what was important in terms of religion, faith, and the meaning of life, a number of important themes come to the fore: faith has its limits; faith is OK but there should be balance between believing and living; and the theme of tolerance of faith. Third, almost half of the respondents said they did not always have the courage to express their faith everywhere. And fourth, music appears to be the main area for inspiration and sacred or religious experiences.

Furthermore, Van Dijk-Groeneboer suggests typifying respondents into four types of youth. In this regard, the author explains: "These are, of course, idealized types of people, but this line of thinking helps to describe the different types of youth found in many different research outcomes. Nevertheless, it is hard to conduct quantitative research in which respondents can specifically be divided into these four groups. Above all, young people themselves do not want to be put into a box."[15] The four types are presented as follows: two types of youth committed to an institute (belonging), the Fortissimos who are believing, active, and concerned with religion in forming their identity, and the Legatos who are non-believing, non-active, and not concerned with religion in

---

13. Van Dijk-Groeneboer, "Youth Ministry."
14. Van Dijk-Groeneboer, "Youth Ministry," 29-30.
15. Van Dijk-Groeneboer, "Youth Ministry," 35.

forming their identity. In addition, there are two types of youth who are not committed to a religious institute (non-belonging): the Spirituosos who are believing, active, and concerned with religion in forming their identity; and the Tranquillos, who are non-believing, non-active, and not concerned with religion in forming their identity.

Subjective Theologies

An article by Carsten Gennerich and Andreas Feige in 2019 is an attempt to propose a couple of concepts related to the subjective theologies of adolescents with which the empirical research on the topic is served.[16] The authors first review the literature on religiously symbolized basic experiences among adolescents and conclude that there are three experiences to be distinguished: "the experience of subjectivity, the question of justice, and the experience of self-discrepancies."[17] Next, the authors report, partly based on an empirical study on the religion and everyday ethics of adolescents, that for each of the three basic experiences, a number of prototypical religious variants might be observed among adolescents.

Another example of an empirical study on the subjective theologies of teenagers is that of Ina ter Avest, Dan-Paul Jozsa, and Thorsten Knautch, published in 2010 in *Religious Education*.[18] This study was part of the European project on "Religion in Education, a contribution to Dialogue or a factor of Conflict in transforming societies in European countries?" (REDCo). Both qualitative and quantitative measures were used to study the subjective theologies of Dutch teenage girls and boys on the role of religion in their life. A qualitative questionnaire with questions on religion, God, religious experience, different religions and religion at school was filled out by seventy-one pupils, aged fourteen to sixteen years. The outcomes of this qualitative questionnaire were used to set up a quantitative questionnaire on the same topics, which was filled out by 565 pupils, aged fourteen to sixteen years from eight secondary schools (higher vocational training level and pre-university training level). In this group of schools both Christian, Islamic, and state schools participated.

The main results of the study can be summarized in three main findings. (a) In general boys and girls do not differ in how they position

---

16. Gennerich and Feige, "Jugend und Religion in neuer Perspektive."
17. Gennerich and Feige, "Jugend und Religion in neuer Perspektive," 45.
18. Ter Avest et al., "Gendered Subjective Theologies."

themselves with regard to religion. For the majority of pupils, God and religion appeared to be of low importance in personal life and religion is not talked about with friends. (b) In girls' subjective theologies, there seems to be more openness toward "the other" and the other's religion. (c) Boys seem to more clearly demarcate the boundaries of their subjective theologies, and, more than girls, tend to "retire from facing differences."[19]

In 2002, Leslie Francis published an article about the relationship between Bible reading and attitude toward drug use.[20] This study was conducted with a sample of 25,888 teenagers in England and Wales, aged thirteen to fifteen years. The study's conclusion is that "Bible reading makes a small but significant contribution to promoting a negative attitude toward drug use among this age group."[21] Also interesting is the outcome that belief in God is a stronger predictor of developing a negative attitude toward drug use than church attendance or Bible reading. In 2001, the same author published a study on the relationship between attitude toward Christianity and dogmatism, based on a questionnaire study among fifteen to sixteen year-old adolescents in the United Kingdom.[22] He concludes there is no relationship between attitude toward Christianity and dogmatism. "Adolescents who hold a positive attitude toward Christianity are neither more closed-minded nor more open-minded than adolescents who hold a negative attitude toward Christianity."[23]

4.2 Faith and Youth Groups

This section discusses the social or communal dimension of faith in relationship to faith development among youth and the importance of youth groups. We start with the review of two articles from the Dutch authors Harmen van Wijnen and Marcel Barnard that explain the importance of youth groups and how groups work in the faith formation of young people.

---

19. Ter Avest et al., "Gendered Subjective Theologies," 389.
20. Francis, "The Relationship Between."
21. Francis, "The Relationship Between," 44.
22. Francis, "Christianity and Dogmatism Revisited."
23. Francis, "Christianity and Dogmatism Revisited," 221.

The Importance of Youth Groups

In 2014, in the *Journal of Youth and Theology*, Van Wijnen and Barnard made a plea for what they call "de-laboratorizing" and de-conceptualizing youth ministry.[24] The authors observed that youth ministry activities had become isolated as a subculture from other church activities on one side and the daily life of young people on the other. This can result in an experienced mismatch among young people between "organized faith" and "faith in action." The article presents empirical research where this experienced mismatch is investigated. The main research question is: "How can the mismatch between faith and adolescents in the environment of church and youth ministry be described, explored, analyzed and (theologically) assessed?"[25]

The study was part of a qualitative research conducted with five small groups of adolescents, aged fifteen to twenty-one years, directly or indirectly related to a protestant local congregation in The Netherlands. As reported in the article, the analysis in the study was directed towards two of these five small groups, both being discussion groups in a youth association. Data were gathered by participant observations and group and individual interviews with both the youth participants and the leadership. The data were then analyzed by both descriptive and *in vivo* coding of activities and behavior in the youth groups. Next, the data were analyzed from the perspective of the faith mismatch of adolescents. The main finding as a result of the analyses was: "it can be said that adolescents need groups that don't have a strategic goal of church or youth ministry. They are searching for groups that are 'just' groups. Or in the words of Root: they are searching for groups that are concrete locations of God's action in the world and not a means of getting them to believe or to obey."[26]

Based on this main finding, the authors draw two conclusions. In the first place, youth ministry needs to de-laboratorize, which means turning away from mainly cognitive oriented, institutionalized youth work towards fresh new concepts of youth work in the midst of everyday life. In the second place, youth ministry needs to de-conceptualize, which

---

24. Van Wijnen and Barnard, "From Organized Faith to Lived Faith."
25. Van Wijnen and Barnard, "From Organized Faith to Lived Faith," 9.
26. Van Wijnen and Barnard, "From Organized Faith to Lived Faith," 17. The reference to Root in this quotation is to the following publication: Root, *Revisiting Relational Youth Ministry*.

means turning away from faith formation on the basis of "faith language as logical grammar system"[27] towards a more narrative approach where the adolescents' own life stories are connected to the narrative of the faith tradition.

In a later article, in 2017, Van Wijnen and Barnard reported on the same study: a qualitative research conducted in five small groups of adolescents, aged fifteen to twenty-one years, directly or indirectly related to a protestant local congregation in The Netherlands.[28] In this report the analysis of the data is directed by the following research question: "How can the communal aspects of youth ministry small groups lead to the development of faith communities?"[29] In the 2017 article, the whole data set of five small groups of adolescents was used in the analysis: in total a group of 148 adolescents and 10 youth leaders. As a first step, the authors provide portraits of two small groups, on the basis of which they present a number of characteristics of communal aspects of faith that function among the adolescents being researched. In a second step, the authors present the results of a coding cycle where they seek to relate the observations in the data with the sensitizing concepts "communal faith" and "faith communities."

The main finding of the analysis is that in comparison with the subject as an individual, the subject in relationship with others (communal) appeared to be powerful in the faith development of young people. The youth group as a natural sociality, a peer group organically connected, is powerful not only for being connected or just being together, but also for developing oneself in terms of faith. This study, thus, shows that youth groups within or outside the church, understood as faith communities or faith tribes, have the potential to balance the individual dimension and communal dimension of faith development of young people. The complete research which formed the basis of the two articles by Van Wijnen and Barnard was published in 2106 in Van Wijnen's dissertation: *Faith in Small Groups of Adolescents: Being Together as a Basic Given*. The main conclusion of this dissertation is that youth ministry needs a twofold turn: a turn from the individual to the communal and a turn from an organized environment to a natural environment.[30]

27. Van Wijnen and Barnard, "From Organized Faith to Lived Faith," 21.
28. Van Wijnen and Barnard, "Faith Tribes as Powerful Communities."
29. Van Wijnen and Barnard, "Faith Tribes as Powerful Communities," 419.
30. Van Wijnen, *Faith in Small Groups*, 136.

Impact of Youth Group Participation

What effects can be expected from youth group participation? This question is the main background for the analysis of a longitudinal quantitative study reported in the *Journal for the Scientific Study of Religion* in 2009 by Patricia Snell.[31] This study examines the effect of youth participation on adult support, church connection, and moral values. The author explains that such an investigation is relevant because congregations have real questions about "whether participation in religious-based youth programs is beneficial for the youth involved."[32] Not just congregations but scholars too should have these questions, because Snell found out that there are only a few empirical studies examining the impact of youth participation.

In her study, Snell examines data from two waves of the National Study of Youth and Religion (NSYR), a longitudinal phone survey in the USA. In the first wave (2001), 3370 English and Spanish-speaking youth, aged thirteen to seventeen, participated. In the second wave (2005), the English-speaking respondents from Wave 1 were contacted again (then aged sixteen to twenty-one): in total, 2604 participated. The analysis in the study concentrated on questions about adult support, church connection, and moral values. What Snell found out is that there is some indication for the hypothesis that youth group participation results in a positive impact on church connection and moral values. Snell's study contributes to research on factors having impact on youth religiosity; it presents data on the relationship with youth group participation, whereas the majority of social science literature is on the relationship with religious service attendance and parental socialization.

The supposed importance of sense of community among young people was one of the backgrounds for Eveliina Ojala's study about Finnish confirmands and their social media use.[33] Ojala conducted a quantitative study (N=468) among Finnish confirmands, aged fourteen to fifteen, who participated in confirmation preparation during the year 2015. Three research questions guided this study: "RQ1: What are an adolescent's perceptions of their parish? RQ2: What kind of social media user types are there among adolescents? RQ3: What do adolescents

---

31. Snell, "What Difference Does Youth Group Make?"
32. Snell, "What Difference Does Youth Group Make?," 572.
33. Ojala, "Finnish Confirmands' Social Media Use."

regard as important when they feel a sense of community?"[34] To answer these questions, a questionnaire was distributed among the confirmands via a random sampling strategy within five parishes. The main finding of the study reads as follows: the research results "draw a picture about young church participants of a certain kind; they are conscious and active in various fields of life. In addition, there are confirmation participants who do not perceive parish as close, they have a lack of enthusiasm to participate in parish activities, use social media cursorily and regard a sense of community as a difficult matter to express."[35]

A Critical Voice

We have already referred to the work of Andrew Root when discussing the findings of the empirical studies by Van Wijnen and Barnard on faith in small groups of adolescents. Root states in his book *Revisiting Relational Youth Ministry: From a Strategy of Influence to a Theology of Incarnation*, published in 2007, that young people are searching for groups not as a means of becoming believers but of experiencing God's action in the world in that particular location. This vision relates to what Root earlier expressed in a journal article in 2004 where he discussed critically the methodology of relational youth ministry: a methodology in which adult (youth) leaders are building relationships with youth with the aim of bringing them to a commitment to faith.[36] Root's critical evaluation reads: "we have appropriated the incarnation as a methodological approach rather than the very centre of our being and source of our ministry."[37] According to Root, relationality should not be a mere tool in youth ministry but, instead, from an incarnational point of view the very purpose of youth ministry.

The communal quality of youth ministry, or in other words, the social dimension or relationality in youth ministry practices is more than once accentuated in the literature. To deepen the understanding of this dimension of youth ministry, both from a theological and an empirical perspective, we suggest two publications for further reading: Andrew Root's article "Relationality as the Objective of Incarnational Ministry: A

34. Ojala, "Finnish Confirmands' Social Media Use," 158.
35. Ojala, "Finnish Confirmands' Social Media Use," 167.
36. Root, "Relationality."
37. Root, "Relationality," 99.

Reexamination of the Theological Foundations of Adolescent Ministry"[38] and Harmen van Wijnen's dissertation "Faith in Small Groups of Adolescents. Being Together as a Basic Given."[39]

4.3 Youth Worship

In this section the theme of youth worship will be discussed on the basis of a number of empirical studies. The quote at the opening of this chapter was taken from the book *Now That Was Worship: Hearing the Voices of Young People* by Steven Emery-Wright. In the book, Emery-Wright concludes on the basis of fieldwork that the worship young people desire is worship in which they create themselves and where the presence of peers is important. These observations are in line with some of the studies we will present in this subsection. We start with a discussion of a study from the Scottish context; after that we discuss two publications on youth worship practices in the Netherlands. Besides studies on youth worship (roughly referring to adolescents and young adults), there are studies on children's worship (roughly referring to kindergarten and primary school age). Two recent examples of these studies are provided by Lydia van Leersum-Bekebrede, Ronelle Sonnenberg, Jos de Kock and Marcel Barnard.[40] These studies will be discussed in more detail in part 3 of the handbook. This is because the perspective of the empirical analyses in these two publications is directed respectively towards the perspective of youth work professionals and policy makers and the perspective of adults acting in worship practices with children in local congregations.

In 2011, Peter Ward and Heidi Campbell demonstrated the usefulness of studying (public) worship events with a view to gaining more insight into the construction of ordinary theology.[41] Their study is situated in the particular study of charismatic and Pentecostal worship. It is part of the SCOT Project, a qualitative research project on the language and expressions used in extempore and informal prayer. During 2002 and 2003, forty hours of youth prayer were recorded at fourteen evangelical youth worship and prayer meetings in different parts of Scotland.

38. Root, "Relationality."
39. Van Wijnen, "Faith in Small Groups."
40. Van Leersum-Bekebrede et al., "Deconstructing Ideals of Worship"; Van Leersum-Bekebrede et al., "Setting the Stage for."
41. Ward and Campbell, "Ordinary Theology as Narratives."

By analyzing the youth prayers recorded, the authors found three main narratives. First, the narrative of *intimacy*. This narrative represents a theological style among youth which has to do with themes like God's presence, worship, prayer, and forgiveness. Second, there is the narrative of *revival*. This narrative refers to references in prayers to geographical locations in Scotland, the theme of restoration, young people or the Church in Scotland being an army or having the theme of reconciling the generations. And third, the authors observe a *doctrinal* narrative. This narrative refers to a cluster of more formal doctrinal metaphors, like metaphors about God, Jesus, salvation, and sin.

In 2014 and 2015, two articles came out in which Ronelle Sonnenberg, Malan Nel, Jos de Kock and Marcel Barnard reported on an empirical study on the participation of youth in worship in Dutch Protestant contexts, respectively in *Questions Liturgiques* and in *HTS Theologiese Studies*.[42] Worship is conceived by the authors as a liturgical ritual gathering. The concept of the participation of youth refers to adolescents being authorities in liturgy: "they negotiate, choose in what they will participate, etcetera."[43] The central question in the *Questions Liturgiques* article is: "How are 'scenario' and 'enactment' in youth worship shaped?"[44] Scenario has to do with the different scenes which describe story, context and action in the youth worship. Enactment refers to putting something into force during the youth worship. The data in the study is informed by fieldwork (including participant observations, interviews, taking pictures) in local worship gatherings in the Protestant Church in the Netherlands as well as at four (inter)national events.

The authors discovered four modes of active participation of youth in youth worship: bricolage, negotiation, eclectic appropriation, and belonging to a plural authority structure. Bricolage has to do with the character of youth worship being a bricolage of contemporary culture and church traditions. Negotiation refers to the dialogical character of authority structures in youth worship, where all kind of actors negotiate in practices: ministers, youth leaders, youth, commercial organizations, etcetera. Eclectic appropriation refers to adolescents choosing groups, forms, and contents in which they want to participate. The authors conclude with regard to young people's appropriation in youth worship

42. Sonnenberg et al., "Shaping Youth Worship"; Sonnenberg et al., "Being Together in Youth Worship."
43. Sonnenberg et al., "Shaping Youth Worship," 220.
44. Sonnenberg et al., "Shaping Youth Worship," 216.

practices: "the eclectic character of appropriation creates room for a momentary character of worship."[45] Finally, belonging to a 'plural authority structure' means there is so single liturgical authoritative elite in youth worship. Authority is the sum of processes of negotiation and appropriation, and of bricolage.

An important conclusion based on the observation of these modes of participation is that for youth worship there is no fixed scenario initially directing youth worship practice. It is "crafted in negotiations and appropriations during the (preparation of its) enactment."[46] In these processes of negotiation and appropriation a plural authority structure is at work. Besides, pre-existing theologies of both adolescents and congregations influence the scenario and enactment of youth worship. The authors draw out the implication that policy making with regard to youth worship has to reckon with these modes of participation as analyzed in this study.

The 2015 article in *HTS Theologiese Studies* is based on the same qualitative research project but is focused on a different research question: "What aspects can be distinguished in the quality of 'being together' in youth worship and how can they be understood sociologically and theologically?"[47] That article starts from the observation that youth worship has "being together" as a primary quality. As such, it understands youth worship as a particular practice in which the communal aspect of faith is central (see 4.1). The authors find four aspects of "being together" in youth worship: (1) community is celebrated through physical presence, in particular the physical presence of siblings; (2) there is an emotional, empathetic experience of unity, trust and equality; (3) there exists the possibility of crossing social and ecclesiological boundaries; and (4) there is the possibility of sharing faith and being in God's presence.

The complete research which formed the basis for the two articles by Sonnenberg et al. was published in Sonnenberg's dissertation in 2015: "Youth Worship in Protestant Contexts: A Practical Theological Theory of Participation of Adolescents." One of the main outcomes of the research for this dissertation has been to distinguish three qualities in the participation of youth in youth worship (albeit with some overlap): being together, recreation, and learning faith. "The distinguished qualities

---

45. Sonnenberg et al., "Shaping Youth Worship," 232.
46. Sonnenberg et al., "Shaping Youth Worship," 235.
47. Sonnenberg et al., "Being Together in Youth Worship," 1.

of participation are categories in which the longings, activities, expressions, convictions, and experiences of adolescents in youth worship are integrated."[48]

4.4 Conclusion

The central question in this first part of the handbook is "Who is the youth?" In this particular chapter we have addressed this question from empirical studies focusing on either the individual or the communal dimension of faith among youth. We learned that it is a complex thing to research faith among youth and saw different examples of how authors classify the different types of faith that can be observed among youth. But under the surface of these typologies we see a large variety of individual or subjective theologies among young people. We began the chapter with an illustration of these subjective theologies, God concepts, and explained that the development of these individual theologies has everything to do with the communal dimension of faith development: characteristics of the social environment in which young people are raised.

The latter issue has been discussed by describing studies on the importance and formational impact of youth groups. In addition, we discussed the formational power of youth worship practices. In these studies, we see that it is not only the social context of young people that influences individual faith development, but it is also true the other way round: individual faith or faith practices influence the broader community of faith in which young people participate. Where this part of the handbook shed light on the individual and communal dimension of faith and faith development, we now turn to the next part that addresses a third dimension: the transcendental dimension. We ask ourselves: Where is God in youth ministry?

---

48. Sonnenberg, "Youth Worship in Protestant Contexts," 196.

Part 2

WHERE IS GOD IN YOUTH MINISTRY?

Where Is God in Youth Ministry?
Introduction to Part 2

THE second part of the handbook draws attention to a question that is fundamental to all theological inquiry: *Where* is God? In the light of the theme of this handbook, the question is articulated in the following manner: *Where is God in youth ministry?* There is no shortage of contemporary attempts to respond to the challenge that this question represents, and it is fair to say that chapter 5 bears witness to a recent theological turn in youth ministry. The chapter therefore offers a comprehensive, lengthy, and in-depth exploration of how a wide range of scholars in youth ministry interpret the presence of God in youth ministry. The focus shifts from spirituality to encounters and relationships, from community and practice to discernment and journeying. Finally, the chapter closes with a section on youth ministry and eschatology.

Drawing on contemporary youth ministry research, Chapter 6 first offers an overview of the research front and different research strategies within this profoundly theological theme. Further, the chapter presents ways of researching the presence of God in youth ministry, by outlining four interpretative models for exploring and investigating the presence of God in youth ministry, arguing in the final section for the importance of a certain theological wiggle room in researching God's presence in youth ministry.

Chapters 5 and 6 identify some common themes, such as the importance of researching and interpreting God's presence in the context of young people's experiences, and assessing what it may imply to research God's presence in community and practice in youth ministry. At the same time research on God's presence in youth ministry is probably best understood as a sort of hermeneutical struggle, at least if we draw on the ancient theological dialectic of apophatic and cataphatic theology. In part 5, chapter 16, framing research as a hermeneutical struggle is an integral part of our proposed practical theological research framework for youth ministry research.

5

God's Presence in Youth Ministry

"Youth ministry is vital to help create such places, places where faith becomes more plausible, more meaningful and more tangible."[1]

"Youth ministry, like all other ministry, is persons meeting persons in relationships bound by responsibility, for it is here that we meet Jesus as other."[2]

THIS chapter elaborates on a key theological question in academic youth ministry: where is God in youth ministry? The theme of spirituality was dealt with in depth in part 1 of the handbook. In this chapter we offer a brief outlook at how the first attempts to ground a theology of youth ministry was rooted in reflections on the spiritualities of youth and youth ministry (5.1). The next part of the chapter explores how different research proposals in youth ministry advocate the importance of encounters and relationships and therefore explore how human experience helps to discover God's presence in youth ministry (5.2). We then move on to discuss how the presence of God in community and practice may be understood (5.3), with the subsequent section exploring God's possible presence in the processes of discernment, questioning, and journeying in youth ministry (5.4). The final section concludes the chapter by exploring the presence of God in youth ministry through the lens of eschatology (5.5).

1. Shepherd, *Faith Generation*, 172.
2. Root, *Revisiting Relational Youth Ministry*, 141.

5.1 The Presence of God in Youth Ministry

In 1983, Charles M. Shelton published *Adolescent Spirituality*, which was one of the first books trying to construct a comprehensive pastoral theology for adolescents. *Adolescent Spirituality* aimed to bridge a theology of youth ministry and insights from psychology with the purpose of creating a theology of adolescent spirituality. Shelton explicitly focused on how the presence of Christ in ministry should be interpreted and how it relates to the spiritual life of young people. Shelton wrote that "the growing presence of Jesus Christ in the adolescent's life and the experience of Jesus in a life of prayer orient the young person to an essential aspect of Christian living."[3]

Many recent contributions in the field of youth ministry have continued this focus on the presence of God in ministry, by exploring different theological avenues responding to the crucial question, "where is God in youth ministry?" In an article from 2009 in *Journal of Youth and Theology*, Andrew Root finds that the question "where is God?" is at the heart of ministry, and that "the core of ministry is the ability to contemplate and articulate the 'where' of God."[4] Bård Norheim has argued that the question "where is Jesus Christ?" is the most fundamental question for any theology of ministry.[5]

How, then, do different scholars try to qualify this interpretative research pursuit to speak of, and perhaps identify, the presence of God in youth ministry. This chapter reviews and assesses the range of research contributions which engages in this discussion, both from empirical, pedagogical, sociological, psychological, and theological angles. In youth ministry scholarship, ecclesiological and theological tensions exist, but they are not very often openly addressed, at least not in a confrontational way. This tendency is also evident in the research material presented here. Possibly this slightly harmonizing tendency comes down to whether theology should define the framework of youth ministry or not. Some scholars would argue that youth ministry needs to cut loose from some of its ties to management theory and pedagogical methods and return to theology as its basic framework.[6] Others would argue for a more empirical approach. Unsurprisingly however, given the research theme,

---

3. Shelton, *Adolescent Spirituality*, 137.
4. Root, "God's Hiddenness, Absence, and Doubt," 60–61.
5. Norheim, *Practicing Baptism*.
6. Muchová and Štěch, "Sustainable Youth Ministry," 69.

theologically informed articles and books dominate the contributions evaluated and discussed in chapters 5 and 6.

5.2 God in Encounters and Relationships

Youth ministry has always had a fundamental sensitivity as to how theology and the practice(s) of the church should relate to cultural shifts to be relevant and authentic. A major shift in youth ministry has been the shift from program-based ministries to an interest in relational youth ministry, where the notion of fostering adolescent discipleship and spirituality plays a major role. In this kind of youth ministry, the focus is on spiritual shaping and formation as the primary vision for youth ministry.

The question of how to interpret the presence of God in youth ministry conjures with another question: how should the role of (religious) experience in youth ministry be evaluated (theologically)? This is an old debate, which goes back to the origins of youth ministry and the two streams within it. Should youth ministry be framed as faith *formation* or should it be understood mainly as a strategic place to facilitate a religious *conversion* experience.[7] One stream or tradition would often emphasize the importance of creation theology and God's durative presence in the ordinary, the other would often highlight God's transcendent presence made available to the individual through the punctual act of conversion.

It is interesting here to note the findings of an empirical study of young people's interpretations of Christ's presence. American scholar Jeremy Myers finds that the young people's experience of Christ's presence and activity may be interpreted as "times of increased awareness of one's humanity—dependent upon God, a steward of Creation, and responsible towards one's neighbor." Myers therefore articulates a theological criterion for God's presence in youth ministry, namely that Christ is present and active within "experiences of *proleptic vocational recapitulation* through God's creation, the law, the gospel and the church."[8] Some scholars, on the other hand, would emphasize the importance of distinguishing between different God concepts as we try to identify how young people perceive the presence of God in youth ministry. Using attachment theory as theoretical framework, Simone A. de Roos argues that God concepts "allude to subjects' ideas concerning different potential

---

7. Myers, "Adolescent Experiences of Christ's Presence," 27.
8. Myers, "Adolescent Experiences of Christ's Presence," 41.

behavioral characteristics of God, like God as a caring, loving, potent, and/or punishing entity."[9] Based on the findings of an empirical research project interpreted with the help of attachment theory, de Roos shows how young people's God concepts are influenced heavily by religious socialization in the home as well as in the school, and have strong effects on children's images of God.[10]

Christ in the Encounter

The strong relational vibe in many theologies of youth ministry underscores the encounter as the place where the presence of God is revealed. In an article from 2002, Erlinde De Lange and Bert Roebben boldly proclaimed: "If Christianity implies an encounter with God, such an encounter will be mediated through human persons." However, the presence of God cannot be guaranteed, some would claim. De Lange and Roebben argue, against an instrumental approach, that the sacraments cannot guarantee the presence of God, rather the desire of God's presence is there in the encounter as a potent possibility, as an open question. The sacraments, they claim, remind us of the fact that God is remote. De Lange and Roebben also propose that "meaningful sacramentality presupposes a profound correlation between faith and life." The framework of this argument is the practice of catechesis, in which they argue that "a biblically inspired sacramentality presupposes an adult Church."[11]

In an article from 2005 Bert Roebben continues this focus and argues for a down to earth theology as a way of unwrapping the presence of God in ministry. The theology proposed by Roebben is a theology of the embrace, where the living God "qualifies himself in a fully qualitative encounter with people who long for a 'life in abundance' and who are willing to share this in community."[12] By appealing to theology's relevance for young people's life experiences, Roebben argues for what may be labelled a weak ontology for youth ministry. God is not out there, but in here. God is the god of life, and immanence is the mode of god reflections for young people, aversive to "immense theological projects" and hungry for "the fountain of life." This "is immanent, hidden in daily

---

9. De Roos, "Young Children's God Concepts," 84.
10. De Roos, "Young Children's God Concepts," 101.
11. De Lange and Roebben, "Seven Propositions."
12. Roebben, "Light of Day," 30.

acts of brother- and sisterhood, in the desire for a more humane world." Basically, this presupposes an anthropomorphic image of God.[13]

Quite in contrast to Bert Roebben and others who advocate a weak ontology showcasing God's being in the ordinary, Andrew Root claims that the practice of youth ministry has over-emphasized the everywhere-ness of God. Both Roebben and Root start their reflections from the experience of fear. Roebben departs from young adults' fear of shame and the fear of the tests and tribulations of the future. Root departs from his son's fear of the monster in the closet and the experience that the parental assertion Jesus is here did not help. The interesting twist is that both also advocate a *diaconal* telos for youth ministry. Their theological axioms serve to safeguard a conception of youth ministry which ensures an engagement with the problematic, the experiences of despair, pain, and suffering, rather than growth and success. Therefore, Root argues that "the hiddenness and absence of God, encountered in the cross, may be a richer theological perspective for youth ministry to stand upon than the all-too-common North American attention to (or obsession with) God's *everywhere-ness*."[14] Root finds that the obsession with God's immediate presence and everywhere-ness serves as a way of rationalizing God and faith:

> When God is bound in God's *everywhere-ness*, then faith is bound in rationality. When we say God is everywhere, but are unable to say concretely "where," we clothe God in a rational system. Not sure theologically "where" to say God is, we must defend that God is somewhere.[15]

Root finds that the problem with committing to God's everywhere-ness, is that a youth ministry bound up with such dispositions will necessarily extract doubt from young people. More fundamentally, the problem is that if we emphasize that God is everywhere and connect the everywhere-ness to the revealed, near, and rational, then "God can only be discovered in growth, advancement, and attention to preparation."[16]

Root's 2009 article in *Journal of Youth and Theology* serves as a sort of preamble to a more comprehensive theological engagement with the presence of God in ministry, in both *The Theological Turn in Youth*

13. Roebben, "Light of Day," 32.
14. Root, "God's Hiddenness," 62–63.
15. Root, "God's Hiddenness," 64.
16. Root, "God's Hiddenness," 65, 67.

Ministry (2011) and in *Christopraxis: A Practical Theology of the Cross* (2014). Here Root engages critical realism, a Lutheran theology of the cross, and other theologians such as Jüngel, Barth, and Zizioulas to argue: "The God of ministry that gives us union with Godself by joining in ministry is a God whose ministry starts in death and breaks it through with life—most fully in the Christopraxis of cross to resurrection, of ascension to Pentecost."[17] In the rather dense and extensive treatment of God's presence in ministry wrapped in the dialectic of possibility and nothingness, Root draws on German theologians Eberhard Jüngel and Jürgen Moltmann to maintain that God's presence in ministry is revealed in the paradoxical: "In paradoxical nature hiddenness, absence, and the absurd are pathways to speak of God's concrete "where," because they touch directly our ontological state, a state that God, through Christ, now shares."

Root uses these theological underpinnings of God's presence in ministry to argue for a new direction for youth ministry, where success and growth are no longer the key criteria, rather we are to search for God in "the emptiness of honest yearning." This shapes a theological "program" for a youth ministry that seeks to encounter the crucified God within nothingness. Ultimately, the heart of youth ministry "becomes seeking to stand with young people between possibility and nothingness." Quite radically, then, Root claims that God is not everywhere, but rather specifically there, "up against your pain, there up against your questions, there upon against your broken dreams." Root also criticizes the sort of youth ministry that rests too heavily on the claim that God is everywhere for being prone to focusing ministry on growth, advancement, and preparation, and making the Christian faith about control, finality, and certainty, and convincing young people "to somehow trust in this nebulous God." As in his book on *Revisiting Relational Youth Ministry* (2007), Root argues for a relational conceptualization of the presence of God in ministry. Christ is revealed in the encounter, where someone bears the burden of reality with young people.[18]

---

17. Root, *Christopraxis*. 110.
18. Root, "God's Hiddenness," 70, 72, 74–75.

Relationships and the Presence of Christ

What Andrew Root does, is to relocate the presence of God in the context of relationships in (youth) ministry. To ground this theological pursuit, he draws on the Christology of Dietrich Bonhoeffer to rethink the presence of God in youth ministry within the context of relationships as encounters. Root argues that Bonhoeffer's theology helps to discover that "Jesus Christ is concretely present to us in our relational lives, in our person-to-person encounters, in the *I* and *you*."[19] Root claims with Bonhoeffer that within the relational encounter Christ is concretely present: "Christ is not present as the other person, but because Jesus is the person *who* is incarnate, crucified and resurrected, he stands in between my person and the person I meet in the world."[20]

Root employs Bonhoeffer's use of Luther's theology of the cross to advocate that Christ is "in between because he stands for and alongside the other, just as he stands for and alongside me (*pro me*)."[21] Therefore Root makes the claim that "relationships with others lead to our mutual transformation into the new humanity of Jesus Christ,"[22] and that "we partake in and taste the reality of Jesus Christ through person-to-person social relationships of place-sharing."[23] In *Relationships Unfiltered*, Root maintains, again with Bonhoeffer, that "Jesus is a living person moving in the world, calling us to himself, calling us into relationship, just as he did with the first-century disciples."[24]

For Root, youth ministry is therefore *not* "about "using" relationships to get individuals to accept a "third thing." Root argues that ministry is about connection, and about sharing in suffering and joy, about persons meeting persons with no secret motives. Therefore youth

---

19. Root, *Revisiting Relational Youth Ministry*, 15. Root writes that "Bonhoeffer's theology alerted me to the possibility that the relationship is the 'end.' It is the place where Christ is present, the place where the adolescent (and I, for that matter) encounter Christ."

20. Root, *Revisiting Relational Youth Ministry*, 111.

21. Root, *Revisiting Relational Youth Ministry*, 111. Root claims that Bonhoeffer "asserts that God in Christ is concretely present in the church and the world, where persons meet persons in being with and for each other in the construct of I and you" (140). And "Jesus Christ is the *who* that encounters others through his own person, standing *pro me* for all humanity" (170).

22. Root, *Revisiting Relational Youth Ministry*, 141.

23. Root, *Revisiting Relational Youth Ministry*, 171–72.

24. Root, *Relationships Unfiltered*, 113.

ministry is not about helping kids to be better Christians; it is about helping them become what God created them to be—human.[25] Root claims that a youth ministry that understands relations as a means for influence represents the Christological heresy of docetism, "which believed that Jesus only *appeared to be* human in order to influence us."[26] Root proposes a ministry of place-sharing.[27] In the practice or ministry of place-sharing, Root underlines, "I take the self of the other into my own self," and he continues, stating that "place-sharing demands that I be completely *other* than the other (closed) while being completely for the other (open)."[28]

Root does not offer a comprehensive and nuanced theological criterion for speaking about the presence of Christ. Root just simply states that "for Bonhoeffer, Jesus Christ, and therefore God, is not locked in the past but is present among us now,"[29] and that "when we assert that God is present in Jesus Christ in relationship (not in where we take relationships), we are free, because God's presence is not dependent upon us—it's already a reality."[30] The question that remains unanswered after Root's theological assessment is what kind of presence this relational Christological presence is, and what qualifies it theologically. Fundamentally, Root finds that "youth ministry, like all other ministry, is persons meeting persons in relationships bound by responsibility, for it is here that we meet Jesus as other."[31]

Later, Andrew Root engages with Charles Taylor's assessment of the secular age and draws on Orthodox theology of *kenosis* and *theosis* and hypostatic union, and the so-called new Finnish interpretation of Martin Luther, to suggest a new vision for faith formation—and youth ministry—in a secular age:

> Faith and its formation, then, is something radically different from a program for making our institutions effective by making them youthful. Rather, through the authenticity of our experiences of death we find an encounter with a person that comes to us as a humble minister, giving us his own being as the healing of our brokenness, sending us back into the world as new beings

25. Root, *Revisiting Relational Youth Ministry*, 15.
26. Root, *Revisiting Relational Youth Ministry*, 79.
27. "Place-sharing" is Root's creative translation of the German *Stellvertretung*.
28. Root, *Revisiting Relational Youth Ministry*, 127.
29. Root, *Relationships Unfiltered*, 113.
30. Root, *Relationships Unfiltered*, 115.
31. Root, *Revisiting Relational Youth Ministry*, 141.

(2 Cor. 5:17). This new being is manifest in us not through power and intellect but as the humble embracing of our neighbor as her minister.[32]

How then should the presence of God within relationships be interpreted in the context of youth ministry? Another approach to qualifying relationships as a place of God's potential presence is offered by Helen Blier and Graham Stanton. Drawing on Maxine Greene and the quest for meaning-making, Helen Blier and Graham Stanton argue that "Christian discipleship finds transformation in inter-personal relationships that announce and embody the presence and promise of Christ. Youth ministries that follow the way of Christ take on Greene's vision of wide-awakeness in the world by being places of generous offering, inclusive welcome, and Christ-like service."[33] Some scholars would even envision the presence of God in youth ministry with "intimacy" as a theological lens, arguing that intimacy even "takes place within the embrace of Jesus Christ whose suffering love redefines the intimacy between us." This implies, Kenda Creasy Dean argues, that "authentic intimacy requires the presence of a transcendent Other who sheds light on us from beyond ourselves, illuminating human relationships in new way."[34]

God in the Virtual Encounter?

This chapter deals with the fundamental question, "where is God in youth ministry?" It is important to remember that youth ministry, both as a practice and as an academic discipline, very early on identified a need to explore possible theological avenues that could open to allow the interpretation of the presence of God outside of the actual physical place. Might God be present in the virtual? If yes, on what grounds? Theologians interested in the junction between theology and ministry have long been concerned with interpreting God's possible online presence. A more creative take on this issue would be to try to identify how the church could use internet-mediated interactions to create *virtual spaces* for a wide variety of activities, like Bible study, theological discussions, or virtual worship.

---

32. Root, *Faith Formation in a Secular Age*, 180.

33. Blier and Stanton, "Wide-Awakeness in the World," 17. For a more comprehensive assessment of this theme, see Stanton, *Wide-Awake in God's Word*.

34. Dean, *Practicing Passion*, 130.

The more tabloid way of asking the same sort of questions would be to ask if virtual church can be real, and if God may be present online. Julie Ann Lytle draws on Karl Rahner's theology to argue that we may recognize God in all of creation, and therefore even in virtual spaces. Lytle argues that God's presence is not confined to a single moment. Rather, we may recognize God in all creation. Therefore, in addition to God's tangible presence in Jesus Christ, creation may reveal God "through mediated forms."[35] Engaging theologian Catherine LaCugna, Lytle maintains that as "Story-Keepers, Christians make God present every time we repeat the stories of our faith and remind each other of the future God intends for creation." Similarly, as "Story-Makers, we become God's Gospel reinterpreted and proclaimed in our words and actions."[36] So, where is God in youth ministry? For Lytle, the Trinitarian and incarnational theology of Rahner and LaCugna mandates a theological exploration of Christian community and the presence of God in midst of us, through relationships and experiences.

5.3 God in Practice and Community

God in Practice

Thirty years after Charles Shelton's book on *Adolescent Spirituality*, American Tony Jones wrote a book called *Soul Shaper*. Jones advocated a renaissance in youth ministry, with youth ministry departing from the personality-driven entertainment model of the late twentieth century, moving into a ministry where the focus is on ancient practices of faith and disciplines in a way that is relevant to young people's lives. According to Jones and other youth ministry theologians, such practices are of particular interest because they have been tested and they are therefore the most coherent way of approaching the spiritual seeking of young people and the adolescent desire for an encounter with the divine in youth ministry. So, where is God in youth ministry? According to Jones, God is in "ancient spiritual disciplines," which "have the ability to enfold an adolescent in God's love while fulfilling her desire for spiritual exploration."[37]

---

35. Lytle, "Virtual Incarnations," 399.
36. Lytle, "Virtual Incarnations," 401.
37. Jones mentions several examples of such ancient faith practices: sacred reading, silence and solitude, the Jesus prayer, centering prayer, meditation, the Ignatian Examen, Icons, Spiritual Direction, the daily office, the labyrinth, stations of the cross,

What, then, are the practices, or even things and objects, in ministry that may "facilitate" an encounter with God in youth ministry? Is the only place we can meet God in the personal encounter, or the relationship, or is there still a role for activities, objects, things? Based on an empirical study of young people's participation in youth worship, Sonnenberg and Barnard draw on the term recreation, as in free time and free choice, to argue with American Lutheran liturgical theologian Gordon Lathrop that "recreational 'things' in themselves, when used as part of the liturgy, are not at the centre of what should be celebrated. However, when these 'things' receive specific meanings, because they are juxtaposed to the Word of God and vice versa, they become core elements in the participation of adolescents in youth worship gatherings." Sonnenberg and Barnard's study emphasizes that God may be found in recreational things and activities when these things receive meaning insofar as they are juxtaposed to the Word of God and vice versa. They suggest an understanding of youth worship that implies turning a party into a faith party, an assembly into a Christian assembly.[38]

In an increasingly secular culture, looking for God's presence is not a given. Many youth ministry scholars have therefore argued for re-thinking faith formation with young people. Drawing on his empirical study of youth groups and Kathryn Tanner's approach to Christian practices as "meaning-making," Nick Shepherd argues for creating "distinctive Christian places" with the help of plausibility practices, identity practices, and reliability practices.[39]

Back in 2004, focusing on the importance of rituals, Jonny Baker argued that the church, and her youth ministry, needs to reshape its practice to connect with contemporary culture: "The construction of genuine, meaningful, dynamic, multisensory, embodied rituals, both old and new, in church and out in the marketplace is an important part of that process."[40] Later, in 2006, Mike King maintained that practices are important as "learning to practice the presence of God in their lives will sustain adolescents in their journey long after they are gone from the youth group."[41] Similarly, in Mark Yaconelli's book *Contemplative Youth*

---

pilgrimage, fasting, the sign of the cross and other bodily prayers, Sabbath, service. Cf. Jones, *Soul Shaper*, 26–27.

38. Sonnenberg and Barnard, "Youth Worship as Recreation," 162–63.
39. Shepherd, *Faith Generation*, 129–31.
40. Baker, "Ritual as Strategic Practice," 95.
41. King, *Presence-Centered Youth Ministry*, 179.

Ministry: Practicing the Presence of Jesus even the title reveals that the notion of the presence of Christ plays a crucial role in a theology of youth ministry—and of practices. Yaconelli claims that "through his words and actions, Jesus communicates that this Presence of love can be trusted."[42] Yaconelli enfolds and explicates several contemplative practices for youth ministry—like contemplative prayer, centering prayer, lectio divina, and discerning your calling. Yaconelli then goes on to claim that "we practice contemplative prayer so we might become aware and receptive to the reality of life—even further, so we might become more in touch with God's presence in the middle of life, the Real within the real."[43]

In an article on how to focus youth ministry through Christian practices, Yaconelli claims that to determine if a practice is Christian one has to take four relationships into consideration since "all Christian practices begin in prayer, invite personal confession, take place within the worshiping community, and bear fruit in solidarity with the poor in communion with the Spirit of Jesus Christ."[44] Yaconelli maintains that "all four elements of Christian practices—prayer, confession, the presence of the worshiping community, solidarity with the poor—are present in any one practice." Yaconelli also underlines that these practices seek to foster growth, sanctification, and conformity to the image of Christ. Yaconelli also advocates that "youth ministries can best facilitate growth in conformity with Christ when they focus on helping youth experience and develop practices of faith."[45]

David F. White also underlines the importance of practices as young people seek to discern the presence of God in their everyday lives. He underlines, that "just as dance requires skills that must be practiced in order to be improved, so does our dance with the Holy require practices for attuning to God." He mentions a list of practices that have been crucial for Christians, like Bible study, prayer, worship, living in community, feasting, fasting, extending hospitality to the stranger, keeping the Sabbath, living simply, and seeking justice. White argues, that "we need not treat practices as rules to keep, but as ways to attune to our Partner and invite others into the dance." The purpose of the practices is to "move us deeper into the heart of God's reign of fullness and beauty, for which we

---

42. Yaconelli, *Contemplative Youth Ministry*, 71.
43. Yaconelli, *Contemplative Youth Ministry*, 90.
44. Yaconelli, "Focusing Youth Ministry," 157.
45. Yaconelli, "Focusing Youth Ministry," 163–65.

were created."⁴⁶ White finds that "Christian practices are concrete ways of inviting God's presence among us and of seeking partnership with God's work in the world."⁴⁷

Similarly, Kenda Creasy Dean has engaged in the practices-conversation and proposes the following definition of how Christian practices relate to the presence of God: "Practices, like signs and sacraments, are human actions that point to the promise of God, and that often serve as a context for divine-human encounter. . . . Practices are the ongoing actions of the Christian community that the Holy Spirit uses to mark us as, and shape us into, followers of Jesus Christ."⁴⁸ She has also argued that Christ's sacrificial life is attainable for us through sacramental practices. However, Dean distinguishes sacramental practices from social practices.⁴⁹ However, sometimes it remains a bit unclear whether some youth ministry scholars actually advocate a theology of real presence or a more symbolic understanding of the sacrament of the Lord's Supper, as "expressions" or "activation" of the Divine.⁵⁰ Later, Dean has highlighted three other practices to help young people encounter God's presence in their lives, namely translation, testimony, and detachment. She argues that these practices throughout Christian history "have served as vehicles that carry God's saving grace into the world "incarnationally"—i.e. through human lives—as we cross geographic, cultural, and even generational boundaries with God's infinitely abundant love."⁵¹ Dean also argues that "the Holy Spirit empowers us to consciously participate in the life of God."⁵² Drawing on the Celtic notion of "thin places," Dean finds that "thin places act as holy reminders of Christ's presence, and we return from them slightly askew."⁵³

---

46. White, *Practicing Discernment with Youth*, 141.

47. White, *Practicing Discernment with Youth*, 162.

48. Dean, *OMG*, 75.

49. Dean, *Practicing Passion*, 226. The idea of sacrificial, self-giving love is also used to criticise the inherent Christology in the What Would Jesus Do-movement. She criticizes the movement by emphasizing that "it implies that Jesus is no longer with us and fails to convey Christ's life as sacrificial—thereby missing the point of self-giving love altogether" (166).

50. O'Gorman, "Imagination Embodied," 437, 442.

51. Dean, *Almost Christian*, 23.

52. Dean, *Almost Christian*, 88.

53. Dean, *Almost Christian*, 166.

Theologically, it is important to note that the term "practice" bears affinity to the Biblical notion of the "fruits of the spirit." One could also consider speaking about the "use" of faith instead of "practicing" one's faith. The term use, or *usus* in Latin, is a term coined theologically by Martin Luther. In chapter 6.3, we will look at the way in which Martin Luther's notion of the three modes of Christ's presence, rooted in the Jesus-narrative, might serve as an interpretative lens as we embark to research the presence of God in youth ministry.[54]

Finally, when looking at God's presence in different practices in youth ministry, it is worth considering how God's presence in worship music may be interpreted. The following examination is closely connection to the treatment of youth worship in chapter 4. After all, the use or practice of worship and music plays a key role in many youth ministries. Christopher Demuth Rodkey addresses what he labels "worship wars," or the argument about what role contemporary music should play in worship. What sort of theological take would vouch for the use of a certain type of music? Rodkey understands music as a practice, which "concerns how young people meet God and which God they meet." When we consider music as a practice thematizing God's presence, Rodkey moves on to argue that God's spatial relation to the world is best understood as a linguistic problem. Here he maintains that religious language is at the "*edge* of language itself." Therefore, Rodkey finds that both transcendent and immanent categories may be found to be incomplete or even inadequate for any description of the divine.[55]

Steven Emery-Wright claims, based on a case-study of young Methodists' (dis-)satisfaction with traditional worship, that for young people "the dominant idea of the God they worship is that of a powerful friend who loves you, accepts you and sets you free to be your best self."[56] Emery-Wright advocates what he labels "fun worship," as that sort of worshiping with friends in the presence of God gave the young people of his study "a sense of satisfaction and contentment, which made them happy. Emery-Wright concludes that "*fun worship* therefore has the potential of relating the worship to their culture, strengthening the bonds between friends, and encouraging their relationship with God."[57] The notion of

---

54. For a lengthy assessment of how to interpret the presence of Christ in Christian practices, cf. Norheim, *Practicing Baptism*; and section 6.3.

55. Rodkey, "The Practice of Music," 47, 59.

56. Emery-Wright, "A Qualitative Study Construction," 71.

57. Emery-Wright, "A Qualitative Study Construction," 75.

God as "friend" implies an image of God as someone who will always be there and not let young people down.[58] Emery-Wright therefore argues for developing youth worship as fun youth experience in which young people may respond to the presence of God.[59]

God in Community

The focus on practice is closely connected with the question of how we may perceive of God's presence in communities of practice, like youth ministry, or the church. We then need to consider the following key theological question: Is the church a phenomenon on the level of creation, or is the work of God's saving activity in the world? Some youth ministry contributions seem to have somewhat ambiguous relationship to this question.[60]

Some scholars would emphasize the communal nature of church, or perhaps church as a communal practice, as a source to discover the purpose of youth ministry. Drawing on the key New Testament term, *koinonia*, the presence of God is expressed in and through community. The pinpointing of koinonia, as the key term for a Christian theology of community, even holds a pilgrimage motif, which we will explore in more depth in 5.4. Where, then, is God in youth ministry? The answer here would be that God is revealed in community. Church as koinonia even contributes to the attractiveness and persuasiveness of the Christian community for young people. Patrick C. Höring has suggested that making koinonia the Church's fundamental concept may help to develop youth ministry towards "a habitat that corresponds to the gospel and to the needs of people."[61]

Others again would highlight the communal nature of youth ministry, by drawing on Eastern Orthodox theology and more contemporary theories on identity and personhood. The outcome is quite similar to those who focus on *koinonia* and bridges the God-in-community-focus with God-in-relationships: "Community is the place of relationships, and relationships with others are the means by which a person is confronted

---

58. Emery-Wright, *Now That Was Worship*, 131.
59. Emery-Wright, *Now That Was Worship*, 179.
60. Brelsford, "Educating for Formative Participation," 323.
61. Höring, "Koinonia," 56. We will assess Höring's article in more depth in chapter 14 on the role of the youth minister in community.

with their own uniqueness."[62] But yet another theological and philosophical motif enters the stage here, otherness as a sort of prerequisite for true personhood, even in youth ministry. The argument goes as follows: The *imago Dei* sort of presupposes that human beings' relatedness must be both vertical and horizontal.[63] According to this approach, God is present in youth ministry through Christ, which enables a recovery of the *imago Dei*, maintaining that it is only through Christ that one can have unbroken relationship with the Father. Interestingly, for Hudson the emphasis on communal personhood is combined with a revised, soft version of conversionism: "The primary objective of youth ministry is to present the Person of Christ and call young people to make, and live out, a personal commitment to him."[64]

Another strand in the attempts to vouch theologically for the presence of God in youth ministry as community is the undertaking to appeal to family metaphors and images when conceptualizing God's presence. More specifically, some scholars would advocate the key importance of acknowledging the role and position of the child in the biblical visions of the kingdom of God. This vision of a familiar, ecclesial community, includes even what we in the next subchapter will identify as looking for God's presence in questioning, discerning, and journeying, perhaps even struggle. Robert J. Parmach argues that the divinity and the humanity of Christ "comes to us in the human struggles and doubts of daily family life, in the wounds of distrust, disappointment, and seemingly insurmountable obstacles."[65] Working with the family as a leitmotif, reminds us of the importance of the other. The openness to the other, some theologians would argue, is even a model for receiving Christ as the Other. The Christian family, conceptualized in this fashion, then becomes a teaching model for ministry in general.[66]

God in Communal Practice? The Practice of Welcome

Looking for God in relationship within youth ministry (5.2) and looking for God in particular practices (5.3) may of course coincide. Very often

---

62. Hudson, "Community, Identity, & Youth Ministry," 25.
63. Hudson, "Community, Identity, & Youth Ministry," 26.
64. Hudson, "Community, Identity, & Youth Ministry," 30.
65. Parmach, "Christian Families," 66–67.
66. Parmach, "Christian Families," 80.

in youth ministry the meaning of being a Christian is defined by pointing at how a fellowship is recognized by the way in which people are included." The "conversion stories" that are shared by the young people in such youth ministries are often stories which showcase the importance of the practice of welcome. The practice of welcome also seems to define the understanding of grace. Grace becomes a community practice which includes the freedom from demands to achieve or perform anything, and if you mess up, there is always a second chance. Such narratives of the practice of welcoming grace trumps a culture of performance at school and in other spare time-activities. Theological engagements with the practice of welcome in youth ministry often draw on theological resources such as Tanner (2002), Ducksworth (2013) or Volf (1996).[67]

5.4 God in Journeying and Discernment

Christ of the Journey

Another way to interpret the spatial location of God in youth ministry is through the framework of journey or pilgrimage metaphors. Such a framing of God's presence would often emphasize that God is present in the encounter, as we saw in section 5.2. Often the encounter is situated outside the "spatial borders of the institutional church," and such encounters may even be viewed as "church" in itself.[68]

In 1999, in *God at the Mall*, Pete Ward emphasized that the fact that the incarnation was located within "a defined cultural setting," implies that "we have no knowledge of God outside of culture."[69] In 2002, following up the interest in locating God and encountering God outside the traditional, spatial borders of the institutional church, Pete Ward wrote the seminal book *Liquid Church*, which basically argued that the church is more of a fluid entity, drawing metaphorically on Zygmunt Bauman's concept of liquid modernity.[70] Later (2008), Ward argued that we know of God's presence through participation and mediation. Looking at the Taizè community, Ward finds that "the divine presence flows

---

67. Tanner, "Theological Reflection and Christian Practices"; Ducksworth, *Wide Welcome*"; Volf, *Exclusion and Embrace*.
68. De Kock, "Being a Church," 228.
69. Ward, *God at the Mall*, 101.
70. Cf. Ward, *Liquid Church*.

as mediation," which enables "transformation" beyond the (youth) community in the small village in Burgundy.[71]

The journey-motif is therefore a rather widespread approach when scholars try to elaborate on the presence of God in youth ministry. Jos de Kock writes about how the young person, as a learner, "is journeying through life, which is a pilgrimage leading to the narthex."[72] Employing the journey metaphor, Jos de Kock argues that religious learning at the street level in youth ministry in some ways may be contrasted with Church life, "which takes place in the space of the institute, within boundaries and inside buildings."[73]

By envisioning God's presence in the encounter of the journey, some scholars apply a pedagogy of accompaniment. This implies taking note of the God-with-us motif (Immanuel) as a model for ministry. Hosffman Ospino has proposed that "God is present as the one who journeys with humanity, the one who comes to our encounter in the everyday, the one who never abandons us, and the one who better understands our human nature because we are "little less than a god" (Psalm 8:6)."[74]

A ministry of accompaniment is committed to a theological legacy which asserts that the God of the Revelation is simultaneously the God of the Encounter (5.2), and that God continues to call both women and men to enter that relationship. Obviously, therefore a theological plea for a ministry of accompaniment effectively highlights a theology of vocation. Fundamentally, the God of Revelation, "who freely and lovingly comes to the encounter of humanity in history, continuously calls women and men to be in relationship."[75] Here we arrive at the theme of adolescent spirituality, suggested by Shelton, framed by a sense of vocation that is at the heart of Christian spirituality. Even Kenda Creasy Dean links her interest in "the historic practices of the Christian community" with the pilgrimage tradition. She finds it fruitful to use pilgrimage metaphors as she elucidates a theology for adolescent faith development. Through this approach she posits God's presence in youth ministry through the

---

71. Ward, *Participation and Mediation*, 185.
72. De Kock, "Being a Church," 222.
73. De Kock, "Being a Church," 228.
74. Ospino, "Theological Horizons," 418.
75. Ospino, "Theological Horizons," 421.

metaphor of faith as a journey, a pilgrimage following the footsteps of previous travelers.[76]

Trying to decipher the presence of God in the world may be described by other scholars as a pilgrimage through a labyrinth, where the classic Greek understanding of beauty as virtue serves as the guide through the world.[77] It is important here to keep in mind that the virtues, such as beauty and goodness, were communal virtues to the Greek. In short, "there is only one standard of true *areté*—the common good of the polis. Whatever helps the community is good, whatever injures it is bad."[78] Muchova and Štěch focus on discernment when exploring the presence of God in youth ministry. They have suggested that the three values: *beauty*, *goodness*, and *meaning*, are an expression of the spiritual core of the human being. These values may therefore be understood as "keys enabling people to unlock the sacred in their lives, allowing them to discern that our world is not only ours, but it is also the world of God and the world of other people."[79]

God in Discernment

A sort of theological "sibling" theme to the journey motif is the emphasis on discernment and process as a locus of God's presence in youth ministry. David F. White focuses on discernment in youth ministry and envisions youth ministry speaking up against oppressive political agendas. He claims, that "the Christian story cultivates an alternate perspective of the world, a dream in which the world is being reconciled." The focus is on encountering God in discernment, emphasizing that "the Christian story helps youth to connect their stories to the story of God, giving a context for faith that extends backward to creation and forward to creation's completion."[80]

David White, based on the commandment of love suggests a four-step circle for the practice of discernment:

---

76. Dean, *Practicing Passion*," 203.
77. Cf. Muchová and Štěch, "Sustainable Youth Ministry."
78. Jaeger, *Paideia*, 92.
79. Cf. Muchová and Štěch, "Sustainable Youth Ministry," 65.
80. White, *Practicing Discernment*, 143.

1. Listening: Loving God with your heart (Ortho-Pathos)
2. Understanding: Loving God with your mind (Ortho-Optomai)
3. Remembering/Dreaming: Loving God with you soul (Ortho-Doxy)
4. Acting: Loving God with your strength (Ortho-Praxis)[81]

Similarly, Graham Stanton and Helen Blier appeal to Maxine Greene's pedagogy and imagines the presence of God in the discerning community. They make a plea to invite "young people to imagine how things could be otherwise opens the way for empathy and moral action." According to Blier and Stanton, youth ministries born out of this vision "will be places of dialogue and mutual care."[82] Some scholar who focus on discernment as a mode of God's presence in youth ministry situate this quest within a *creatio continua* theology. Theodore Brelsford argues that creation is "not a completed event from the distant past, but an ongoing action, an unfolding process of which we are all a part." Like many other theological contributions in youth ministry, Brelsford emphasizes that human beings are created in the image of God and therefore participants in God's continuous creation, even actively "forming what is yet to be," as calling for discernment in the world. Like Blier and Stanton, Brelsford also draws on Maxine Greene, highlighting that a primary goal of education is liberation, which includes freedom from bonds of ignorance and from the victimization of external determination."[83]

Yet, another avenue from which to interpret the presence of God in youth ministry is that of narratives as motifs for discernment of God's presence in youth ministry and beyond. What sort of narrative framework can give a comprehensive and nuanced account of the presence of the triune God? Some scholars would argue that the human body plays a key role in our conception of ministry and should serve as an organizing plot for the exploration of God's presence in youth ministry. The simple but basic point of departure is that every human is born with a body. This approach would consider youth ministry as a system directed towards a *telos*, a future goal. Bård Norheim argues that in the light of death, which is the ultimate human experience of transition, the Christian story of the body may be presented as a threefold movement. "The body is moving from creation, through death, to the hope of resurrection." Norheim

---

81. White, *Practicing Discernment*, 88.
82. Blier and Stanton, "Wide-Awakeness in the World," 17.
83. Brelsford, "Educating for Formative Participation," 312.

maintains that this implies that Christian youth ministry has to "embrace the created body as the home of youth ministry, not just a point of departure."[84] Norheim's basic point is that the Christian story of the body as created, finite, and living under the hope of resurrection should serve as "a ritual plot in youth ministry."[85]

5.5 Youth Ministry between Hope and Fear: Youth Ministry as a Utopia for God's Presence?

Several theologians engaged in re-thinking youth ministry in a shifting world have focused on the importance of hope, maybe because being young is intrinsically bound up with looking "with expectation to the future."[86] Most theologians would subscribe to the idea that hope is not a supplementary part of the Christian gospel. Rather it is a counter plot to a world where death often seems to have the final word. The hope of resurrection and eternal life in Jesus Christ is the embodiment of the gospel here and now, and already, but not yet. How we relate to fear, may be a particularly interesting topic to explore as we try to identify ways to understand how we perceive of God's presence in the world and in youth ministry. Bert Roebben indirectly hints at this theme with his appeal for a prolegomena for youth ministry, where he argues that young people are balancing on the fine line, or cutting edge, of hope and fear.[87]

Kenda Creasy Dean ends her book *Almost Christian* (2010) by making a case for hope. The book and the epilogue of the book, focusing on hope, is a response to the National Study of Youth and Religion (2005) and the default Christian faith, which that study portrayed, Moralistic Therapeutic Deism (MTD). According to Dean, MTD "set our sights on ourselves, not the stars." In other words, she interprets MTD as a sort of *amor sui*, self-love. Against this, Dean envisions the hope of a missional imagination inspired by the gospel, which encourages to embody self-giving love. This requires the church to think big, to set her hope on Jesus Christ, who "established the church for the world, nothing less ... which means that we are not here, any of us, for ourselves."[88] At the very end

---

84. Norheim, "The Christian Story," 94–95.
85. Norheim, "The Christian Story," 104–1.
86. Roebben, *Seeking Sense in the City*, 209.
87. Roebben, "Light of Day," 28.
88. Dean, *Almost Christian*, 192.

of the book, Dean hints at, without developing it any further, that living out this hope—embodying, if you like—is rooted in "a particular story."[89]

Steve Griffiths, on the other hand, has argued in *A Christlike Ministry* (2008), that hope is not so much passion for the possible, rather it should be understood as passion "for the Promised." Like many other youth ministry theologians, he draws on the theology of Jürgen Moltmann, supporting his appeal to ground eschatology, and therefore hope, in the person and work of Jesus Christ. Griffiths ends by warning that Christian eschatology should not be hi-jacked by oppressive political agendas, since a Christian eschatology, with hope at its heart could be "immensely liberating."[90] One may perhaps ask if Griffiths' reformed, theological proposal ends with a somewhat simplistic approach to Christ's presence in (youth) ministry as Griffiths ends with a rather provocative dictum: "If we teach a 'present Christ', we rob our young people of hope since the return of Christ is that upon which all hope is founded."[91]

We see that focusing on hope in youth ministry also relates to fear, but often with a sort of constructive purpose.[92] Youth ministry may serve as a laboratory of hope, embedded in a larger narrative of the human body as created, finite, and, through the body of Christ, inscribed in the hope of resurrection. Another approach to the eschatological understanding of God's presence in youth ministry is found among the many scholars who draw on Jürgen Moltmann's theology of hope, rooted in the philosopher Ernst Bloch's principal of hope. Wesley Ellis has argued that the focus on eschatology enables us to look for God's active presence in all the places it may not seem to belong, even within the context of youth ministry. Ellis argues that "central to an eschatological praxis is an epistemic humility." This may be understood as a posture of listening, along the lines of what Moltmann calls "patience." In the light of an eschatological approach to interpreting God's presence in youth ministry, the young person is no

---

89. Dean, *Almost Christian*, 196. To this see also how Walter Brueggemann emphasizes that symbols of hope cannot be general nor universal but must be known concretely in a particular story; cf. Brueggemann, *The Prophetic Imagination*, 64.

90. Griffiths, *A Christlike Ministry*, 94–96.

91. Griffiths, *A Christlike Ministry*, 85.

92. Cf. how the Hungarian Philosopher and Sociologist Elemér Hankiss claims that "Anxiety and creative power: these may be the two poles of human existence." Hankiss, *Fears and Symbols*, 37.

longer just "a potential adult, a human *becoming*, but as a human *being*," rooted in the practice of story-listening.[93]

In other words, there is an *eschatological* emphasis in much of contemporary youth ministry research. For Helen Blier and Graham Stanton, in their article on "wide-awakeness" in youth ministry, the argument seems to be that Christ is present in the kingdom vision of shalom, in a hope grounded in the resurrection of Christ. They therefore advocate the role of martyrdom as testimony in youth ministry "the way of martyrdom has the power to be transformative, not as an act of personal persuasion by the youth minister, but as an act of testimony to Christ. They suggest that Christian discipleship finds transformation in interpersonal relationships that announce and embody the presence and promise of Christ.[94] Blier and Stanton's emphasis on the future hope of the in-breaking of God's kingdom through discipleship as martyrdom resonates with much of the theological sentiment in contemporary youth ministry scholarship. Much of the theological engagement in youth ministry is geared towards change and to the future. Theologically, this often seems to add an eschatological flavor to things.

The focus on the future and the need for change seems to create a dialectic current in much of youth ministry theology. This dialectic is also present in other contemporary theological streams, like liberation theology in different fashions, and other theological movements directly or indirectly influenced by the Marxist legacy of change. Marx's eleventh thesis on Feuerbach, claiming that the philosophers have only *interpreted* the world, in various ways and that the point is to *change* it, could even apply as an axiom for much of the theological ambition that stems forth from contemporary youth ministry scholarship in its theological and ecclesiological engagement.

Perhaps it would be more accurate to align the theological and ecclesial legacy of many youth ministry studies with German philosopher Theodor Adorno's idea of *utopia*. For Adorno the concept of utopia is philosophically important, since a conception of another world in the future enables the political activity of trying to change the world here and now. Although Adorno accepted the Marxist analysis of the social, he reversed Marx' thesis, as he would not subordinate thought to practice. Rather Adorno and the Frankfurter School advocated the use of critical

---

93. Ellis, *Human Beings and Human Becomings*, 135–36.
94. Blier and Stanton, "Wide-Awakeness in the World."

thought to bring about change in society, in the light of a future utopia.[95] Similarly, the theoretical elaboration of the church as a community in youth ministry is often conceptualized as a sort of *utopia*. The practice of community in youth ministry, at least in theory, appears as an appetizer of God's eschatological kingdom feast, a laboratory of hope[96] which represents a foretaste of things yet to come.

5.6 Conclusion

How then does the practice focus of section 5.3 relate to the eschatological lens of the final section (5.5)? Although many practices and rites of passage, and the religious socialization that follows with it, often support the socioeconomic status quo of a society, this is not necessarily always the case. Religion practices religious rites and symbols may also be some of the most important drives for change, as they might be effective in uniting people's beliefs with their actions and making their ideas relevant for their social lives. This has to do with how religious symbols often present an *image* of future change.[97] So although religious rites and symbols appeal to tradition and continuity, they may also play an important role in a group's desire for change.[98]

Among many youth ministry scholars it is common to claim that "youth work is only as good as its underpinning theology."[99] For a youth ministry scholar, it is essential to reflect on how you discover and explore the "underpinning theology" of a particular youth ministry. Doing this, it is key to reflect on the theology as a *glocal* practice, being both fundamentally a global and globalized endeavor and fundamentally local and contextual at the same time.[100] It is therefore well worth noting that, some youth ministry scholars also offer critical perspectives of traditional and potentially hegemonic interpretations of God's presence, like Anthony Reddie, who critiques Black Christianity's tendency to be embedded in Eurocentric thought forms, and even the adherence to the version of

---

95. Benzaquèn, "Thought and Utopia."
96. Cf. Dean, *Almost Christian*.
97. McGuire, *Religion*, 245.
98. McGuire, *Religion*, 243, 249, 251.
99. Savage et al., *Making Sense of Generation Y*, 129.
100. For further reflections on youth ministry as a glocal practice, cf. Norheim, "Naming Glocal Fear."

nineteenth-century biblicism. Reddie therefore issues a warning against a too individualistic approach to interpreting God's presence, even taking socio-political contexts into account when developing modes to interpret God's presence in youth ministry.[101]

---

101. Reddie, "Re-thinking," 176, 181, 184–86.

6

Researching God's Presence in Youth Ministry

"We offer presence."[1]

"In order to conduct good research, you need both: the roughness of the practice and the cleanness of the theory."[2]

THIS chapter elucidates how to research the presence of God in the context of youth ministry. In a way, it serves as a prelude to the more extensive treatment of research methodology in part 5 of the book, which asks about how to do research on youth ministry (practice). At the same time, chapter 6 and part 5 offer different takes on youth ministry research methodology, based on an assessment of contemporary youth ministry research. Whereas part 5 will present a research framework and research design mainly oriented towards the empirical, the current chapter presents a comprehensive typology for a theologically informed interpretation of empirical and more theoretical research projects on youth ministry practice. In 6.1, we start by offering a research outlook on the theme. 6.2 discusses what it might imply to research God's presence in the context of young people's experiences. Section 6.3 examines what it might imply to research God's presence in community and practice in youth ministry. The discussion will here make use of Lutheran Christology to offer

---

1. Kageler, *Youth Ministry in a Multifaith Society*, 178.
2. Van Wijnen, *Faith in Small Groups*, 150.

a nuanced and at the same time complex exposition of what it might imply that the triune God reveals Godself in practice and community. The following section (6.4) envisions the research of God's presence in youth ministry as a struggle, drawing on the ancient theological dialectic of apophatic and cataphatic theology. In the final part of chapter (6.5), we close by arguing for the importance of theological wiggle room in the research of God's presence in youth ministry.

6.1 Introduction: A Research Design for the Presence of God?

Like in other disciplines more or less associated with practical theology, there has been a widespread shift towards research of what we might call "lived experience" in youth ministry over the last decades. This might be coined as an "empirical turn," but it simultaneously acknowledges that a reorientation and re-envisioning of what it means to engage doctrine in ministry, is needed. It represents a turn to the lived, which has brought a new appreciation of the place of theology and divine encounter in the study of religious communities.

How may one then research the presence of God in youth ministry? What theological presumptions, underlies the notion that empirical, qualitative research is able to say anything about the presence of god or God in youth ministry? Traditionally, the mandate for empirical research in ministry has been authorized by creation theology in some fashion. As God is the god of creation, and Christians tend to believe that God has "not left the building," theological research may employ qualitative methods and use human reason to explore and investigate human experience as a possible arena for encountering the Triune God in ministry.

One way to categorize these attempts to interpret the presence of God, or more precisely the presence of Christ in youth ministry, would be to suggest four *models* for reflection, or hermeneutical concepts, which offer a way to comprehend and make claims about the presence of Christ in and through human experience:

- Model 1: The presence of Christ in the *youth minister*
- Model 2: The presence of Christ in the *encounter* and *practice* of youth ministry
- Model 3: The presence of Christ in the *experience (of the youth)*

- *Model 4:* The presence of Christ in the *question*: Youth ministry as hermeneutical struggle[3]

A basic presumption for any research engagement with God's presence in youth ministry is of course the fundamental theological conviction that God reveals himself in Scripture, and through tradition and with the help of reason. At the same time, the four models are rooted in the theological assessment, that by reading Scripture and studying the tradition, and even examining reason, we are confronted with the possibility that God may reveal Godself in the empirical world.

This implies that when we research God's presence in ministry, we also need to evaluate the different conceptualizations of God's presence—or Christ's presence, to be exact—in youth ministry theologically. Simultaneously, we also we need to consider human beings' position before God (*coram Deo*). This includes making an account of how the matrix of sin and brokenness, into which human life is intertwined, should inform the interpretative limitations of any research on the presence of God, in youth ministry or elsewhere. This corresponds to an understanding of theological dogmatics, which consists in ever anew discerning and distinguishing between God's revelation and human religion, God's Word and man's own word.[4]

This approach to theological research is rooted in the fundamental conviction that theology is about seeing. Such an assessment is related to what Alistair McGrath finds to be the primary task of practical theology, which is to enable theologians to see situations and individuals from the standpoint of the Christian tradition, "so that we may evaluate them and behave toward them in an authentically Christian way."[5]

It is here also important to take note of how Jos De Kock distinguishes four layers of normativity: (1) the layer of discourse in religious practice; (2) the layer of professional theory of practice; (3) the layer of academic theory of practice; and (4) the layer of the metatheoretical foundation of the research project. Drawing on Deborah Court's book *Qualitative Research and Intercultural Understanding—Conducting Qualitative Research in Multicultural Settings*, de Kock argues for the positioning of qualitative research as a personal encounter of the researcher with the other and with otherness: "In qualitative research the researcher is a

---

3. This model is adopted and adjusted from Norheim, "The Presence of Christ."
4. Schlink, *Theology of the Lutheran Confessions*, 27.
5. McGrath, "The Cultivation of Theological Vision," 115.

research participant no less than those whom s/he is studying. Qualitative researchers collect and analyze data through the lens of who they are.[6]

All in all, research in the context of youth ministry obviously has to consider carefully the relationship between theology and qualitative research, when God's presence in youth ministry is the research theme and research context. This includes the ambition to connect research methods and fundamental epistemological reflections to the shape of each research project, and by reflecting on the relationship between theology and qualitative research. What is needed is a nuanced reflection on how theology shapes the design of the focus of the research project and to further reflect on how the relationship between theology and qualitative research shapes the research project as a whole.

The purpose of the following sections is to offer theological reflection on this research area, God's presence in youth ministry. Which theologically informed hermeneutical and epistemological underpinnings are key as we embark on researching where God is in youth ministry? Articulating confessional and contextual implications of this research theme, the intention of the following reflection is to foster a deeper understanding of how contextual and confessional considerations and framings shape the theological design of research projects trying to interpret the presence of God in youth ministry. Although youth ministry as both an academic and practical discipline performs and holds a profound ecumenical quality, it sometimes lacks an awareness of the confessional and socio-geographical context of youth ministry. The following section will hopefully contribute to a more comprehensive approach here.[7]

6.2 Researching God's presence in Young People's Experiences

Let us start by asking the following question: What does it mean for research on religious experience among young people that the church is an interpretative community? Bert Roebben, complains that "the answer of the official churches on the crisis of religious experience tends towards a renewed and increased focus on the small group of core believers." We have seen in chapter 5 that many researchers strive to conduct research

---

6. De Kock, "Wait a Minute in Stressful Times," 38.
7. Cf. Norheim, "Confessionality."

with relevance beyond such a core group. Roebben also mourns that "a church who withdraws itself, who doesn't risk or dare itself to be scorched by the dynamics of the world and its future generations, will lose her correlative power, her vision on how faith and life relate, and on how God wants to exceed himself in this world."[8]

Roebben argues for engaging with young people in finding fresh theological vocabulary and new approaches to religious experience, which may in the long term contribute "to the development of new Christian doctrine." On the other hand, this re-imagining and re-living of the gospel is not about conforming the gospel to our present culture, but it is about bringing "the Gospel closer to itself, where it belongs, namely into the realm of friendship where God happens."[9]

In other words, if we are to imagine the presence of God in young people and their experiences, theologically speaking we need to keep in mind that the Christian self is a decentered self. This means that theologically speaking the self is constituted by another, by Christ. Simultaneously that self is a self, which is constituted for others, for the neighbor and the world.[10] So, when we research human experience, that experience, as being together in Christ, is *gifted* in a certain sense. This gift is not an inherent quality in each person, but rather a gift to uncover the mystery of the presence of Christ in and through human experience as relationships and encounters. As young people and those who accompany them see and receive the world, they may become gifted to see the world as God's world and use that insight to serve the neighbor.

6.3 Researching God's Presence in Community and Practice

Moving from section 6.2 to 6.3 it is worth paying attention to how it may be possible to combine the focus on human experience and human relationships as a place for God-encounters with a turn to practice(s). American theologian Martha Ellen Stortz claims that "the faith practices of Christianity develop as disciples seek to stay close to the One whom

---

8. Roebben claims that "beneath the *Tradierungskrise*, the crisis that makes it difficult for churches to connect the Christian faith with everyday life, lies an *experiential crisis*." Roebben, *Seeking Sense in the City*, 202–4.

9. Roebben, *Seeking Sense in the City*, 216–17.

10. Mattes, "The Thomistic Turn," 80.

they love, the One whom they follow."[11] How do we access the presence of God, then?

One way to respond to the dilemma of the question above would be to advocate that researching God's presence in youth ministry implies, in a postmodern fashion, a sort of reclamation of imagination as *a* or *the* human bridge to a sacramental encounter with the Divine. The question is how a different framework of human knowing enables different conceptions of God. In the premodern era, the believer experienced the world as mysterious or enchanted, as Charles Taylor puts it. With the modern era, the printing press can be said to have captured mystery and put the mystic experience on paper with the help of technology, and this enabled that experience to be objectified—analyzed, manipulated, and perhaps even controlled. Some scholars would advocate the postmodern era reintroduces and reclaims mystery as a hermeneutical category. The mode of research, then, is imagination, which is "the bridge by which we *stretch* from the everyday to the mystery."[12]

This approach connects well with another strand of research, namely the study of young people's participation in worship. Worship turns the person towards the triune God, and fundamentally therefore, research on worship practice(s) would imply an explicit or implicit research interest in how to interpret the presence of God (in youth ministry). An interesting Dutch study of young people participating in youth worship events thematizes this question. The study collected data from four different youth worship events, amongst them a Christmas event and a worship festival events. In the study, Sonnenberg et al found that the concept of "being together" was crucial. They researched four different worship events, namely:

1. a national Christmas event for the youth organization of the Protestant Church in the Netherlands (JOP), called *X-Mas Proof*;
2. a day arranged by the Evangelical Broadcasting Company, the so-called *EO youth day* (studied twice in different years);
3. the *XNoizz Flevo Festival*, a worship festival organized by Youth for Christ together with the EO and JOP organizations already mentioned;
4. a *European Taizé* event in the Netherlands.

11. Stortz, "Practicing Christians," 3.
12. O'Gorman, "Imagination Embodied," 434.

It turned out that some respondents in the study, particularly girls, connected the experience of being together with an experience of God's presence. More programmatically put, "in the presence of others, also the presence of the Other may happen."[13] For a more nuanced account of a research design of this sort, Ronelle Sonnenberg expands reflections on these themes in her dissertation (2014) and argues that for some of these young people the presence of God was a conviction, but also an experience.[14]

For a more comprehensive theological assessment of the pursuit of researching God's presence in youth ministry practice, it is worth paying attention to the fact that sometimes even the respondents of an empirical research project in youth ministry may express ambiguity in identifying God's presence, even though worship songs and preaching themes suggest that God is immediately, and immensely present. Then it is key for the researcher to be attentive to the young people's reflections and experiences. A research project on young people's participation in worship preparations identified a certain need among the youth to safeguard God from being framed by what was seen, heard, felt, and tasted. God was at once both powerfully present, but ultimately beyond sensation. If they were to speak of God as clearly present, many of the young people identified God with something in the past, perhaps in their home church, or in a cathedral in a foreign land. The young leaders demonstrated a clear reluctance, or hesitation, to speak about their shaping of a place of worship in relation to the presence of God.[15]

The evaluation so far has left us with a range of questions when it comes to developing a nuanced theological hermeneutics for researching the presence of God in youth ministry. With the aim of developing a more comprehensive, theological framework for research on the presence of God in youth ministry, the following sections offer a historical exposition of how Martin Luther and the Lutheran tradition interpreted the presence of Christ. We will focus particularly on the sacramental controversies with the left wing of the Reformation, and these theological discussions may offer an interpretative lens to better understand the presence of Christ in youth ministry.

---

13. Sonnenberg et al., "Being Together in Youth Worship," 7–9.
14. Sonnenberg, "Youth Worship in Protestant Contexts," 194.
15. Norheim and Tveitereid, "Stemning."

First, let us start with the term "practice" in itself. Obviously, Luther does not use the term "practice" in the way MacIntyre and other contemporary Neo-Aristotelian thinkers do, as well as many contemporary youth ministry scholars. However, Luther on several occasions uses the word "practice."[16] It is, however, crucial to place Luther's understanding of the presence of Christ in the context of his theology of the incarnation and his theology of the sacraments. Already in 1527, in *This is My Body*, Luther rejected Zwingli's assumption that the risen Christ is located only at the right hand of God, which is confined to one heavenly location. Rather, as the right hand of God is everywhere, Christ is everywhere.[17] In other words, "Christ is near, and not confined to one spot in heaven."[18] The implication of this is that God may manifest his power everywhere. In general, Luther questions any attempt to confine Christ (only) to one particular place. Luther celebrates both the universal presence of Christ in creation, and the particular presence of Christ in the sacraments, or the church's core practices. Therefore, Christ is both in the midst of all human experience—in, with and under it. At the same time Christ is there for us in a particular way in the places to which he has promised his saving presence. These theological underpinnings may serve as a preamble for any research on the presence of God in youth ministry.

Further, Luther argues in *Confession concerning Christ's Supper* (1528) that there are three modes known to us in which Christ is present. Luther develops his interpretation of these three modes based on his reading of Scripture, and the Jesus-narrative in particular, and in critical dialogue with medieval Ockhamist philosophy.[19] The first mode, or the circumscriptive mode, is the mode where Christ walks bodily on earth, occupying and yielding space according to his size. This is the mode ascribed to Christ from nativity until crucifixion. The second mode, or the diffinitive, uncircumscribed mode, is where Christ "occupies nor yields space, but passes through everything created as he wills." This is the spiritual mode ascribed to Christ from resurrection until ascension. This is also the mode Luther applies to the presence of Christ in the Lord's Supper. The third mode, or the repletive mode, is the divine or heavenly mode, and is ascribed to the way the exalted Christ seated to the right of

---

16. In German, Luther uses the verb "treiben" or "üben"; cf. Kolb and Wengert, *Book of Concord*, 466; Luther, *Martin Luther Studienausgabe*, 593.

17. Luther, *Word and Sacrament III*, 47, 55, 207.

18. Luther, *Word and Sacrament III*, 280.

19. Luther, *Word and Sacrament III*, 214–31, esp. 214–15.

the Father, is present. In this mode, created things "cannot measure or circumscribe him but they are present to him so that he measures and circumscribes them."[20]

If we combine the distinctions Luther here makes with the categorization of the *notae ecclesiae* in *On the Councils and the Church* we are able to discern between different circles of practices. In the first circle, there are those practices, which are by necessity Christian. These are practices on the economy of salvation, which offer the salvific presence of Christ, or Christ according to his *diffinitive* presence. They may be labeled "first-tablet (Christian) practices," parallel to Reinhard Hütter's term, "the church's core practices." In the next circle, you find the "second-tablet practices." These are practices on the economy of creation, through which Christ may be present according to his *repletive* presence, which is a sustaining presence. These practices are not by necessity Christian. What then might make these practices of the second tablet "Christian"? Luther, in different treatises, used a variety of words for the marks of the church, using terms like colors, markings and signs. In a sermon from 1538 on the foot-washing on Maundy Thursday in John 13, Luther saw it necessary to include "love" as a fruit of faith created by word and sacrament.[21]

This is in many ways parallel to how Luther towards the very end of *Confession concerning Christ's Supper* introduced the term "the common order of Christian love," which is lived out within the daily calling of the Christian by serving every needy person, offering the thirsty something to drink, forgiving enemies, and praying for all men on earth.[22] Based on this, we see that what may make second-tablet practices "Christian," is their *diaconal* telos; the love for the other, the neighbor. These second-tablet practices may therefore be "Christian" insofar as the "common order of Christian love" is practiced through them—for the benefit of the neighbor and all creation, as the *telos* of the second-tablet practices is diaconal. This is very-well summed up in Luther's *The Freedom of the Christian* (1520), where he highlights that a Christian lives in Christ through faith, and in the neighbor through good works. He or she is therefore a perfectly free lord of all, subject to none, and that a Christian is simultaneously a perfectly dutiful servant of all, subject to all.[23]

20. Luther, *Word and Sacrament III*, 222–23.

21. See here Lathrop and Wengert, *Christian Assembly*, 83.

22. Luther, *Word and Sacrament III*, 365.

23. Luther, *Career of the Reformer*, 344. For a comprehensive account of how to employ Martin Luther's Christology in the theological engagement with practice(s) in (youth) ministry, see Norheim, *Practicing Baptism*.

We will therefore argue that the church—for the research purpose(s) that we here try to assess theologically—could be defined in a strict sense as the place where sins are forgiven. However, more needs to be said, and written. If the church is the place where one may encounter the presence of Jesus Christ, the Son of God, who offers unconditional forgiveness, the church is the place where one may come to know God. However, here we encounter a true and inescapable paradox: The gospel of the presence of God's grace and love through Christ serves as a promise, not as a mere statement of human experience. This paradox must be considered as a sort of theological *aporia*: When researching human experiences in community and practice(s) in youth ministry, the research practice itself is a sort of open paradox, a contradictory riddle, or a "hermeneutical struggle," a term that will be introduced in the next section. What does this imply? Theologically speaking, trying to identify the presence of God in practice and community therefore remains embedded in the dialectic of the revealed God and the hidden God, in the dynamic of apophatic and cataphatic theology, which we will explore in more depth in the next sections. In his book, *Christopraxis: A Practical Theology of the Cross* (2014), American Youth Ministry Scholar, Andrew Root, offers a set of practical-theological hermeneutics that in many ways continues and develops the Lutheran, Christological legacy presented above and expands its implications for contemporary practical theological research—and research on the presence of God in youth ministry.

In the introduction to *Christopraxis*, drawing on critical realism, Root makes the case for "a realist practical theology." He finds, when investigating human experience in and through (youth) ministry, that identifying "divine action is always a real possibility." At the same time, there is always a need for judgment and evaluation:

> It is possible that our experiences of God are truly that, but it is also possible that we are confused or misguided. I claim, with critical realism, that parts of reality exist outside the human mind, that there is a real world that human minds cannot possess. But because this is so, we are always in need of judgment and discernment of our experiences. Because reality is more than us, there is the possibility that we do have real encounters with God.[24]

---

24. Root, *Christopraxis*, xiv.

There are of course other ways to do explorative research on God's presence in and through practices: A more interactive, and action-focused way of exploring God's presence in practices in youth ministry is found in the book *Way to Live: Christian Practices for Teens*. Here, eighteen teens and eighteen adults investigate ancient and more contemporary Christian practices to deepen awareness of God's presence in the lives of young people.[25]

6.4 Researching God's Presence in Ministry: A Hermeneutical Struggle

In chapter 5 we saw how Andrew Root criticized what he found to be much of theology's obsession with the everywhere-ness of God. But how then should the hermeneutical challenges of the *Deus Semper Major*-axiom be assessed theologically as we try to investigate how to interpret the presence of God in youth ministry? Accepting the inscrutability of the divine, implies that it is not possible to argue from a presumption of knowledge. As we have already emphasized above, it is thus important to consider the apophatic-cataphatic dialectic when we research the presence of God in youth ministry. This implies insisting on the appropriateness of not knowing and an apophatic mode in any such research attempt is a fundamental mode for theological hermeneutics and research on the practice of God's presence in youth ministry.

The benefit of making use of the apophatic-cataphatic distinction as we research the presence of God in youth ministry and insisting on an apophatic mode next to a cataphatic mode of research, is that it reminds us that human experiences do not necessarily fully coincide with who God is and how God may reveal Godself. Doing research on God's presence in youth ministry therefore means cultivating vision. However, this vision, is always contested. The danger in researching the presence of Christ in youth ministry is therefore to become a theologian of glory, someone who favours a direct approach to God.[26]

Robert W. Jenson suggests that theological hermeneutics should be understood as a *struggle*. Similarly to McGrath, Jenson argues that theology has to do with the practices and language of a discerning

---

25. Bass, *Way to Live*.

26. Norheim, "Cultivating a Vision of the Unseen"; De Kock and Norheim, "Youth Ministry Research."

community.²⁷ Both place the hermeneutics of theology not merely in the academic classroom, but in the life of the church, founded in the concrete practices of preaching and worshiping. But Jenson seems less optimistic as to whether it is possible to gain a clear, theological vision. He therefore emphasizes that doing theology, and reading Scripture in particular, is a *struggle*, "because lives and behaviour are at stake and folk are not going to let us off with evasions." Therefore "the struggle itself is the hermeneutical principle," according to Jenson.²⁸

This implies that our seeing is always somewhat distorted. Both when working with empirical data from ethnographic research, and working with ecclesiology dogmatically, and particularly as we *struggle* to manoeuvre between the two, we need a balanced dialectic between the cataphatic and apophatic mode. The negotiation between those two modes of theological interpretation, is a constant struggle, a *tentatio*. Researching God's presence in youth ministry should therefore be interpreted as a *tentatio*, a hermeneutical struggle. This hermeneutical principle also seems to correspond well with a critical realism-epistemology.²⁹

The hermeneutical struggle that follows from interpreting human reception of divine agency through the incarnation and the on-going work of the triune God in the empirical context of youth ministry, is always something contested. This is true, not just from the perspective of human experience, but even from the perspective of the revelation of God's presence, since the revelation of the gospel of the church, God's love in Jesus Christ, is hidden under the cross as a *tentatio*. Viewed from the perspective of the triune God's gradual revelation history, the church is even in an "already-not-yet" state. Our image of the church is fundamentally rooted in a theology of God's hiddenness. In other words, the concept of God hidden under weakness is an aspect of a *theologia crucis*. Radically understood, the implication here is that "the faith of man corresponds to the hiddenness of God," as "the struggle for faith—*of* faith—arises from the free choice of God that he is to be found under the cover

---

27. Jenson, *The Triune God*, 18.
28. Jenson, "Hermeneutics and the Life of the Church," 94–95.
29. To this, see for instance how Andrew Wright argues against the Cartesian-driven quest for epistemic closure, which holds that knowledge of reality is either absolutely certain (modernity) or absolutely uncertain (postmodernity), and by this that both modernity and postmodernity commit "the epistemic fallacy of reducing ontology to epistemology and restricting reality to the extent and limits—whether greater or lesser—of human knowledge." Wright, *Christianity and Critical Realism*, 10.

of weak external things."[30] In part 5, and particularly in chapter 16, these hermeneutical insights and considerations are embedded in the research framework and research design we propose.

6.5 Conclusion: Theological Wiggle Room?

In conclusion, how should we research God's presence in youth ministry? One thing seems obvious, we need to take the otherness of God, the appropriateness of speaking about the triune God's presence in both cataphatic and apophatic terms. As we embark on this research pursuit, it may even be worth reflecting on the presence of God in ministry by considering which character Jesus Christ is represented by in a particular youth ministry. Andy Stirrup has argued that portraying Jesus as something of a superhero is problematic: "When we think of modern superheroes and when we consider Jesus and his mission in the light of their stories, we run the risk of suggesting that Jesus is somehow remote and detached, which would not do justice to the reality of the incarnation. We also run the risk of presenting the salvation he offers as a weak and limited thing, a sort of spiritual first aid; but the reality is better explored in terms of a new creation." The presentation of God must therefore remain firmly anchored in the primary world.[31]

Yet another way to look at the persona or ethos of Christ as a way of interpreting the presence of God in youth ministry is by engaging postmodern thought and contemporary theology, particularly Jürgen Moltmann's three-dimensional Christology (the eschatological, the theological, and the social Christ), in conversation. Richard James argues that "in a decentered age where identity and meaning is often sought through the acquisition of goods and shallow consumerism telling and sharing God's (small) stories encourages the postmodern young person to associate with Christ, and helps them find much needed meaning. Christ then soon becomes their 'identity expert.'" James further finds that "contrary to popular opinion postmodernism does not discourage young people from discovering Jesus Christ, it actually encourages that discovery to become real and personal."[32]

---

30. Trigg, *Baptism in the Theology of Martin Luther*, 28–29.
31. Stirrup, "Is Jesus My Superhero?," 74–75.
32. James, "Discovering Jesus," 63, 68.

Research on God's presence in youth ministry is usually empirically qualified on one level or another and theologically informed in some fashion. Perhaps one way forward for any research of this sort would be to operate with a kind of "theological wiggle room" as the language of the research, both the data and the metatheoretical reflections, is produced. As theology is an art of performance, both in the social, the personal, and the theological, a language for the approximate and imprecise nature of theological reflections is required, hence the need for a theological wiggle room.[33]

---

33. Tveitereid and Norheim, "*Theological Wiggle Room*," 2.

Part 3

WHAT IS THE PURPOSE OF YOUTH MINISTRY?

What Is the Purpose of Youth Ministry?

Introduction to Part 3

THIS part of the handbook focuses on the following key question: *What is the purpose of youth ministry?* It provides a variety of research-based insights on what youth ministry might aim for. Reflection on the purpose of youth ministry is important because setting goals is instructive for how youth ministry practices are performed and perceived. Part 3 will explore both aims and typologies of aims that resemble categories used in general educational settings, and aims and typologies of aims that are theologically loaded, rooted in church and youth ministry contexts. And of course, we will discover a range of theories about this.

The question of the purpose of youth ministry is discussed in two chapters. Where chapter 7 focuses on the broad width of different types of goals and typologies of goals found in youth ministry literature and youth ministry research, chapter 8 addresses what might be labeled "theologically loaded goals," i.e., goals that are formulated and understood primarily in theological language. Chapter 7 highlights typologies of religious learning goals, catechetical learning goals, and sets of youth ministry goal types in relation to church paradigms. The chapter presents a multi-colored picture of what youth ministry practices might ultimately aim for.

Following from this, chapter 8 shows how theological language functions in the area of goal setting in youth ministry. Theological language can be helpful because youth ministry practices are functioning in theologically loaded contexts of faith communities, but at the same time, theologically loaded goals are challenging. Although rooted in theology and/or Scripture, such goals necessitate reflection on their practical application in concrete contexts of youth ministry. The chapter sheds light on goals such as finding God, encountering God, salvation, being in relationships, and living as disciples.

7

Typologies of Goals

"Hope-centered agenda targets youths' discovery of content and meanings of the Christian faith that give them handles on how faith connects with their present and future lives. . . . A helpful way of considering goals is to take renewed notice of the characteristics of youth in our youth ministry and ones we seek to reach. When we take seriously these characteristics, we also make holistic ministry central. Include goals of spiritual development, cultural awareness and affirmation, social learning, environmental and political awareness and response, cognitive development and educational preparedness, emotional well-being, and physical development."[1]

SETTING an agenda for youth ministry begins with setting goals. Setting goals in youth ministry is the main theme of this part of the handbook. If we examine the literature on different approaches to youth ministry, we can detect various kinds of goals, although they are not always made explicit. Therefore, the current chapter reviews particular publications in which typologies of goals are presented. These typologies help us to understand the breadth of possible goals of youth ministry and how to navigate them.

The authors of *Youth Ministry in the Black Church: Centered in Hope* illustrate this breadth by summing up goals for holistic ministry that vary from spiritual development to emotional well-being, from cultural awareness to physical development. This chapter tries to categorize the

1. Wimberly et al., *Youth Ministry in the Black Church*, 119–21.

different types of goals and typologies of goals found in youth ministry practices and youth ministry research. As a first step, section 7.1 will draw a broad perspective from the angle of spirituality outcomes. Next, in section 7.2 main categories of religious learning goals will be discussed. Next, our discussion of typologies of goals is continued by describing sets of youth ministry goal types in relationship to church paradigms (section 7.3). Section 7.4 will focus on types of goals in the particular context of catechetical learning environments. The chapter closes with a conclusion in section 7.6.

7.1 Spirituality Outcomes

In chapter 3 we already observed that the concept of faith development is sometimes linked up with spiritual type theories. A spiritual type theory is at the core of a publication by Samuel Baker on spirituality type outcomes. In a study on assessing catechetical models of adolescent faith development, Samuel Baker analyzes data collected over seven years among late adolescent students at a private Christian university in the US.[2] In the article in 2015 in which the results of the study were published, Baker interpreted the results in terms of the theory of spiritual types and argues that this theory can be applied to both the context of youth ministry and the context of Christian colleges. The theory broadens the often more restricted catechetical perspectives by including a broad range of approaches to faith formation, incorporating both kataphatic and apophatic approaches to spiritual growth. The dimension kataphatic—apophatic spirituality is one of the two axes in the *Circle of Sensibility* originally presented by Urban Holmes, which Baker takes as a basis for his understanding of goal orientations in youth ministry and Christian education.[3] The second axis is the axis of heart-directedness—mind-directedness.

According to Baker, kataphatic spirituality describes the revealed God (by using images and symbols referring to one's relationship and union with God) where the apophatic spirituality is about the mystery of God (going beyond images and words, with a place for silence, more directed towards a mystical union). When it comes to the second axis: a mind-oriented type of spirituality is oriented towards thinking, cognition, and intellectual activity (to know God), whereas the heart-oriented

---

2. Baker, "Raised a Teenage Kataphatic."
3. Holmes, *A History of Christian Spirituality.*

type of spirituality is oriented towards feeling, sensation, and emotion (to sense God). In the research data Baker analyzes, a tendency towards a kataphatic orientation was observed; against this background Baker pleads for a more balanced approach that also includes apophatic orientations. This is important to the author because Baker presumes the orientation to a particular type of spirituality in catechetical models functions like a "goal orientation," influencing the faith development of late adolescents. Combining the two axes of spirituality type orientations leaves the youth minister the choice for goal orientations in terms of (1) thinking (Mind-Kataphatic orientation), (2) feeling (Heart-Kataphatic orientation), (3) being (Heart-Apophatic orientation), and (4) doing (Mind-Apophatic orientation).[4]

Whole-Making

Earlier, in chapter 1, we addressed the theme of spirituality and quoted Kathleen Engebretson who describes spirituality as "apprehension of a sacred dimension in life, and the implications that this has for the way one lives."[5] In chapter 3, we argued that the term spirituality is used in many different ways in youth ministry literature: sometimes, the term is more or less used as a synonym for (religious) identity or faith; sometimes, the term spirituality is reserved for the aspect of (religious) beliefs; sometimes it is set aside for the aspect of experience; and sometimes it is seen as synonym for "lived faith." In 2002, David Hindman argued for spiritual development as a core goal for colleges engaged with students. The title of his article, "From Splintered Lives to Whole Persons: Facilitating Spiritual Development in College Students," reveals how the author conceives the aim of spiritual development. It has to do with becoming whole persons. Becoming a whole person is related to the development of a healthy spirituality which is "a dynamic expression of who we are, truly."[6]

Becoming a whole person, or the notion of 'whole making,' is referred to in the youth ministry literature, as also by Reginald Blount in his article, "Toward Whole-Making: The Power of Voice in the Faith Formation of Black Youth." Blount defines the concept of whole-making, with

---

4. Baker, "Raised a Teenage Kataphatic," 50.
5. Engebretson, "Young People, Culture, and Spirituality," 6.
6. Hindman, "From Splintered Lives to Whole Persons," 165.

reference to the theologian Howard Thurman,[7] as arriving at community on the interpersonal and intrapersonal levels. Interpersonal community refers to connectedness and relationship with one another; intrapersonal community refers to a sense of self-worth and the allowance of fully actualizing one's own potential. Blount states: "I believe this process of whole-making that includes the work of Intrapersonal Community building is essential for the faith formation of Black youth."[8] Blount's contribution is embedded in the discussion on the distinctive characteristics of youth ministry among African-American youth in the confrontation with racism and conflicting cultural forces. According to Blount, the church has an important task to make space for the process of whole-making for these youngsters who yearn "for a healthy and liberating theological anthropology."[9]

Spiritual Development and Spiritual Maturity

The previous subsection discussed whole-making as a particular theme within the general aim of spiritual development. The current section addresses the goal of spiritual development and becoming spiritually mature in general. For example, Melissa Ann Brandes sees the healthy spiritual development of youth as an important goal for religious communities.[10] In her study, she explored a summer camp of the Reformed Church in America that took place in New York State's Adirondack Park. Interviews were conducted with twelve participants, aged eighteen to twenty-eight. Through these interviews, the author identified seven aspects of spirituality. Brandes states: "When these aspects of spirituality are nurtured and develop in positive ways, they seem to counter some of the detrimental effects of the pressures of the larger culture and fill in the gaps left by a weakened Church."[11] The seven aspects are Identity, Purpose, Belonging, Sense of Worth, Capacity to Care, Reflectiveness, and Integrity. Based on these seven aspects, Brandes proposes an integrated spiritual development model that nurtures positive growth in the spiritual lives of young people.

7. See, i.e., Thurman, *Disciplines of the Spirit*.
8. Blount, "Toward Whole-Making," 46.
9. Blount, "Toward Whole-Making," 47.
10. Brandes, "Integrated Spiritual Development."
11. Brandes, "Integrated Spiritual Development," 193.

The aim of spiritual development is often linked up with the aim of more social-oriented goals. This is one of the outcomes of the following study. The central research question in an article from Naomi Thompson and James Ballantyne on Christian detached youth work in the *Journal of Youth and Theology* is: "How do Christian detached youth workers articulate the social and spiritual purposes and impact of their work with young people in the communities they serve?"[12] To answer the question, the authors conducted narrative research interviews via email with seven youth workers volunteering as detached youth workers for churches or Christian organizations. Six of them were based in England, one in Scotland. The findings suggest the youth workers' main purpose is "the formation of trusting relationships with young people, starting from their concerns and leading to young-person-led impacts, both social and spiritual."[13] The authors conclude that these relationships are catalysts for both the exploration of spiritual issues and the identification of social needs. These two areas are inter-linked and have overlap and are achieved within an incarnational approach to Christian detached youth work.

Spiritual development and spiritual maturity as dominant goal orientation in youth ministry is also critically encountered in the literature. Wesley Ellis, for example, critiqued this dominant approach in a contribution in *Journal of Youth and Theology* in 2015.[14] The main problem as observed by the author is the normative orientation in the concept of development in terms of progress, and the pathway towards spiritual maturity being seen in terms of a stage model. Ellis argues that youth ministry needs to be determined theologically rather than developmentally. An important theological interpretive corrective the author introduces is based on the eschatological theology of Jürgen Moltmann. "In an eschatological praxis, the object and center of ministry is not the Christian adulthood into which adolescents are developing, but the youth themselves in their encounter with God in the depth of lived experience. . . . Growth may follow but the success of our ministry does not depend on it. So, the pragmatic question of youth ministry is not 'how can I develop them?' but 'how can I love them?' And 'how can I participate in God's ministry in their life?'"[15]

12. Thompson and Ballantyne, "Being Church," 91.
13. Thompson and Ballantyne, "Being Church," 111.
14. Ellis, "Human Beings and Human Becomings."
15. Ellis, "Human Beings and Human Becomings," 134–35.

Ellis' critical reflection on the developmental perspective in youth ministry partly corresponds with that of Brett Webb-Mitchell which was already discussed in chapter 3.[16] Webb-Mitchell criticizes theories of developmental psychology for being too much influenced by Enlightenment ideals and religious education in churches for being too much influenced by developmental psychologist theories. To correct this, Webb-Mitchell does not propose to skip the growth normativity in youth ministry ideals, however, but instead to see growth more in terms of community and obedience to authority, with a vision of the interconnection of mind, body, and spirit in Christ and an accent on both the particularity of Christianity and the particularity of contexts and individual lives. This proposal can be understood as replacing a developmental psychology perspective on growth with a theological perspective on growth rooted in Old and New Testament accounts on pilgrimage.

In what follows, we will observe quite a bit of variety in this distinction between thinking-feeling-being-doing orientations. Whether in the discussion of religious learning goals (7.1), youth ministry goals and church paradigms (7.2), or catechetical learning goals (7.3).

7.2 Religious Learning Goals

In 2015, Jos de Kock published an overview article on the concept of learning in practical theological studies. In the article, the author analyzes different (empirical) research projects and educational and religious education literature in which the concept of learning is used. The article provides an overview of "descriptions of learning, (theological) interpretations of learning, normative positions regarding learning, and strategic considerations toward (the promotion of) learning."[17] Within the framework of his overview, De Kock also discusses the aspect of learning goals in the context of religious education and youth ministry. Referring to De Kock (2014),[18] the author distinguishes between learning goals in terms of (a) cognition and affection, (b) emotions and experiences, (c) the formation of one's own opinion and social interaction, and (d) identity development. He also points at the role of theological and biblical normativity in formulating goals for practices of religious learning. De

---

16. Webb-Mitchell, "Leaving Development Behind."
17. De Kock, "What about Learning?," 1.
18. De Kock, "A Typology of Catechetical Learning Environments."

Kock states that setting goals can be understood as an area of theological interpretation: the goal one sets for a learning situation expresses the way in which one expects religious learning to be theologically enhanced.

Where De Kock[19] presents cognitive and affective oriented learning goals in one category, the article from Richard Rymarz (2011) focuses on the different orientation of affective goals in comparison with cognitive goals.[20] The background to Rymarz' article is the context of Canadian Catholic schools where, in the educational discourse, a distinction is made between religious education and catechesis. "This distinction is based on the assumptions of faith commitment on the part of catechesis and the focus on cognitive outcomes on the part of religious education."[21] In many official Canadian Catholic Church documents, religious education is conceived as primarily catechetical, or the distinction between educational goals and catechetical goals is not made clearly.

The author argues that in contemporary culture, where the function of religious education for working towards faith commitment is no longer valid, an emphasis on educational cognitive goals in religious education is more appropriate at Catholic schools in Canada. Parents choose Catholic schooling for their children for reasons of familial link, proximity, and the general moral environment available, much more than for reasons of faith tradition and faith formation.

Rymarz, thus, distinguishes between cognitive coals and affective goals in religious education, based on the influential Bloom's taxonomy.[22] He does not see cognitive and affective learning goals as opposite or in tension with each other. But in the classroom a knowledge focus should prevail: for students who are part of a faith community, this knowledge can be an important instrument of catechesis; for other students, it serves to provide a firm understanding of Catholic religious claims. At the same time, Rymarz explains that the school as a whole, as a community, has its function and opportunities to foster catechesis.

In the distinction between different religious learning goals in the article by De Kock[23] we found the contrast between thinking-feeling-be-

19. De Kock, "What about Learning?"
20. Rymarz, "Catechesis and Religious Education."
21. Rymarz, "Catechesis and Religious Education," 537.
22. Bloom, *Taxonomy of Educational Objectives*; Anderson and Krathwohl, *A Taxonomy for Learning.*
23. De Kock, "What about Learning?"

ing-doing orientations of Baker[24] reflected. The contribution of Rymarz concentrated on the subcategories of affective and cognitive goals.[25] The 2012 contribution of Ronelle Sonnenberg and Marcel Barnard in *HTS Teologiese Studies* distinguishes five so called learning products, which is another angle from which we can discuss religious learning goals in relationship to youth ministry practices.[26] The article is based on empirical research on the participation of youth in worship in Protestant Dutch contexts. The data in the study is informed by fieldwork (including participant observations, interviews, taking pictures) during local worship gatherings in the Protestant Church in the Netherlands as well as at four (inter)national events. The main research questions in the article are: "How do young people, in a late-modern context, participate in youth worship? . . . How are youth worship and 'learning faith' related? And, what are the qualities of learning faith in youth worship?"[27]

Sonnenberg and Barnard, in their article, show what adolescents learn in youth worship gatherings. They identity five learning products or in their words "learning contents," mainly derived from the interviews with adolescents: (1) Information and support, referring to new knowledge, clarity on questions and topics, and receiving encouragement and challenges; (2) Knowledge about and insight into God, referring to both affectively and cognitively gaining new or renewed insight into who God is; (3) Religious and social-ethical applications, referring to "what to do" in relationship to God and in relationship to daily life; (4) Relevance of tradition, referring to the translation of something old (biblical texts or church practices) to a new context; and (5) Rules and freedom, referring to "things you *have to do* in life and faith or the release from this 'having to' obligation."[28]

A main conclusion of the study is that youth worship is an educational function and that, in report with Asteley (1984), the language of worship is "performing non-cognitive."[29] "The learning process in liturgy does not, in the first place, include cognitive elements, but primarily it creates a basic attitude towards being a Christian. We agree with Astley

24. Baker, "Raised a Teenage Kataphatic."
25. Rymarz, "Catechesis and Religious Education."
26. Sonnenberg and Barnard, "Educating Young People."
27. Sonnenberg and Barnard, "Educating Young People," 1.
28. Sonnenberg and Barnard, "Educating Young People," 6.
29. Astley, "The Role of Worship in Christian Learning," 245.

that within that spiritual framework there can be explicitly cognitive aspects."[30] We end this section by giving two particular examples of religious learning goals: moral development and reconciliation.

Moral Development

In 2002, Rian Prins stressed the importance of churches and youth ministers paying attention to the moral development of youth.[31] Apart from morality in general, congregations are directed towards Christian morality in particular. Prins describes "Christian morality" as the result of one's relationship with God and the quest to know and act according to his will. Furthermore, "through identification with the congregation, identification with the congregation's values and norms takes place."[32] Against this background, after having discussed a couple of factors hampering the formation of values among youth, the author describes four aspects of the congregation's task in facilitating moral education. In the first place, the congregation should support parents, because the primary place for moral development is the family. In the second place, the congregation should be an intergenerational community, in which youth is recognized and accepted and where they find role models that embody convictions, values, and norms. In the third place, moral decision-making activities should be included in congregations, in catechesis and youth ministry in particular, to facilitate youth in practicing dealing with moral issues in day-to-day life from a Christian perspective. In the fourth place, youth should be engaged in a reciprocal process with adults with regard to discourse on the content of the values of the community of believers.

One specific example of moral development as a goal attributed to youth ministry can be found in Stefan Gärtner's article on sex educational concepts in the pastoral care of youth.[33] This article has already been discussed in chapter 1 in the context of society being pluralized and individualized as a social condition which forms children's and adolescent's sexuality in postmodern society. Gärtner argues that in this condition both youth and adults are challenged to make their own choices in the midst of multiple (formerly) existing traditional models. The author

30. Sonnenberg and Barnard, "Educating Young People," 7.
31. Prins, "Values to Be Caught and Taught."
32. Prins, "Values to Be Caught and Taught," 23.
33. Gärtner, "Education through and to Love."

argues that "the development and consolidation of the ability to love and to build relationships is *the* fundamental aim of sex education in ecclesial youth work.... From this main aim to teach young people how to love and build reliable relationships, ecclesial youth work could, using its own particular strengths, play an important part in the project of sex education from a Christian viewpoint, in cooperation with the other agents of socialization."[34]

Reconciliation

In 2003, Christo Thesnaar put the spotlight on reconciliation as a goal of youth ministry in post-apartheid South Africa.[35] He pleads for the church to be a safe place for young people to share their stories, to bring in their personal hurts and to experience being accepted. The church and youth ministry should help young people on their trajectory towards healing and reconciliation. In his article, the author proposes practical approaches in this regard within the context of South Africa; at the same time the plea for reconciliation to be one of the goals of youth ministry has a far wider reach. Thesnaar mentions the examples of conflict situations in Northern Ireland, Rwanda, Sudan, Israel-Palestine, Afghanistan, and Congo, and more.

"In almost all of these conflict areas divisions between opposition groups are so huge that sporadic armed conflicts erupted, and in some cases full-scale war is still continuing. The effects of these political, religious or cultural conflicts, though initiated by the convictions of adults, are not limited to adults. They also have tremendous effects on young people. These conflicts deeply divide young people on different grounds, e.g., religion, race, sex, ethnicity, culture, politics, etc. In many cases these young people were directly involved, either as victimizers or as victims of war."[36] This observation underlines and situates the need to work for reconciliation among young people. In addition, Thesnaar argues that the divisions mentioned occur not only as a result of armed conflicts but also in peaceful contexts where they function mainly below the surface. "The fact of the matter is that suppressing, denial or even prosperity does

---

34. Gärtner, "Education through and to Love," 101–2.
35. Thesnaar, "Facilitating Healing and Reconciliation."
36. Thesnaar, "Facilitating Healing and Reconciliation," 8.

not protect against the devastating psychological, spiritual and emotional effects they have on young and old alike."[37]

The division of (young) people on the grounds of race is central to a 2011 article in the same journal from Cobus van Wyngaard: "Post-Apartheid Whiteness and the Challenge of Youth Ministry in the Dutch Reformed Church."[38] The author shows how youth ministry directed towards healing and reconciliation is challenged by white primacy in post-Apartheid South Africa. The challenge, in short, is that youth ministry, striving for an encounter which provides the possibility of transcending racialized categories, can, at the same time, turn out to reinscribe "notions of racial superiority and the power relations inherited from a history of colonialism and apartheid."[39] To tackle this ambiguous role of mission, including youth ministry, Thesnaar takes a postcolonial critique of mission into account. Working on reconciliation, healing, and transcending racialized categories demands a huge effort to overcome systems of racial privilege and to lead youth and adults into self-critical reflection.

7.3 Youth Ministry Goals and Church Paradigms

In this subsection we first describe two typologies of youth ministry goals closely related to church paradigms. Both were published in *Religious Education*. The first is derived from a publication by Bert Roebben in 1997, and the second from a publication by Arthur David Canales in 2006.[40] Next, these two empirical studies will be discussed to illustrate parts of these typologies in practice.

In 1997, Bert Roebben provided a cultural-psychological analysis of identity formation of youth in Western Europe in these days.[41] This analysis is informed by West European cultural psychology and youth research. Roebben detects what he calls "three problematic aspects of identity formation of contemporary youth,"[42] that he understands as not only social and moral issues but also as a religious issue: (1) the

---

37. Thesnaar, "Facilitating Healing and Reconciliation," 9.
38. Van Wyngaard, "Post-Apartheid Whiteness."
39. Van Wyngaard, "Post-Apartheid Whiteness," 23.
40. Roebben, "Shaping a Playground for Transcendence"; Canales, "Models for Adolescent Ministry."
41. Roebben, "Shaping a Playground for Transcendence."
42. Roebben, "Shaping a Playground for Transcendence," 332.

commercialization of the environment of young people; (2) the mediatization of the youth period; and (3) the risk of what Roebben calls the "Fall into Insignificance." (See chapter 1 for a more detailed discussion of these three aspects of identity formation.) Here, we turn to a discussion of three paradigms for youth ministry that Roebben observes as a particular appraisal of these aspects of identity formation.

First, there is the secularization paradigm based on the assumption that the relationship between church and youth can be considered as "inside" and "outside" and the main goal is to bridge that gap. There are two ways to do this, both seeing the church as a "counter-story": "by welcoming youth into the church or by going out to encounter them in the real world (ministry *ad intra* or *ad extra*)."[43] Second, there is the reflection paradigm based on the assumption that the church is an exponent of the world and not opposed to the world. One of the important goals in this paradigm is as an authentic church giving room for the liberating gospel to criticize oppressive structures and to inspire solidarity.

The third paradigm is the evangelization paradigm based on the assumption that the church and youth ministry practices should engage in an ongoing dialogue in a spiritual playground for young and old. "The evangelization approach to youth ministry is aiming at a materially qualified and communicative salvific commitment to young people, one in which humankind's love of God can be experienced and become transparent for individuals and congregations."[44] It is evident from the article that Roebben is most supportive to this third paradigm and combines this with an articulation of, from his perspective, the main goal of religious education and youth ministry, the "clarification of the narrative identity of contemporary young people."[45]

In 2006, Arthur Canales presented eight so-called ecumenical examples or models of adolescent ministry, emerging from ministry practices in the United States from both a Catholic and an ecumenical perspective.[46] The eight models "indicate different ways of viewing the church, illuminating diverse aspects of youth ministry in its ecclesial relationship with community and adolescents."[47] As such, each model also

---

43. Roebben, "Shaping a Playground for Transcendence," 342.
44. Roebben, "Shaping a Playground for Transcendence," 345.
45. Roebben, "Shaping a Playground for Transcendence," 332.
46. Canales, "Models for Adolescent Ministry."
47. Canales, "Models for Adolescent Ministry," 205.

includes a goal orientation for ministry among youth. Below we present an overview of the eight models and a brief description of the accompanying goal orientations.

(1) The friendship model is about teaching that Jesus is a friend and is about fostering friendships among youth and between adults and youth. (2) The spiritual awareness model is directed towards promoting spiritual awareness and developing communal adolescent spirituality, e.g., by prayer and worship experiences. (3) The servant-leadership model, with a focus on respect, justice, and honesty, is directed towards the development of youth as servant-leaders in the faith community and embodying Jesus' Golden Rule. (4) The liberation model, with a focus on compassion, justice, and peace, is directed towards "emancipation and transformation, not contained within a vacuum, but one that moves beyond self to community, this is conscientization."[48] Liberation is conceived as an evangelical term, with the goal of youth taking responsibility for their own lives and for their environment. (5) The biblical-hermeneutical model's goal is interpreting the Bible for contemporary (church) practice by exegesis, criticism, and appropriation. (6) The liturgical-initiation model has a focus on sacred rites, liturgical events and the sacraments and aims at "creating and empowering young Christian disciples."[49] (7) The social justice model is a model in which youth ministers embody service and social justice and has the goal of nurturing youth in terms of service and justice that is rooted in faith in Jesus Christ, and of empowering them to address causes of human suffering. (8) The Christian discipleship model, with a focus on being attuned to the presence of God in your life, is directed towards Christian formation and transformation of the Christian life according to the essential aspects of the Christian faith.

In 2010, Ruth Webber et al. compared youth ministry approaches in different denominations in Melbourne (Australia) with the eight models as proposed by Canales.[50] They found out that to some extent every model could be observed, but four models were found to be most prominent in both Catholic and Protestant ministries: the social justice model, the Christian discipleship model, the friendship model, and the liturgical-initiation model. In part 4 this empirical research will be discussed in more detail.

---

48. Canales, "Models for Adolescent Ministry," 214.
49. Canales, "Models for Adolescent Ministry," 218.
50. Webber et al., "Models of Youth Ministry in Action."

In 2019, in the *International Journal of Children's Spirituality*, Lydia Van Leersum-Bekebrede et al. published a qualitative study (participant observations) of liturgical rituals involving children from fifteen congregations of the Protestant Church in the Netherlands.[51] In total, twenty-one distinct liturgical rituals were witnessed once and accompanied by at least one individual or group interview. The main research question was how adults shape liturgical rituals with children. This question also involved the question of adults' intentions in creating liturgical rituals for the particular group of children. Intentions reveal something about goals that function among adults, in this case often children's workers in faith communities. Among other results (more detailed information will follow in part 4 of the handbook), four specific intentions of adults in the context of liturgical rituals with children were found.

First, the category of intentions related to faith: this category reflects the hope of adults that children's faith will grow or their spirituality will develop. Second, the category of intentions related to liturgy: this category reflects adults' intentions such as initiating children in liturgical practice and them gaining liturgical knowledge. Third, the category of intentions related to community: this category reflects the hope of children becoming part of the community and the church continuing to exist. Fourth, the category of intentions related to experiences. Within this category a distinction can be made between children's experiences and adults' experiences. The sub-category of children's experiences reflects intentions like promoting children's well-being, their joy at attending church, their self-belief, etcetera.

In a 2013 article in *Journal of Youth and Theology*, Mark Cannister holds a critical mirror up to church communities when stressing the importance of providing young people with opportunities to wrestle with their faith.[52] In terms of the Identity Status approach of James Marcia, this can be understood as a plea to give space to the status of *moratorium*.[53] The status of *moratorium* is about "exploring various faith constructs through theological reflection."[54] Churches should provide for a healthy environment, sufficient space, time, and opportunities for adolescents to dwell in this status. Moratorium should be valued by every

51. Van Leersum-Bekebrede et al., "Setting the Stage."

52. Cannister, "Moratorium Matters."

53. Marcia, "Development and Validation"; Adelson, *Handbook of Adolescent Psychology*.

54. Cannister, "Moratorium Matters," 27.

faith community and should be part of the process of faith formation of youth. "Such a community allows space for questions, doubts, and identity reformation, and maintains authentic relationships with students, supporting them through the challenges of transitioning environments as they move from middle school into high school and high school into college or the workplace."[55]

Typologies of youth ministry goals, thus, are closely related to church and youth ministry paradigms. A book that helps both youth ministers and youth ministry scholars to reflect on possible paradigms and their own views on youth ministry is *Youth Ministry in the 21st Century: Five Views*, edited by Chap Clark. Five authors each discuss a particular view. Greg Stier discusses the gospel advancing view, Brian Cosby elaborates on the reformed view, Chap Clark presents the adoption view, Fernando Arzola reflects on the ecclesial view and Ron Hunter discusses the D6 (Deuteronomy6) view of youth ministry.

7.3 Catechetical Learning Goals

In 2012 and 2014, Jos de Kock published three articles on catechetical learning environments, two in the *International Journal of Practical Theology* and one in the *International Journal for the Study of the Christian Church*.[56] In these articles, special attention is paid to the aspect of goals in catechesis practices. In the 2012 article, "Promising Approaches to Catechesis in Church Communities: Towards a Research Framework," De Kock describes three educational models of catechetical learning environments and confronts these with the modern and cultural landscape of the time.[57] De Kock argues the third model, an apprenticeship model, is most promising for church communities willing to serve a next generation with faith education. We will now briefly discuss the three models and how these relate to three sets of goal orientations in catechesis.

The first model as distinguished by De Kock is a behavioral model. Catechetical learning environments that follow a behavioral model are "accentuating the passing on of the religious tradition onto the next generation in conjunction with what families and schools are aiming at in

---

55. Cannister, "Moratorium Matters," 42.

56. De Kock, "Promising Approaches to Catechesis"; De Kock, "A Typology of Catechetical Learning Environments"; De Kock, "Catechists' Conceptions."

57. De Kock, "Promising Approaches to Catechesis."

raising their youth."[58] The main goal of catechesis practices corresponding to this model is to pass on knowledge and skills to a young generation: knowledge and skills rooted in the faith and church tradition that are needed to live the Christian life. The second model De Kock distinguishes is the developmental model. Catechetical learning environments following the developmental model make the catechumen central to the learning process: lessons are strongly dependent on what the person wants to learn and the model supports catechumens to construct personal religious outlooks. The main goal in these catechesis practices is independent critical thinking on the part of the catechumens and personal reflection on their own experiences in the light of the Christian faith.

The third model is the apprenticeship model that has been mentioned already. Catechetical learning environments that follow this model are about participation in a shared world, a shared faith community and practice. In these learning environments it is "neither the content, nor the young person's challenging questions but the person of the catechist, - who he or she is and does -, which directs the learning process of young people."[59] The main goal in catechesis practices that fit the apprenticeship model is that young people experience the Christian faith and life, incorporating elements of worth from tradition but at the same time actively putting new elements into the faith community that are derived from their own religious outlooks. De Kock argues that the apprenticeship model is promising for contemporary church communities because it meets young people's need for identity formation based on the lived experience of model figures in the faith community, and because it meets the need for community in a highly individualized world.

In 2014, in the same *International Journal of Practical Theology*, De Kock presented a typology of catechetical learning environments in which the distinction between the three instructional paradigms or models as described above plays a significant role.[60] At the same time, the models are much more conceived as models for role division between catechists and catechumens and not so much as indications of goal orientations in catechesis practices. The article presents an elaborate literature review of studies about catechetical learning environments and learning processes. Based on this literature review, the author comes up

58. De Kock, "Promising Approaches to Catechesis," 185.
59. De Kock, "Promising Approaches to Catechesis," 186.
60. De Kock, "A Typology of Catechetical Learning Environments."

with a typology of catechetical learning environments including twelve types of learning environments that are the result of combinations of categories reflecting two aspects: (1) the aspect of role division between catechist and catechumens and (2) the aspect of learning goals. The first aspect has three categories within it: a role division according to (a) a behavioral model, (b) a developmental model, and (c) an apprenticeship model. The second aspect, of learning goals, is decoupled from the three aforementioned instructional models and contains four categories. In 7.1 we summed up these categories when discussing the theme of religious learning goals.[61] They comprise (a) cognitive and affective goals, (b) emotions and experiences, (c) the formation of one's own opinion and social interaction, and (d) identity development.

Taking each in turn: (a) Learning goals in terms of cognitive and affective goals aim, among other things, "to accept (cognitively) what the Bible teaches and then coming to trust God (an affective goal)."[62] The cognitive domain in this goal category has to do with acquiring knowledge and gaining learning skills, whereas the affective domain reflects attitudes and affective learning skills. (b) Learning goals in terms of emotions and experiences refer to emotions such as love and religious experiences in the sense of encounters with God. (c) The goal category dealing with formation of one's own opinion and social interaction refers to stimulating the evaluation of the practices and beliefs of one's own and the surrounding faith community: this goal is helped by the intention to exchange viewpoints in catechetical learning environments. (d) The goal category of identity development refers to the aim of developing or forming whole persons. In the discussion of this category, De Kock distinguishes between a material dimension and a formal dimension of identity. What is at the core of this goal category is that catechesis is not just about acquiring knowledge, skills, opinions, or having experiences but is about the formation of 'selves': identities that develop during a whole life.

In a following stage, De Kock in 2014 reported an interview study with catechists to investigate "whether the types of catechetical learning environments drawn from the typology are reflected in catechists' conceptions of their catechetical practices."[63] The interview study was a

61. De Kock, "What about Learning?"
62. De Kock, "A Typology of Catechetical Learning Environments," 269.
63. De Kock, "Catechists' Conceptions," 54.

small-scale study with seven catechists from different parishes within the Dutch Protestant Church, two of them were youth workers and five of them were parish pastors. The interview guide that was developed was based on the aspects of learning goals and role divisions. The outcomes of this empirical study will be discussed in more detail in part 4 of the handbook. Here, we will focus on the particular theme of learning goals catechists mention and how these relate to De Kock's original typology.

The respondents mentioned a wide variety of learning goals, ranging from "to talk about something" to "to find truth," and from "to know Jesus" to "to prepare for partaking in Holy Communion." This variety was not only a variety of goals among catechists but individual catechists also appeared to vary the goals they set. De Kock points out that there are parallels among the goal orientations of the different catechists but there are as many nuanced differences that can be observed. Despite a couple of matches between the goals mentioned by the catechists and the goal categories in the typology, De Kock observes "many formulations of goals do not fit into the categories of the typology."[64] Good examples are goals expressed as "learning to know Jesus," and "finding truth." In the end, De Kock concludes that the typology has its usefulness in *developing* catechetical learning environments but misses the nuanced language needed for *accurately describing* catechetical learning environments.

7.4 Conclusion

This chapter has offered a broad overview of the different types of goals and typologies of goals found in youth ministry practices and youth ministry research. These typologies help to understand the breadth of what might be set as a goal in youth ministry but also help to make explicit what often is implicit: ambitions, motivations, and the convictions of youth ministers or churches that are rooted in theological, psychological, and/or pedagogical perspectives. We agree with the authors of *Youth Ministry in the Black Church: Centered in Hope*, who were quoted at the very beginning of this chapter: setting goals is an important beginning in setting an agenda for youth ministry. This chapter showed a variety of starting points: types of spirituality outcomes and types of religious learning goals; a reflection on church paradigms that have consequences for goal setting in youth ministry; and types of catechetical learning goals

---

64. De Kock, "Catechists' Conceptions," 66.

in educational oriented youth ministry practices. Having established this broad perspective on goal setting, we now can continue in chapter 8 with a specific focus on theologically loaded goals in youth ministry practices.

8

Theologically Loaded Goals

"The healing needed among youth demands that we introduce them to practices of discernment that engage their whole selves. In the deliberate practice of discernment, young people will seek to be faithful in the hundreds of minute decisions that face them. As a young oak is nurtured, one decision at a time, into fullness, so discernment creates an incrementally adequate environment for growth in Christian vocation, or love of God and neighbor. One decision at a time, the orange crate of culture that limits our young people's growth can be dismantled and discarded, and youth will finally find more appropriate—and genuinely real—ways to support their flourishing as disciples and saints."[1]

WHAT does it mean do be a disciple, and what role should youth ministry take in shaping young people as disciples? David White makes a plea for supporting youth with practices of discernment in youth ministry. What is it that underlies this invitation to practices of discernment that is youth ministry's aim—as envisioned by White—in inviting young people as Christian disciples? Practices of discernment help to work towards this goal by giving opportunities to young people to use the gospel to confront their questions and circumstances in life and culture. In chapter 7 we focused on the broad range of goals that youth ministry might aim at and that are reflected in the literature in different typologies of youth ministry goals. The current chapter is on what might

1. White, *Practicing Discernment with Youth*, 82–83.

be called "theologically loaded goals," i.e., goals that are formulated and understood primarily in theological language.

Although theological language can be helpful because youth ministry operates in a theologically loaded context of faith communities, theological language can also be confusing when it comes to practical consequences. The quote from David White is a good example. The aim of supporting young people to be Christian disciples or even saints is both attractive and confusing at the same time. Attractive, because it reflects the language of the church and refers to biblical words and themes. Confusing, because it leads to a question of what it actually means in concrete youth ministry practice, and what meeting such a goal actually looks like. In other words, theologically loaded goals are challenging. Although rooted in theology and/or Scripture, they leave us with a couple of questions about how to apply these goals in the concrete settings of youth ministry.

This chapter distinguishes five types of theologically loaded goals. Section 8.1 thematizes the goal of discovering identity, finding oneself, and finding God. Encountering God is the theme of section 8.2. In section 8.3, faith and salvation as goals are discussed. Section 8.4 will address the goal category of "being," both being in God and being in relationships. Next, we will discuss the goal of living as disciples (8.5). A concluding section will end the chapter (8.6)

8.1 Discovering oneself, God, and Christ

This subsection thematizes from different angles the goal of discovering identity, finding oneself, and finding God. This goal not only refers to a final discovery or a completed identity at the end of a searching process. It also refers to the process of searching itself. With respect to the latter, Steve Griffiths, for example, with an eye to Anglican youth ministry practices, developed the notion of *orthoyatra*, the process of becoming, or, in other words, the journey we are embarking on as Christians. Young people are on this journey and adolescence is one stage of it and youth ministry should encourage young people to go on this journey.[2] In a later publication of 2013, Griffiths published *Models for Youth Ministry: Learning from the Life of Christ*, in which he describes a Christological

---

2. Griffiths, "Negotiating *Orthoyatra*."

approach to youth ministry that serves young people who are on their journey.³

In 2002, in the *Journal of Youth and Theology*, Chris Hudson stated that besides "community," the word "identity" is a buzz word often used in the setting of youth ministry.⁴ In his contribution, "Community, Identity, & Youth Ministry," Hudson attempts to explain theologically what is meant by both words. It becomes clear that Hudson believes that young people finding their identity in terms of who they are in Christ is the main goal of youth ministry. That said, the nature of a (young) person is found only through relationships with others. As a consequence, "for humanity to be created as the *imago Dei* is to be made as a person who is found in relationship."⁵ At this point, the concept of community comes in: to be united with the community of believers is to be united with Christ. Hudson argues that community with others is not a sociological option but a theological reality. "We discover our identity through self-giving relationships with others only by participating in the community of Christ."⁶

In chapter 1 we referred to Richard James who in 2004 published on postmodernism and its relationship to young people discovering Jesus Christ.⁷ For James, an ultimate goal for youth ministry is to support young people to discover Jesus. With reference to the Christology of Jürgen Moltmann,⁸ James explains this process of discovering in three different directions: discovering the *eschatological* person of Christ, the *theological* person of Christ and the *social* person of Christ. Discovering the eschatological person of Christ means young people associating with Christ by being attentive to Christ as revealed in God's story in the world. Discovering the theological person of Christ means young people being involved in contemplative life with attention to the transcendent and the expectation of God's acts in spiritual, supernatural ways. Discovering the social person of Christ means young people experiencing togetherness and relationship just as Christ sought to be a brother for others, especially vulnerable others.

3. Griffiths, *Models for Youth Ministry*.
4. Hudson, "Community, Identity, & Youth Ministry."
5. Hudson, "Community, Identity, & Youth Ministry," 25.
6. Hudson, "Community, Identity, & Youth Ministry," 28.
7. James, "Discovering Jesus as a Postmodern Young Person."
8. Moltmann, *The Way of Jesus Christ*.

In chapter 1, we discussed Russell Haitch's 2011 contribution in which the author describes a particular characteristic of youth culture at that time, namely the desire for freedom, by comparing youth on three continents: America, Europe, and Africa.[9] How this core value of freedom turns out in America, Europe, and Africa is explained along the lines of a couple of global forces, a few "isms," that attach themselves to freedom as a core value: individualism, postmodernism, consumerism, proteanism, and fundamentalism. Against this background Haitch proposes a vision for leading youth towards freedom in Christ. Freedom in Christ as an ultimate goal for youth ministry is grounded in a sacramental theology that the author partly grounds in the work of Karl Barth and John Howard Yoder. "Freedom in Christ corrects the distortions of liberty found in the global forces just named. It could even be said that these global forces are themselves corruptions of a Christian view."[10] Christian ministry (and youth ministry) according to Haitch, should thus explain and exemplify what freedom is *not*; at the same time, it should explain and exemplify what freedom *is*. "In the Christian tradition, the negative paradox that freedom leads to a certain caughtness or bondage is met by the positive paradox that union with Christ is the path to genuine liberty."[11]

An author who links up the discovery of God or Christ with a more developmental psychological perspective is Gary Davis, who in 1986 proposed spiritual direction as a model for adolescent catechesis.[12] Davis draws the adolescent as one in an "identity crisis," forced to discover a new sense of self. According to the author, little attention is paid in general to the spiritual components of this crisis in adolescence. Therefore, he pleads for youth catechesis or a youth ministry which integrates spiritual direction. Spiritual direction is defined "as an ongoing relationship between the director and adolescent directee, in which, during regular one-on-one meetings (or which possibly include one or two other directees), the discussion centers on the issues which are affecting the directee's life, with a goal of seeing how God may be present and working in them."[13] Spiritual direction as the church's ministry has the goal, on the one hand,

---

9. Haitch, "Free as a Bird."
10. Haitch, "Free as a Bird," 18.
11. Haitch, "Free as a Bird," 17.
12. Davis, "Spiritual Direction."
13. Davis, "Spiritual Direction," 268.

of discovering God's presence in one's own life, and on the other, of supporting young people to resolve their spiritual crises.

When it comes to discovering one's identity, Bard Norheim challenges the idea of producing identity as a voluntaristic process.[14] In an article in which Norheim rethinks ecclesiology in the context of Nordic youth ministry, he sees discipleship when understood as practicing baptism as a main goal orientation in youth ministry. Or more precisely: be(co)ming a Christian through the art of practicing baptism. This process of identity development is not a production process on the part of humans but, instead, is a gift from God trough His Spirit: "Through the art of *practicing baptism* The Holy Spirit acts through us, and frees us to see this world as god's world and receive our life and god's world as a gift—and to trust in god as God."[15] In this light, the direction of youth ministry is to support young people to be conformed to Christ, which is a process of "becoming human under the sign of the cross."[16]

Let us now have a brief look at an empirical study in which finding God is at the core of the reflection. In 2016, Kevin Flatt and Millard Haskell reported on a case study of a large Catholic youth rally in Toronto in which they compared the organizer's intentions with the actual experiences of participants.[17] The youth rally studied was the Lift Jesus Higher youth rally held on April 9, 2011, at the Metro Toronto Convention Centre, organized by Catholic Renewal Ministries (CRM), an American based para-church organization. The organizers of the rally appeared to have the following goals: "The first goal was that the youth in attendance would have a personal experience of God leading to a deeper relationship with God. . . . The second, closely related, goal was that the youth in attendance would take a step of personal commitment to Christ."[18]

As part of the case study, the authors and research assistants conducted interviews with the organizers, conducted observations during the rally, and conducted semi-structured interviews with a sample of rally participants (twelve interviewees, aged sixteen to eighteen). The analysis of the data resulted in the conclusion that the first goal of the organizers, youth having a personal experience of and a deeper relationship

14. Norheim, "Practicing Baptism."
15. Norheim, "Practicing Baptism," 47–48.
16. Norheim, "Practicing Baptism," 49.
17. Flatt and Haskell, "Participant Experiences."
18. Flatt and Haskell, "Participant Experiences," 141.

with God, was met for most of the interviewees. Furthermore, the second goal, taking a step towards personal commitment to Christ, had not been met for the interviewees. An important explanation for these results according to the authors can be found in the religious socialization of these particular youth: "Our interviewees' involvement in Catholic churches seems to have left them attuned to the more familiar, traditionally Catholic elements of the rally and less engaged by the quasi-evangelical elements."[19]

8.2 Encountering God

Some authors put the encounter with God in the middle when discussing the goal orientation of youth ministry. In this subsection three perspectives will be presented: a sacramental perspective, a pedagogy of accompaniment perspective, and a contemplative perspective.

Against the background of what the authors call the "religious homelessness of young people," Erlinde De Lange and Bert Roebben in 2002 presented seven propositions on sacramental youth catechesis that are important corner stones for the future of religious congregations.[20] The article concentrates particularly on the context of the Roman-Catholic church in Flanders and The Netherlands. These seven propositions are as follows:[21]

1. "If Christianity implies an encounter with God, such an encounter will be mediated through human persons." (p. 48)

2. "The human person is open to the encounter with God in rituals and symbolic actions. For Christians, the sacraments constitute a focal point of this encounter." (p. 49)

3. "Rituals and sacraments are always rooted in the life of a community and only exist by grace thereof." (p. 51)

4. "Meaningful sacramentality presupposes a profound correlation between faith and life." (p. 53)

5. "Our present day and age is confronted with the challenge to understand and develop the correlation between faith and life." (p. 55)

---

19. Flatt and Haskell, "Participant Experiences," 147.
20. De Lange and Roebben, "Seven Propositions."
21. De Lange and Roebben, "Seven Propositions," 48–59.

6. "Biblical catechesis strives to provide a response to this challenge." (p. 57)
7. "A biblically inspired sacramentality presupposes an adult Church." (p. 59)

It becomes clear from the first two propositions that the encounter with God is at the heart of the ministry among young people. The rationale for this "goal setting" is the author's theological perspective of the God of Christianity revealing Godself in the lives of persons who can live in a relationship with God. The person, also the young person, is conceived as reaching out to God to fulfill the ultimate desire of the human heart. In this respect, rituals, symbolic actions, and the sacraments are important aspects of the faith community to support young people in this "reaching out" and encountering God. In this respect, it is interesting to see that the empirical work of Sonnenberg et al. (2015), in a Protestant context, concludes in the same direction: the experience of community or "being together" among young people participating in (protestant) youth worship "has social and psychological connotations and is open to something of God that may be revealed."[22] (see also chapter 4.)

A comparable theological perspective is found in a contribution from Hosffman Ospino in 2010, "To Educate Christians in the Faith Is an Art Deeply Rooted in Our Relationship with the God of Revelation Who Comes to Us in History as a Divine Companion, Particularly in Jesus Christ."[23] Where De Lange and Roebben (2002) elaborate implications in the direction of sacramental youth catechesis or youth ministry, Ospino elaborates a pedagogy of accompaniment in religious education. This pedagogy contains three principles. Teachers and learners (1) being companions on an educational journey, (2) as human beings on this journey, they yearn for fulfillment of personal projects, and (3) the journey's end is an encounter with what is ultimately true and good. The third principle shows the encounter with truth and goodness as a central goal of religious education, also in youth ministry practices. It becomes clear from Ospino's argument that this encounter should be understood in terms of deeper relationships with God and others.

The same theme of encountering God is taken up by Michael Hryniuk in his article, "Creating Space for God: Toward a Spirituality of Youth Ministry." The main background of the author's argument is research

---

22. Sonnenberg et al., "Being Together in Youth Worship."
23. Ospino, "Theological Horizons," 427.

conducted by the *Youth Ministry and Spirituality Project* (YMSP), an ecumenical research and teaching initiative (Protestant, Roman Catholic, Mennonite, and Brethren traditions) in Canada. Hryniuk explains the need to integrate contemplative practices into youth ministry, contrasting such an approach with two predominant approaches in youth ministry. In the first place, there is the entertainment approach which assumes youth are not ready for nor interested in deeper engagement with their own faith tradition. The entertainment approach "focuses its attention largely on the planning and coordination of church-based recreational programs, events, and activities that will attract the largest number of young people into church life."[24]

In the second place, there is the catechetical approach focusing on the transmission of the faith and church tradition, in terms of beliefs, practices and values to a next generation. This approach is comparable to what Brelsford (2001) observes as "assimilation to tradition" in traditional forms of confirmation that include providing proper answers to questions, and learning to behave in the proper way in church practices (see section 8.3).[25] In contrast to these entertainment and catechetical approaches the YMSP project emphasizes the need for cultivation of contemplative consciousness in young persons. The goal of youth ministry in this approach is to "respond first to young people's desire for spiritual experience as the foundation of a religious life."[26] Hryniuk pleads for youth ministry to have the goal of young people having real and meaningful experiences of the sacred. These experiences, according to the author, will help young people to find meaning, to experience belonging and wholeness in their lives. Youth ministry should be directed towards the experience of God and a spirituality of living in relationship to God.

8.3 Faith and Salvation

In chapter 2, we already discussed the article from Ulrich Schwab on the theme of transmission of faith across generations.[27] The author approaches the transmission of faith as "dialogue between generational

---

24. Hryniuk, "Creating Space for God," 143.
25. Brelsford, "Educating for Formative Participation."
26. Hryniuk, "Creating Space for God," 146.
27. Schwab, ". . . try and find the thread . . ."

perspectives and practices."[28] This dialogue implies the church being a church *im semper reformanda*, where young people do not just receive the faith as handed over by a former generation, but actually perform faith and transform faith practices. Here, we see faith as a central aspect in the direction of youth ministry. But what does a drive towards faith mean? Andy Goodliff relates faith to the concept of salvation, and discusses this concept as a central goal in youth ministry.[29]

Against the background of a postmodern culture, Goodliff published an article in which he evaluates the traditional evangelical model of salvation and describes an alternative evangelical model of salvation.[30] According to the author, an understanding of salvation lies at the heart of Christian youth ministry. "The implication being that the basic aim of Christian youthwork is to see young people saved."[31] The traditional evangelical model of salvation is rooted in the concept of "justification by faith": the death of Jesus Christ is a substitute for us, and salvation as benefit of His death is accessibly by faith, and this is an individual decision. This individual decision comes with a conviction about who Jesus is, confessing your sins and asking forgiveness.

The author then evaluates this model by pointing at a variety of problematic elements, such as salvation presented as an escape route from Hell instead of a free undeserved gift, salvation made dependent on a moral shift by a person, having a contractual structure revealing tendencies of individualism and rationalism, and the model having nontrinitarian tendencies. Next, an alternative evangelical model of salvation is described by Goodliff, usually described as "apocalyptic" or "participatory." "At the heart of this model is a narrative that tells the story of Jesus and his death and resurrection. However, so far, the model has only described the story of Jesus, without reference to a soteriology that saves the rest of humanity. . . . [I]t is pneumatology that allows humanity to be saved."[32] In this model it is the Spirit who makes people Christians and make salvation accessible. The concept of grace, in this way, is unconditional and covenantal. As a result, Christians participate in the person of Christ and salvation should thus be understood relationally: Christians

---

28. Schwab, ". . . try and find the thread . . . ," 10.
29. Goodliff, "Can the Christian Gospel Speak."
30. For a discussion on culture and postmodern culture, see Part 1 of the handbook.
31. Goodliff, "Can the Christian Gospel Speak," 41.
32. Goodliff, "Can the Christian Gospel Speak," 48.

are in relation to the Father, through the Son, in the Holy Spirit. Salvation is thus an experience.

In relation to youth ministry, Goodliff observes the danger of a traditional model of salvation: "We've held on to a version of the gospel that resembles more the story of the Enlightenment than the story of Jesus Christ."[33] The author believes the soteriology of the alternative model of salvation provides a more robust theological soteriology for postmodern times in which young people live: it puts emphasis on experience of real change in life and a dependency on the Spirit. According to the author this will speak more clearly to the experience of young people.

8.4 Being in God and in Relationships

In 2001, Theodore Brelsford made a plea for formative participation as a central goal of education in the church.[34] "[I]nviting formative participation in a community entails inviting and empowering others to participate in shaping and defining a community's very identity."[35] Doing so, a church community empowers itself and empowers its members to participate in the wider communities. Theologically, Brelsford understands this process as a formative participation in God's ongoing creation. In the article, Brelsford offers images and possibilities for such education in the church that enhance formative participation. With an eye, in particular, to youth and newcomers, Brelsford contrasts formative participation with assimilation to tradition.

Brelsford observes assimilation to tradition in traditional forms of confirmation that include providing proper answers to questions, and learning to behave in the proper way in church practices (compare the catechetical approach as described by Hryniuk (2005) focusing on the transmission of the faith and church tradition in 8.1).[36] Full participation in the church community is a result of proper assimilation to tradition. Thus, here, the goal of education among youth and newcomers is assimilation, and is a prerequisite for full participation. In contrast, Brelsford sketches the need for formative participation as an educational goal in the function of bringing new generations into the church's identity. The

---

33. Goodliff, "Can the Christian Gospel Speak," 51.
34. Brelsford, "Educating for Formative Participation."
35. Brelsford, "Educating for Formative Participation," 324.
36. Hryniuk, "Creating Space for God."

experiences of young people are often different from the experiences of past members; according to the author, churches need not to assimilate youth into old patterns but invite them to participate together with older members in "shaping orienting patterns and practices that are faithful to the community's tradition—its past identity—as well as to the reality of its present—current experiences of God's unfolding creation."[37] The latter is in correspondence with what Jos De Kock calls apprenticeship learning in church communities: "In apprenticeship learning, thus, the learner (novice) does not merely take on the established culture, principles, knowledge, and ideals. The novice, of course, develops toward expertise by acquiring existing wisdom, but at the same time, the novice brings into the practice or community new, creative habits, solutions, and vision."[38]

The very idea of young people participating together with other members in the faith community is sometimes related to the idea of relational youth ministry: a methodology in which adult (youth) leaders build relationships with youth with the aim of bringing them to a commitment to faith. In 2004, Andrew Root wrote a critical piece on this methodology that presents itself as a form of incarnational ministry.[39] (See also chapter 4.) Root's critical evaluation reads: "we have appropriated the incarnation as a methodological approach rather than the very center of our being and source of our ministry."[40] According to Root, relationality should not be a mere tool in youth ministry but, instead, from an incarnational point of view the very purpose of youth ministry. Root presents the theological idea of God becoming incarnate, not as a model but as a reality and power. "Now, through the incarnate Christ, humanity is embedded within the Trinity, and the Trinity within humanity." For relationships within youth ministry practices this means that there is an inner reality of relationality which is all about the power of God.

8.5 Living as Disciples

In *The Theological Turn in Youth Ministry*, American youth ministry scholar, Kenda Creasy Dean, makes a plea for youth ministry that is

37. Brelsford, "Educating for Formative Participation," 321.
38. De Kock, "Challenges to Apprenticeship Learning," 234.
39. Root, "Relationality."
40. Root, "Relationality," 99.

directed towards spiritual formation and discipleship over Christian education and membership. As Dean sees it, this is an implication of youth ministry being *ministry*, and thus a need for Christian communities and churches in which youth can participate and where young people can encounter and incarnate Christ. Living as disciples is a goal of youth ministry that can be broadly recognized in youth ministry literature.[41]

From an Indian context, in 2003 Jerome Vallabaraj made a plea for a regnocentric youth ministry starting from the principal of God's reign that contrasts with an ecclesiocentric youth ministry with the church as its starting point.[42] Vallabaraj argues that it is not the church but the reign of God that should define the mission of the church and the mission of youth ministry. Youth ministry's mission is to bring about the Kingdom of God in the world of the youth. "Such Youth Ministry truly becomes a sacrament of the Reign of God."[43] The purpose of youth ministry in this perspective is to live the great commandment of love: love of God, love of neighbor, and love of self with all one's mind, heart, and strength. For Vallabaraj, this purpose is a theological way of saying that youth ministry supports a journey towards human maturity: "to help the young to accept life in its totality, as both gift and duty, and live it well. It seeks to form a person who can confront him/her self, others and society at large with the wealth of values and meaning."[44] Faith should become integral and central to youth's life and their worldview, resulting in taking responsibility for one's own life and the welfare of the community and society.

A comparable plea for not taking the church as a starting point in youth ministry (ecclesiocentric youth ministry) can be observed in a contribution of Jeffey Kaster in *Religious Education* in which he presents the development and testing of a Christian Discipleship Scale which seeks to measure Christian discipleship as an outcome of adolescent catechesis.[45] Kaster's article presents a case study of a program evaluation of a Youth in Theology and Ministry curriculum in Minnesota. One of the four core learning outcomes of this curriculum is to apprentice Catholic leadership youth to live as disciples of Jesus Christ. The main background to this study is the observation of many Catholics leaving the Catholic

---

41. Root and Dean, *The Theological Turn in Youth Ministry*.
42. Vallabaraj, "Youth Ministry."
43. Vallabaraj, "Youth Ministry," 54.
44. Vallabaraj, "Youth Ministry," 50.
45. Kaster, "Evaluating Adolescent Catechesis."

Church in the US, this giving birth to the question of what is working and not working in adolescent catechesis. Kaster states that the Catholic Bishops stress religious literacy as an answer to the question of how to get young people to stay connected to the faith. But one of the implications of the case study of Kaster is that catechetical leaders "need to look more deeply into the connection between religious literacy and Christian discipleship."[46] For Kaster, fostering Christian discipleship a crucial aim for adolescent catechesis and at the same time, in itself, an important means for denominational affiliation.

8.6 Conclusion

This chapter addressed many examples of theologically loaded goals in the context of youth ministry. For a further reflection on theologically loaded goals as part of a holistic vision for youth ministry, the following publications are an interesting read. First, *Passing on the Faith: A Radical New Model for Youth and Family Ministry* written by Merton Strommen and Richard Hardel. The authors present a paradigm for faith formation containing desired outcomes in terms of ten characteristics that mark a life of commitment to Jesus Christ and a life of witness and service. Examples are: (1) trusting in a personal Christ, (6) demonstrating unprejudiced and loving lives, and (9) participating in the rituals of a Christian community. And second, *The Vision of Catholic Youth Ministry: Fundamentals, Theory, and Practice*, edited by Robert McCarty and Laurie Delgatto. This edited volume contains seventeen chapters written by a variety of authors. After a chapter on theology and Catholic youth ministry, the second chapter of the publication, authored by Greg "Dobie" Moser, addresses "A Vision of Catholic Youth Ministry," presenting three overarching goals: (1) to empower young people to live as disciples of Jesus Christ in our world today; (2) to draw young people to responsible participation in the life, mission, and work of the Catholic faith community, and (3) to foster the total personal and spiritual growth of each young person.

"As a young oak is nurtured, one decision at a time, into fullness, so discernment creates an incrementally adequate environment for growth in Christian vocation, or love of God and neighbor."[47] These words of David White were quoted at the beginning of this chapter. Growth in

---

46. Kaster, "Evaluating Adolescent Catechesis," 80.
47. White, *Practicing Discernment with Youth*, 82–83.

Christian vocation. Love of God and neighbor. These are two examples of theologically loaded conceptualizations of goals or "the goal" of youth ministry. This chapter addressed many more, among which are finding God, encountering God, faith and salvation, or being in God. These goals challenge youth ministry: Though being theologically or biblically rooted, these goals at the same time leave us with questions about how to actually apply these goals in concrete contexts. For those who take up this challenge, one first step can be to mirror what was presented in chapter 7 with what has been presented in the current chapter: How do pedagogically or psychologically envisioned goals relate to profoundly theologically loaded goals? This step brings us to the very heart of what it is to be a youth ministry scholar: to continuously combine these different perspectives in such a way that more understanding and more practical wisdom with regard to youth ministry will develop.

Part 4

WHO IS THE YOUTH MINISTER IN YOUTH MINISTRY?

Who Is the Youth Minister in Youth Ministry?

Introduction to Part 4

THE fourth part of the handbook does not ask *what* youth ministry is or should be, but rather *who is the youth minister?* In one way it is a response to the first *who*-question of this academic handbook, namely *who* the youth in youth ministry are. There is an interpretative and reflexive relationship between the two *whos*. Who we imagine young people to be, influence how we conceptualize the role of the youth minister, and how the role of the youth minister is modelled, influences who young people are found to be.

Chapter 9 offers an overview of the theme, presenting how the role of the youth minister is challenged as the position of the church in society changes. To re-imagine the role of the youth minister implies examining what it means to be an ecclesial leader in a secular age and highly pluralized society. Chapter 10 focuses on theological, or perhaps more precisely, Christological approaches to the role of the youth minister: To what extent may it be possible to understand the role of the youth minister as an imitation of Christ? Investigating this theme, it is crucial to evaluate what it may imply if youth ministry takes its cue from incarnational theology and the incarnation as event. The rest of the chapter focuses on other key theological *loci*, like baptismal theology and the encounter with God through relations.

Chapter 11 elaborates on pedagogical, educational, and partly psychological approaches to a research-based conceptualization of the youth minister as *teacher*. Drawing on the elaborations in chapter 9 on the shifting terrain for the church and her youth ministry in a secular age, the chapter starts by identifying how the context of learning is in flux.

The rest of the chapter examines a wide range of themes related to the youth minister as teacher, such as learning as socialization, learning as dialogue and the youth minister as dialogue partner, the youth minister as a potential spiritual director or a liturgical coach. Chapter 12 imagines the youth minister as *pastor*. Examining the paradigmatic shift in youth ministry from programs to practices, and from events to relationships, the chapter evaluates different models for youth ministry and how they might envision the role of the youth minister as a pastoral role, characterized by listening, guidance, and welcoming.

Chapter 13 discusses whether the youth minister may be understood as a *prophet*. Many youth ministry scholars emphasize youth ministry as a sort of prophetic practice, engaging both with church and culture. Drawing on theories on the liminal, prophetic imagination and holistic ministry, the chapter assesses different aspects of the prophetic role in youth ministry. Chapter 14 concludes the fourth part of the handbook by examining the role of the youth minister in the light of youth ministry as community. Drawing on *koinonia*-theology and theories on the relationship between youth ministry and the church, the chapter presents research focusing on youth ministry as a community and portraying the role of the youth minister as a communal role.

Part 4 examines how the youth minister may explore multiple roles in times of change, and throughout the chapters it is possible to identify some overarching themes in contemporary youth ministry research focusing on the role of the youth minister. First, the research engages a wide range of theological motifs, such as the imitation of Christ, encounters with the divine, and ecclesiological models. Second, a guiding principle in much of youth ministry scholarship and practice is an emphasis on the relational. The focus is on the youth minister as a *relational* teacher, a *relational* pastor, and a *relational* prophet. It is no surprise, therefore, that a key asset for a youth minister is to take on the pastoral role of safeguarding the practice of welcome in youth ministry.

9

The Youth Minister as a Leader in Times of Change

"We are called to participate in the imagination of a sending God, which is different from reinventing the church through our own creativity."[1]

This chapter, and the following chapters, elaborates on a key "pastoral" question in academic youth ministry: who is the youth minister? We first look at (9.1) how the role of the youth minister is challenged as the position of the church is challenged, moving on to look at how we should interpret the role of the youth minister in the public sphere, at the agora (9.2). Further, the chapter discuss how the youth minister may explore multiple roles in times of change (9.3). Then we explore what it means for the youth minister to be a leader in a secular age, drawing on contemporary leadership theory (9.4). The final section concludes by presenting how the following chapters will make use of youth ministry scholarship to investigate different roles the youth minister may take on to face the current challenges for youth ministry (9.5).

9.1 Being a Youth Minister when the Position of the Church Is Changing

The question "who is the youth minister?" is a context-sensitive question. In times of contextual change, the question must be explored over and

1. Dean, *Almost Christian*, 195.

again. The ecclesial terrain, particularly in the Western world, is changing rapidly. The role of the church in society, particularly the traditional churches of the North and the West, is in flux. Put bluntly, the church has lost her hegemonic position and no longer defines the public sphere or tells people what time it is in the same way as it used to when the church structured the way people ordered their lives. Previously, the rhythm of the church defined public life. In an increasingly secular era this is no longer necessarily the case.

The point is that the church has lost its hegemonic influence on this public sphere, particularly in the Northern and the Western hemisphere. The vertical understanding of the world has disappeared as our modern idea of social order or imaginary presupposes a "horizontal" reality, to which everyone has direct access. This order is both "created and sustained by common action in a secular time, as we see it in forms such as the public sphere, the market economy, the sovereign people. By contrast, the earlier "vertical" vision presents society as articulated into hierarchically ordered parts, which determine the identity of those who make them up, so that they relate to the whole only mediatedly, through the part."[2] It seems fair to claim, that this has left us with a flat(ter) world, where the church has lost her authoritarian hegemony of the Christendom era. The power to define the discussion in the public space is now a democratic value, principally open to all. This makes any plea to "vertical" arguments a tougher call.

The church and her representatives, such as the youth minister, must therefore rethink how they "position" themselves as they meet with people on the agora—in the open space at the marketplace—to proclaim the gospel and serve the needs of the community. As the context is becoming increasingly plural, the church and her youth ministry need to find her "voice" in the "jungle" of multiple voices. In other words, the role of a representative from church, like a youth minister, is no longer necessarily a given. It must be articulated and constructed anew. The role of the youth minister is in many ways up for grabs, and the church must renegotiate its role after the loss of hegemony. Faced with the fear of losing privileges at the agora, the church and her ministries may be tempted to react by either fleeing or fighting the change. This sort of reaction to the shifting dynamics of the increasingly secular agora, may be labelled

---

2. Taylor, *A Secular Age*, 392.

ecclesial agoraphobia.³ The phenomenon of ecclesial agoraphobia may also be a way to understand the challenges contemporary youth ministry faces, particularly with regard to re-shaping the role of the youth minister.

Leaders in church also need to negotiate how inherited modes of church may interact with new modes of church to make the gospel known to groups of people and cultures increasingly estranged from the traditional modes of being church. However, as a post-Christendom culture is not the same as pre-Christendom culture, patient "sowing" of the gospel message in youth ministry, "will often involve reconnecting our culture to its own heritage."⁴ Who is the youth minister amidst all of this? What sort of leadership or what role should a youth minister seek to develop to address these changes and challenges to serve young people and the church? In a study on young adults in the US and their relationship to the church, the author suggests a few virtues for leaders who want to encourage church growth—namely courage and charity and sharing the gospel with flexibility and fidelity.⁵

9.2 The Youth Minister at the Agora

What does it mean to be a leader in youth ministry in an era where the church no longer defines the marketplace (the *agora*), and where a certain ecclesial *agoraphobia* may prevail? What does missional leadership look in such a context? Perhaps an essential role of the youth minister in an increasingly secular society is to prepare youth for "participation in the public sphere by more intentionally forming them *for* and *through* deep reflection on classic religious symbols"?⁶

The fact that the church and its offers is no longer a given, implies that the church is one of many alternatives on an increasingly plural religious marketplace. Obviously, this implies that youth ministry activities are also offered on a competitive marketplace alongside other leisure time activities. In many countries, the space for leisure activities also shrinks as schools become all-day schools, which is a relatively new phenomenon in a European context. German youth ministry researchers, Claudia Gärtner and Karin Kempfer, have investigated how all-day-schools collaborate

---

3. Cf. Norheim, "Den norske kyrkjas," 408–11.
4. Savage et al., *Making Sense of Generation Y*, 159.
5. Carroll, *The New Faithful*, 278–92.
6. Manning, "Engaging Our Symbols," 452.

with extracurricular organizations—like church-based or para-church youth ministries—to enhance their extracurricular programs. They explore the chances and limitations that cooperation projects between the "systems" school and youth ministry may have, finding that it is crucial for local youth ministers to reflect on the obstacles to simply copying and pasting a classical youth ministry model into a school context. Further, it is necessary that contextual factors, like cooperation based on parental consent, the topography of the school (urban, suburban, rural), and how the owner of the school relates to cooperation of this sort, are considered.[7]

Every leader in youth ministry must at some point speak: a sermon, a devotion, a Bible lesson, a Facebook post, or another speech of some sort. But *why* should young people listen to you when you speak? Speaking to an audience is an act of public communication. It engages both the context of the listener and the world at large, the context of the church and the life of the speaker.[8]

Being a leader in church, like a youth minister, is therefore a public ministry.[9] When the leader appears in public every aspect of her appearance is exposed: The church or youth club in the basement, not to mention the Facebook page or Instagram account of the youth ministry, is not a private place. As a leader you cannot really hide. As a leader you are on display. This implies that your whole life is on display, and this becomes particularly evident when the leader speaks. The perceived role that a youth minister or another leader in the church takes on when speaking publicly is not a defined role, but the role of the youth minister, the *who* of the youth minister, is shaped as the youth minister appears before the public, like a group of young people. As we continue to investigate how different youth ministry scholars articulate and construct the *who* of the youth minister, it is wise to keep this essential aspect in mind: that the role of the church and that of the youth minister is in flux and will be re-constructed and de-constructed as the church and her ministry struggle to position themselves in the public sphere.

---

7. Gärtner and Kempfer, "Jugendverbände in die Schule?," 26, 49–50.

8. Cf. Haga and Norheim, "The Four Speeches."

9. For a wider assessment of this theme, see Volf and McAnnaly-Linz, *Public Faith in Action*, 3.

9.3 Exploring Multiple Roles in Times of Change

According to Bert Roebben, the task of youth ministry is to shape "a playground for transcendence in a world of difference." The question is how the role of the youth minister should be shaped by this task. Should the youth minister act as a project developer or hope generator? Or is the youth minister more like a fellow pilgrim? Roebben argues that the role of the youth minister is to involve young people in "journeys of longing and perspective, let them experience what it is like to have hunger and thirst, what it means to endure when one is on the way, what it means to look forward to getting home in the life of a pilgrim."[10] Roebben underlines that when the youth minister takes on the role of a fellow pilgrim, the aim of youth ministry ultimately centers developing resilience with young people.[11]

Reading Roebben and other youth ministry scholars makes it clear that the youth minister needs to explore multiple roles to meet the challenges and changes that the church and her ministry face. One may even ask if the youth minister should take on the role of coach or personal trainer, or even of captain. Perhaps the youth minister may even act as a sort of clown at the agora, as the old French legend has it.[12]

The catalogue of roles for a youth minister is wide and open, and in times of ecclesial change, the youth minister is challenged to rethink and reconstruct the role of youth minister in multiple ways. Perhaps the youth minister should rather consider the role of the guide or the expert. Bert Roebben has explored the different roles a youth minister may take on in this shifting ecclesial terrain and argues that the youth minister who acts as a guide or expert draws on theological-heuristic competence and learning in youth ministry that happens mainly through information. The youth minister could also act as a mentor or moderator. Roebben writes about how this implies drawing on theological-communicative competence, which in turn implies learning through communication. The youth minister could even pursue the role of the witness, Roebben finds. Then, the youth minister draws on theological-existential competence, and learning happens through confrontation, Roebben points out.[13] According to David White, the role of youth minister is to practice

10. Roebben, *Seeking Sense in the City*, 234.
11. Roebben, *Seeking Sense in the City*, 220–26.
12. DePaola, *The Clown of God*.
13. Roebben, *Seeking Sense in the City*, 180.

theological and social discernment with youth.[14] Like Roebben, White draws on the liberation theology scheme of change: "see, judge, act."

Perhaps the youth minister could even try to take on the role of the friend. For Bert Roebben this has to do with bringing "the Gospel closer to itself, namely into the realm of friendship where God happens."[15] The obvious problem with identifying the youth minister as a friend is the blurring of the dynamics of symmetry and asymmetry. The question is whether the youth minister could also take on the role of a more parental figure. This sort of role intensifies the symmetry/asymmetry-dilemma. We will return to these dilemmas shortly.

In the following chapters and sections, we will investigate and discuss how youth ministry researchers over the last decades have explored and constructed the *who* of the youth minister. What roles should a youth minister take on—when teaching, speaking, meeting young people, and in the minister's discernment of the biblical tradition?

Assessing the role of the youth minister, also forces us to reflect in more depth on the purpose of any youth ministry. In other words, asking *who* the youth minister is or should be, inevitably pokes the question *what* is youth ministry? If youth ministry is like a pilgrim refugee camp, like Noah's ark, who then is the youth minister? If youth ministry, like Kenda Creasy Dean suggests, should be like a laboratory for hope,[16] who then is the youth minister? A lab assistant? Or, if youth ministry should be like a city on the hill or like the salt of the earth, who then is the youth minister, other than the guy with the WWJD-armband?

9.4 The Youth Minister as a Leader

The following section offers an exposition on the role of the youth minister in times of change, drawing on contemporary leadership theory with relevance for the challenge at hand. The act of leadership is by its very essence, directed towards the future. It may be understood as a process of influencing others to commit and dedicate themselves to future visions and goals.[17] Charting a course, however, into the emerging future

---

14. White, *Practicing Discernment with Youth*.
15. Roebben, *Seeking Sense in the City*, 217.
16. Dean, *Almost Christian*.
17. Cf. Yukl, *Leadership in Organizations*, 9.

envisioned by the leader, like the youth minister,[18] implies building on an assessment of an organization's past, both of its story, value, and legacy.[19] Gary Yukl defines leadership as "the process of influencing others to understand and agree about what needs to be done and how to do it, and the process of facilitating individual and collective efforts to accomplish shared objectives."[20] Departing from that definition, it is evident that a youth minister is a leader. But what does that mean? If leadership is about the future, and the youth minister is a leader, in which way may the youth minister then act as a visionary leader? How is the youth ministry's vision of the future shaping the image and identity of the youth minister? And: What role does the youth minister play in the dynamic process of "facilitating individual and collective efforts to accomplish shared objectives."

First, it is important to note that leadership in a late-modern world has become a more ambivalent enterprise because of the ethics of an inwardly defined authenticity.[21] It makes the leader's appeal to the feelings of an audience, what in classical rhetorical theory is called *pathos*, more complicated. This implies that the credibility of a leader, like a youth minister, is constantly at stake in a whole new way, as it is often very difficult to "distinguish self from role."[22]

In times of great insecurity, leaders are often challenged to perform *adaptive change*. With adaptive problems, establishing authority as a leader does not necessarily mean looking for authoritative solutions.[23] Often the leaders are expected to develop and appear with an informal authority that derives its strength from its ability "to meet expectations that are often left implicit."[24]

Studies in what makes leadership appear authentic in times of change emphasize the importance of *consistency* in words, actions, and values. Such leadership may even increase the followers' trust. This may include beliefs about the leader's integrity and honesty.[25] This insight is

---

18. Cf. Scharmer and Kaufer, *Leading from the Emerging Future*.
19. Heifetz, *The Practice of Adaptive Leadership*, 15.
20. Yukl, *Leadership in Organizations*, 22.
21. Cf. Taylor, *The Ethics of Authenticity*.
22. Heifetz, *Leadership without Easy Answers*, 264.
23. Heifetz, *Leadership without Easy Answers*, 87.
24. Heifetz, *Leadership without Easy Answers*, 101.
25. Yukl, *Leadership in Organizations*, 344–46.

an important one to take note of, even for a youth minister re-negotiating the role of the youth minister.

9.5 O, Youth Minister, Who Art Thou?

These initial reflections on the many roles of the youth minister prove that there is a need to reflect on the authority of the youth minister. What constructs the public authority of a youth minister as something authentic and credible? Perhaps that authority is best understood as a narrative authority. Bert Roebben writes that "young people have a right to stories that testify to the human struggle with life's major questions and to the tentative and vulnerable nature of the answers."[26] Roebben underlines that "nobody can live without a narrative."[27] When the role of youth minister is no longer a given, there is an urgent need for self-reflexivity. Terry Linhart writes about the self-aware leader and emphasizes the importance of discovering your ministry blind-spots.[28]

In times of great change and insecurity, maybe the youth minister is best understood as the one who enters the liminal spheres, who explores the wild, and challenges the boundaries of church by embodying a welcome (to the gospel and to the church), where a welcome may not be expected. To the one at the door this might take on a different meaning as the meaning of church is being challenged. Anyhow, as youth is an exemplary transitional stage in human life, both the welcome and the farewell are essential practices in youth ministry. At a time where many churches in the West experience numerical decay, one way to revise the role of youth ministry and the understanding of the youth minister is to focus on welcoming the stranger. American theologian Jessicah Krey Ducksworth has argued that the catechetical practice of the church must be shaped by the newcomers' questions and experiences to meet the challenges of secularization. Ducksworth, drawing on Kathryn Tanner's theology of the welcome (2002), maintains that the practice of welcome that the minister models must lead to not just a re-articulation of theology and practice, but to a sort of disarticulation.[29] A youth ministry needs to rehearse both the practice of welcome and the practice of bidding young

---

26. Roebben, *Seeking Sense in the City*, 155.
27. Roebben, *Seeking Sense in the City*, 229.
28. Linhart, *The Self-Aware Leader*.
29. Ducksworth, *Wide Welcome*, 30–34.

people farewell, sending them off to work, college, or simply life outside youth ministry.

Similarly, in an article on young people's disaffiliation from the church, James Michael Nagle explores hermeneutics central to the concept of shared praxis for developing the faithful but critical dialogue which is required when young people disaffiliate. He draws on Thomas Groome's theory/method of shared praxis that encourages youth ministers to make the Christian Story and Vision accessible to those inside and outside the community ("learners"), "not as an immutable object from the past but a source of revelation to put into dialog with their own stories and visions."[30] Nagle points out how, Groome's student, Tom Beaudoin (2013), and other scholars (like Jamieson 2002 and Streib 2009) have used the term "deconversion" to illuminate an element of the disaffiliation process, which is both deconstructive and reconstructive as persons learn and discern what is essential and nonessential in a tradition. Nagle's theological and pedagogical point that seeks to revise how leaders in churches conceptualize their role in being with young people, particularly young adults, is articulated in the following manner: "As more and more people choose to leave conventional religious communities, and for some this is a learned and discerned choice, theologians and educators must also learn to seek the divine being revealed in those lives and stories."[31]

9.6 Conclusion

In the chapters to come we will assess how to understand the *who* of the youth minister by looking at the youth minister as a person, as someone placed so serve in a public role in the world, and as a representative of the church. In the next chapter (chapter 10), we will discuss to what extent it may be meaningful to interpret the role of the youth minister as an imitation of Christ, by discussing theologically informed conceptualizations of the role of the youth minister. In the following chapter (chapter 11), we will look at the many attempts to understand the youth minister in the capacity of a teacher or pedagogue. Chapter 12 returns to more theological ground, exploring scholarly contributions that see the youth minister as a pastor. In chapter 13, we discuss the contributions posing the role of the youth minister as a sort of imaginative and prophetic role.

30. Nagle, "Learning to Leave," 536.
31. Nagle, "Learning to Leave," 540.

In the final chapter of this part (chapter 14), asking *who* the youth minister is, we briefly explore the role of the youth minister from a communal perspective.

10

The Youth Minister as *Jesus*?

"Leaders can make or break a ministry. A youth ministry without adequate leadership can never be healthy, but one with an abundance of quality leaders will always have the potential for health."[1]

IF Doug Fields is right in the quote above, that without adequate leadership a youth ministry can never be healthy, whatever "healthy" means, what does it imply for the conceptualization of the role of the youth leader in the context of Christian ministry with young people? Does it mean that the leader should try to be perfect, perhaps try to be like Jesus? This chapter examines key theological themes which are essential as we discuss to what extent it may be possible to understand the role of the youth minister as an imitation of Christ. We first look at how the theological motif of *imitatio Christi*, the imitation of Christ, seems to be a guiding principle in much of youth ministry scholarship and practice (10.1). We move on to discuss how the concept of imitation relates to another important strand in youth ministry scholarship, namely the claim that youth ministry should take its cue from incarnational theology and the incarnation as event (10.2). In the next section we explore how yet another influential current in youth ministry thinking, relational youth ministry, portrays the role of the youth minister (10.3). Then we explore other motifs of imitation, drawing on baptismal theology, imitation

1. Fields, *Purpose-Driven Youth Ministry*, 271.

through family relations and imitation in the context of mentorship (10.4).

10.1 Imitation as the Theological Tune of Youth Ministry

To what—or perhaps to *whom*—should a youth minister, and the role of the youth minister, be compared? Why not start at the top, and parallel the youth minister with the Son of God himself? What is better than rooting the conception of the youth minister's service in making Jesus the role model for ministry? After all, to many, youth ministry is all about Jesus. Dave Rahn argues that "the genius of Jesus' servant leadership strategy is that a slave could be expected to influence his or her master through the quality of a well-lived and opportunistic, Spirit-led boldness."[2] Similarly, Andrew Root has argued that the youth worker is a "participant in God's action."[3]

UK youth ministry scholar David Bailey claims that youth ministry has been "infused with the idea of model, pattern and imitation."[4] Bailey has also used the term "theological shorthand" to express how abbreviated catch phrases and short sentences relate to a deeper Christian (theological tradition). The challenge, Bailey finds, is that the connection to the wider, theological tradition is thinly expressed and tends to collapse into the relational. He interviewed six youth ministry practitioners (four male, two female) in the UK, and they were asked to tell stories about their mission amongst non-church young people. Based on the interviews with youth ministers, Bailey argues that the youth ministers mainly rely on a self-understanding of their role as youth ministers of "being there" and "being like Jesus."[5] Bailey concludes:

> *Being there* again acts as theological shorthand and a partial description of the intricacies, of practice and service amongst young people. *Being there* for young people is a performed theological moment in time and space through which the youth ministers act as a symbol.[6]

---

2. Rahn, "Focusing Youth Ministry," 179.
3. Root, *Taking Theology to Youth Ministry*, 100.
4. Bailey, "Enacted Faith," 35.
5. Bailey, "Enacted Faith," 37, 32.
6. Bailey, "Enacted Faith," 34.

Christians throughout the ages have struggled to understand the nature and mode of discipleship. Focusing on *imitatio Christi*—the imitation of Christ—has long been a key motif. To imitate Christ is generally understood as the attempt to live and act as Christ lived and acted. But how should the role of the youth minister be understood in relation to the *imitatio Christi* motif, which runs through the historical veins of Christianity? After all, there are, conflicting strands within Christian theology, in how to conceptualize this idea. Either way, imitating Christ, involves carrying the cross. For this very reason, Martin Luther identified the cross, or discipleship in suffering, as one of the seven marks of the church in *On the Councils and the Church* (1539).[7] Even the gospels as genre may be taken as biographies designed to make the reader and hearer imitate a narrative pattern. In other words, the first disciples were called to imitate Christ whenever the Gospels were liturgically read. So, the *imitatio Christi* motif provided a significant impulse for the writing of the gospels, and concurrently the gospels shaped the understanding of what it meant to follow Jesus.[8]

Today, this pattern continues, as many researchers focus on the role of the Bible (stories) in youth ministry formation and mentoring. Nathan Chiroma maintains that the apostle Paul emphasized that the object of imitation was Jesus Christ, which is a call to imitate him in his self-denying, Christ-enjoying fulfilled life. In other words, in the context of youth ministry, Chiroma argues, this sort of *mimetai* (imitation)-mentoring "provides adolescents with models or examples to follow for shaping their spiritual formation."[9]

David Bailey's finding, that youth ministers tend to display an imitational model in their role as youth ministers, relates to a strong tradition within academic youth ministry, namely, to focus on incarnational and relational ministry and more distantly or indirectly, to a long (theological tradition) of imitation. Throughout the history of the church and her ministry the *imitatio Christi* motif has played a key role in many ways. One of the most and influential famous expressions of this motif is found in *The Imitation of Christ*, which is a Christian devotional book written by Thomas à Kempis. It was first composed in Medieval Latin (as *De Imitatione Christi*) around 1418-27. The book is a handbook for spiritual

---

7. Norheim, *Practicing Baptism*; Hütter, *Suffering Divine Things*.
8. Capes, "Imitatio Christi."
9. Chiroma, "The Role of Mentoring," 83.

life arising from the Devotio Moderna movement, of which Kempis was a member. The classic by Thomas á Kempis is probably the most widely read Christian devotional work next to the Bible. Interestingly, it gained popularity immediately, and was printed 745 times before 1650. Apart from the Bible, at the time no book had been translated into more languages than the *Imitation of Christ*.

10.2 Incarnational Youth Ministry

Many contributions in youth ministry scholarship would stress that youth ministry should be incarnational in its approach to both contemporary culture and to young people. In shaping the role, the youth minister should take a cue from incarnational theology, and perhaps even the incarnation as an event and ongoing reality. Youth ministry contributions drawing on the incarnation and incarnational theology tend to focus on two things:

1. *How* God became flesh in Jesus Christ, and that the way Jesus encountered human beings should serve as a *model* for the way the church encounters young people.
2. To preach and portray *Jesus as a role model* for the young people involved in youth ministry.

Incarnational youth ministry has inspired anything from discipleship, evangelization through friendship, relational youth ministry, holistic, diaconal youth ministry, solidarity in youth ministry etc. In *God at the Mall* (1999), Pete Ward argues that relational youth ministry has to do with meeting young people where they're at and spend time with them to preach or convey a culturally relevant gospel, an incarnated gospel. In the book, *A Christlike Ministry* (2008), Steve Griffiths critically examines the whole concept of "incarnational youth ministry" or "relational youth ministry." He argues that the focus on relationships in youth ministry tends to miss out on crucial aspects of the life and ministry of Jesus. The meetings with Jesus in the gospels, he finds, are first and foremost characterized by their "*kairos*"-character. They are events. Perhaps it is therefore more fitting to speak of the youth minister as someone being shaped by the *story* of Jesus. Pete Ward has argued that "the Christian youth worker

The Youth Minister as Jesus?

looks back to the cross of Christ, engages in the mission of God in the present, and looks for liberation in the future."[10]

In the book *The Godbearing Life* (1998), Kenda Creasy Dean proposes Mary as the role model for youth ministry. In the Orthodox tradition, Mary is often pictured as a *theotokos*, a god-bearer. Dean suggests that Mary serves as a role model to Christians because she accepts God's gift and calling to bear God to the world through her life and ministry. As Christians, Dean argues, we are called to live a god-bearing life: "God invites us all to become Godbearers—persons who by the power of the Holy Spirit smuggle Jesus into the world through our own lives, who by the virtue of our yes to God find ourselves forever and irrevocably changed." The story of Mary is also a role model for how youth ministers should seek to become "midwives" for new births of Christ in the (godbearing) lives of young people.[11]

The problem with some of the models that focus on Jesus as a *role model* is that they do not sufficiently thematize the asymmetric relationship between Jesus as the son of God and human beings. Theologically speaking, human beings are always at the receiving end, and ministry is not just simple mimicry. However, by placing ourselves in the position of Mary it is more evident that we are receivers of God's gift in Jesus Christ.

Anyway, the contributions of Ward, Griffiths, and Dean reveal a need to investigate further the whole concept of imitation in youth ministry. Is it possible to see the role of the youth minister as a way to mimic Christ, as an art of *mimesis*? In other words, is the role of the youth minister defined by an imitation of the Son of God?

Here, perhaps it is worth taking note of French Philosopher Rene Girard's theory on mimesis and imitation. The philosopher's fundamental concept is "mimetic desire." Girard seems to think that when you imitate the desires of others, you may end up desiring the very same things. Furthermore, and if you desire the same things as the others, you (you and the others) may easily become rivals, as you all reach for the same objects. However, Girard usually distinguishes "imitation" from "mimesis." Girard makes the ability to imitate, an ability he labels "mimetism," the fundamental principle in process where human beings are forms as cultural creatures. Girard's basic idea is that human beings are not able

---

10. Ward, *God at the Mall*, 45.
11. Dean and Foster, *The Godbearing Life*, 48.

to desire anything by themselves but need Another to point out what is desirable.¹²

10.3 Relational Youth Ministry

What role should relationships play in shaping the role and self-understanding of the youth minister? Andrew Root has argued that the relationships between adults and adolescents are not means to a greater end but should, in and of themselves, be the theologically greater goal.¹³ Rather, the youth minister should, with young people, contemplate and articulate the "where" of God. Root draws on German Lutheran theologian Eberhard Jüngel's work with *theologia crucis*—the tension in how human existence is set between possibility and nothingness—to outline how youth ministry should attend to the "where" of God by focusing on relationships. Ultimately Root finds, that the vocation of a youth minister is to walk near "the nothingness of adolescents, by being in relationship with them."¹⁴ Furthermore, as the "where" of God is encountered in the cross and in the nothingness, which tells the story of how Christ "joins our own suffering, yearnings, and brokenness," then the vocation of the youth minister centres on *bearing reality* with young people. It becomes essential then for the youth minister to be a "bearer of reality, to be able to see, feel, and attend to nothingness," and to search for God even "in the heavy nothingness of existence," always searching for the "where" of God "alongside adolescents."¹⁵

For a youth minister to seek the will of God, or in the words of Root "discerning Christopraxis," this implies that the youth minister should not seek the role as a church programmer. Rather, the role of the youth minister means to join in the dynamic actions of God in the world, and even in the lives of adolescents. This implies that doing youth ministry "is not about programming events, but about discerning God's continued Ministry in the world and therefore joining it."¹⁶ To the question, "Who is the youth minister?," Root would therefore probably answer simply "a

---

12. Cf. Girard, *Violence and the Sacred*; Girard, *The Scapegoat*.
13. Root, "Relationality as the Objective."
14. Root, "God's Hiddenness," 74.
15. Root, "God's Hiddenness," 75.
16. Root, "Youth Ministry as Discerning Christopraxis," 28.

person." Basically, the youth minister or youth pastor should "support, encourage and assist adult and adolescent relationships of place-sharing."[17]

The plea to conceptualize relationships as the primary context where youth ministry happens seems to have wide support within contemporary youth ministry scholarship. In the next chapter, we will look at how relations are even found to be essential in catechetical learning in youth ministry. It should also come as no surprise that the development of relationships between youth worker and the young person is essential in so-called *detached* youth work, as an empirical study by Naomi Thompson and James Ballantyne shows. Spiritual and social purposes of youth ministry often meet in the relational encounter: As trust increases, youth workers can get to know the young person even better "as well as being able to offer guidance, information or advice."[18]

All in all, the youth minister, particularly within relational and incarnational models of youth ministry, is often portrayed as someone who should seek to encounter young people within a mode of friendship, where encounters happen on equal terms. However, there are some obvious challenges to this way of portraying the role or the youth minister, particularly when it comes to retaining professional boundaries. Peter Hart has investigated this challenge and argues that "as youth ministry is a unique vocation, with a unique *telos* and set of practices, it should approach the limits of appropriate behaviour and relationships on its own terms."[19] Hart explores how the use of professional boundaries is understood within other work-areas and disciplines. Hart refers to how "overly prescriptive boundaries can prevent intimacy and authenticity, despite the personality and character of the worker being essential in good youth work and ministry."[20] Hart also conducted an ethnographic study of four youth organizations, exploring how boundaries were practiced. Hart pointed out that boundaries do not only come from external professional and organizational influence, or from youth workers, rather the young people themselves are active in constructing and negotiating their own boundaries.[21]

---

17. Root, *Revisiting Relational Youth Ministry*, 207.
18. Thompson and Ballantyne, "Being Church," 114.
19. Hart, "Professional Boundaries," 24.
20. Hart, "Professional Boundaries," 27.
21. Hart, "Professional Boundaries," 35.

In conclusion, Hart argues that Christian youth ministry (sometimes) needs a different approach to boundaries from secular youth work, as "allowing space for work in the grey areas of human interaction is not a weakness of youth ministry, but a strength, when the needs of the young person are being prioritized and the worker is seeking to be a positive example." However, youth ministers need to be more articulated and intentional about the boundaries that still need to be set in youth ministry, for the sake of the young people.[22]

10.4 Motifs of Imitation

Another important motif in much of youth ministry research is to conceptualize the youth minister as a fellow pilgrim, a wayfarer, perhaps even a guide. Different theological traditions and loci are used to configure this image of the youth minister theologically. Bård Norheim argues, that even baptismal theology may serve as an entry point and source for a peregrinational conceptualization of ministry by coining the term *practicing baptism* as a model to interpret the life of the Christian in the world:

> In the right meaning of the word, *practicing baptism* is a lifestyle, a lifestyle shaped by the image or the sign of the cross. We are baptized into the image of Christ, the crucified and the risen. In this mystery lies the hidden unity of the true image of humanity. Therefore, the process of being conformed to Christ, which starts in baptism, and which finds its form in a continuous return to baptism throughout life, is really a process of becoming human under the sign of the cross.[23]

In the life of family, imitation plays a key role. A child imitates its parents, or perhaps even its older siblings. Interestingly, Robert J. Parmach points out that (youth) ministers are teachers, and that "the Christian family is a great teaching model to share." However, when adopting that model of teaching, it is important that to learn from how Jesus "urged church leaders and ministers to embrace the frailty and impressionable qualities of the child when leading social ministries of God's people to love one another." In fact, Parmach finds that "Jesus' entire social ministry on earth was a paradoxical, meaningful proceeding: seeking an *in*human

---

22. Hart, "Professional Boundaries," 38.
23. Norheim, "Practicing Baptism," 49. See also Norheim, *Practicing Baptism*.

attained goal by living *in* humanity." Therefore, "Jesus is the best example of faithfulness to the apostolic mission of the family."[24]

In recent youth ministry scholarship, the youth minister is sometimes portrayed as mentor. The role of the mentor also originates, at least theologically, from a theology of imitation. In an article drawing on the findings of research done focused on the critical evaluation of mentoring programs in three ECWA seminaries in Nigeria, Nathan Chiroma first defines mentoring with Anderson and Reese,[25] as "a triadic relationship between mentor, adolescent and the Holy Spirit, where the adolescent can discover the already present action of God, intimacy with God, ultimate identity as a child of God and a unique voice for kingdom responsibility." Chiroma further argues: "Adolescents deeply desire adults in their lives who are willing to help them navigate the journey from adolescence to adulthood."[26] Chiroma continues to emphasize that "The Christian faith is an imitative faith and adolescents are looking for adults with an authentic Christian faith to imitate."[27] Fundamentally, Chiroma finds that "the use of mentoring as a supportive pedagogy in adolescents' spiritual formation employs several concrete steps, namely discipleship, imitation, spiritual direction, modelling and coming alongside adolescents' in their spiritual journey."[28] Similarly, David M. Hindman has offered a broad exploration of how college mentors can facilitate spiritual development among college students by increasing awareness and offering companionship on the, sometimes painful, road towards wholeness.[29]

What characterizes the good mentor, or what should the youth minister who strives to be a good mentor focus on? In a biblical study on mentorship, Andy Stirrup concludes that when we think of a good and wise mentor to young people we should "think of those individuals who are 'living the story' and who are *already* in a family-like relationships with younger others, who want to see them grow, and are excited by the prospect that their protégé might develop a more mature faith than them."[30]

---

24. Parmach, "Christian Families," 81, 66, 76.
25. Anderson and Reese, *Spiritual Mentoring*.
26. Chiroma, "The Role of Mentoring," 80.
27. Chiroma, "The Role of Mentoring," 83.
28. Chiroma, "The Role of Mentoring," 88.
29. Hindman, "From Splintered Lives."
30. Stirrup, "Growing Faith," 74.

10.5 Conclusion

We see that the imitation motif and aspirations to draw on incarnational theology are prominent features in contemporary attempts among youth ministry scholars to chart a course for the role of the youth minister. The focus on mentorship reminds us that imitation is also a sort of learning. This insight serves as a mental springboard to our next chapter, where we will look at different ways to conceptualize the youth minister as a teacher.

11

The Youth Minister as *Teacher*

"I think it is remembering that you are not one of them; that you are there as an adult, not as a child. You've got to keep the line to keep some order." (Volunteer youth minister)[1]

This chapter discusses what it may imply to posit the youth minister in the role of the *teacher*. In the first section (11.1), we look at three words starting with *A* (autonomy, authority, and authenticity) that seems to shape the current context of learning. In the second part of the chapter, we look at scholarly contributions portraying the youth minister as a relational teacher (11.2). In 11.3. the focus shifts to learning as socialization, and the role of the youth minister in processes of socialization. In 11.4. we explore contributions which imagine the youth minister as a dialogue partner in learning, and which focuses learning as dialogue, even in the context of the digital. The next section (11.5) assesses the youth minister's potential role as a sort of spiritual director, which moves into a discussion of how it may be possible to learn with the arts in youth ministry (11.6). Finally, we look at how the youth minister may serve as a sort of liturgical coach (11.7), and to which extent learning should be considered an individual or communal enterprise (11.8). The latter section addresses a theme already introduced in chapter 4: the individual and communal aspects of faith development among youth.

---

1. Hart, "Professional Boundaries," 33.

11.1 Three Words Starting with A: Autonomy, Authority, and Authenticity

New educational paradigms force the youth minister—or any other religious leader—to rethink the role of the youth minister. If teaching no longer simply means telling, and learning no longer means listening, but rather teaching implies listening and learning implies telling, then the role of the youth minister—or any other religious leader—needs to be revised.[2] One might therefore argue that there are three words starting with an *A* that are key terms as one tries to understand the role of the youth minister in an increasingly secular age: autonomy, authenticity, and authority. First, the whole quest for identity and meaning-making is rooted in a particular understanding of self-choice or personal autonomy. Secondly, what vouches for autonomy is a feeling of authenticity, that the young person perceives that choices, encounters, and experiences are real and trustworthy. Any claim to authority must be rooted in these first two premises of autonomy and authenticity. In other words, authority is configured intentionally, not formally. Emotionally, not institutionally.

We see the same pattern once formal bonds of modelling in learning are challenged, the focus shifts towards authenticity. The role of the adult in the religious socialization that takes place in youth ministry is configurated by the perceived authenticity of the person, not their position. This means adults in youth ministry, like teachers and youth leaders, may be involved in this communication process. The authority of the adult youth minister is then not shaped mainly by the position of the minister, but by the extent to which they are taken to be authentic, with a certain charisma if you like, and most importantly "convincingly contribute and participate in the communication process with young people."[3]

But how does a youth minister appear with authority in the encounter with young people in a secular age? With the autonomization of religion (McGuire and Taylor), it seems like the youth minister appears authoritative insofar as they embody what it means to have a relationship with God, and insofar as this embodiment of religious practice inspires young people to identify with this leader. In other words, as a leader in a religious community, the youth minister may become authoritative "authentically showing or expressing their close relationship with God."[4]

---

2. Kelman, "The Rabbinic Leader," 333–34.
3. De Kock et al., "Beyond Individualisation," 336.
4. De Kock and Sonnenberg, "Embodiment," 19.

In short, youth ministry in this fashion offers a sort of tribalistic socialization, where the focus shifts from the oral instruction of a message, given by one with a positioned authority, to a more holistic approach, where showing the message becomes key. Andrew Root argues that in a secular age this religious socialization of "show, not tell," implies that the pastor, or the youth minister for that matter, is simply someone who prays and teaches other people to do the same: "For all the tension we feel in the secular age, and its making of divine action opaque, prayer simply but profoundly directs the pastor's attention back to divine action."[5] Perhaps the youth minister in a secular age is called to teach with the help of *resonance*, also to avoid alienation, as German sociologist Hartmut Rosa argues that "resonance, from an anthropological and phenomenological, neurological and ethnological perspective, constitutes the primary relation to the world from which the subject and the world it encounters first arise as empirical facts."[6]

11.2 The Youth Minister as a Relational Teacher

It seems almost banal to point it out, but even catechesis and teaching—education—is based on relation. Some would even claim relationship is "the dominant theme of any educational process." It comes down to the fact that "no education can take place without relationship between adults and children, adults and adults, and so on."[7] With a phenomenological approach to investigating the lifeworld, particularly that of children and young people, it becomes clear that the fundamental dimensions of relationship are relationship with oneself, with others, with society and history, and with time.[8]

This perspective on teaching and learning in youth ministry is apparent in Urie Bronfenbrenner's social theory of understanding individuals in their social contexts and different social systems:

- the microsystem (face-to-face relationships),
- the mesosystem (encounters on an institutional level, such as neighborhoods, schools, and jobs), and

---

5. Root, *The Pastor in a Secular Age*, 274.
6. Rosa, *Resonance*, 445.
7. Boschki, "Re-reading Martin Buber," 115.
8. Boschki, "Re-reading Martin Buber," 116.

- the macrosystem (political and social situations as represented in the mass media, for example, in television and on the Internet).

Later, Urie Bronfenbrenner added a fourth dimension to his typology, namely: the chronosystem, which relates to biography and history.[9]

How, then, should the relationship between the adult, the youth minister, and the young people be characterized? Many would emphasize the asymmetric character of such a relationship, but, interestingly, educational philosopher Janusz Korczak would maintain that the relationship is an equal one. Korczak does not conceptualize this through a romantic notion of the (innocent) youth or child. Rather, he emphasizes, based on his experience of meeting children in orphanages, that the child is characterized by poverty. Overall Korczak abandons all asymmetrical thinking about education.[10]

The push towards equal relations in processes of learning is, for Korczak, a call to avoid the relationship to become inhuman and destructive. He found that teachers and children must try to live and learn together on the same level, not with those teaching regarding themselves at a superior level. Korczak, thus, wanted to create a pedagogy of radical "respect for the child."[11] Korczak's view here is free of any romanticism and idealization because, to him, children in their everyday life were characterized by "absolute poverty, social disadvantage, and very bad health conditions." All in all, Korczak's educational pedagogy bears many similarities to Martin Buber's educational philosophy. To both thinkers believe that learning and education with young people is rooted in personal encounters and dialogue. Dialogue, however, is not just a conversation, but something that happens based on trust. In many ways, Korczak went further than Buber in emphasizing that the teacher-pupil relationship is something strictly mutual, where the teacher learns just as much from the youth and children, perhaps even more.[12]

Similarly, Sonia Matthaei advocates for the importance of focusing on relationships, structures, and practices to develop a "life-giving ecology of faith formation," which also "celebrates gifts of leadership." However, those who serve as leaders and role models in an "effective" and

---

9. Cf. Bronfenbrenner, *The Ecology of Human Development*; Bronfenbrenner and Morris, "The Ecology of Developmental Process."

10. Boschki, "Re-reading Martin Buber," 120.

11. Referenced in Boschki, "Re-reading Martin Buber," 121.

12. Boschki, "Re-reading Martin Buber," 121–22.

life-giving ecology of faith formation are "models of a faithful life, not in the sense of being perfect, but in their attempt to be faithful through all of life's challenges and opportunities."[13]

11.3 Learning as Socialization

Jos de Kock has argued that a key factor to consider when exploring the role of leadership in youth ministry is the shifting landscape of religious socialization. De Kock starts by criticizing an overstated belief in the role of individualization, arguing that the grand narrative on religious individualization is not entirely convincing: "Firstly, Christian families, schools and churches continue to exist in contemporary society, and they continue to produce believing youth. It is indeed not always known how loyal these youth are to this trio of institutions, yet the picture of flawed religious involvement, inferred by many sociologists, is, to say the least, one-sided."[14]

Looking at the Dutch context, de Kock detects three institutional strategies for dealing with the religious development of Christian youth. The first strategy focuses on restoring or repairing the triangle connection between family, school, and church. The second strategy focuses on catering to the needs of the young person, by offering meaning and by adapting to the lifestyle of young people. The third strategy de Kock calls an "identification strategy." Here the focus is on creating communities where young people may identify with older people.[15]

De Kock also discusses three instructional paradigms, namely the behavioral model, the developmental model, and the apprenticeship model. He describes the differences between the three paradigms in the following way:

> A behavioural paradigm reflecting a social system in which the expert has a high status and the novice has a low status but is expected to acquire more of the expert's expertise; (b) a developmental paradigm reflecting a social system in which the novice learns by developing his or her own personal theories with the support of the expert, who may question, contradict, and challenge those theories; and (c) an apprenticeship paradigm

---

13. Matthaei, "Rethinking Faith Formation,"
14. De Kock, "Promising Approaches to Catechesis," 179.
15. De Kock, "Promising Approaches to Catechesis," 180-81.

reflecting a social system in which the learner must clearly participate in the expert's world to learn (through acculturation).[16]

De Kock finds that more and more Dutch Protestant churches are starting to use versions of the apprenticeship model in their youth ministries. He also argues that a shift from more traditional forms of socialization to more modern forms does not exclude teachers or church youth leaders as actors or role models when it comes to being accepted as religious authority for young people.[17] De Kock concludes with a plea to see teachers and youth leaders, not as mere facilitators of the search of the individual, but rather that they should act as "living representatives of a religious tradition *participating* in the religious development process of young people; thus *participating* in what young people accept as religious authority."[18] De Kock ends the article by offering a research framework for empirical studies on learning in catechetical practices.[19]

In an article two years later (2014), "A Typology of Catechetical Learning Environments," Jos de Kock continues his work on catechetical learning with youth and socialization (learning environments) by offering an overview of key concepts when it comes to religious learning goals, often conceptualized through the triad cognitive, affective, and attitudinal goals. Based on these key concepts and reflections on the nature of catechetical practice, de Kock proposes a typology of twelve typical catechetical learning environments, drawing on three instructional paradigms—the behavioral, developmental, and apprenticeship models. The three paradigms offer different pathways for a youth minister to pursue in setting the stage for catechetical learning with young people.

In yet another article from the following year (2015), De Kock maintains that the encounter between the youth minister and the young person is "the core of religious learning in missionary work." Therefore, "the person of the youth worker is an important 'means' for initiating and guiding religious learning." Put bluntly, the youth minister serves as "an identification figure and someone who embodies the message of the Gospel."[20] Fundamentally, the process of religious learning in this manner is situated in the encounter, an encounter which may encompass the

---

16. De Kock, "Promising Approaches to Catechesis," 184–85.
17. De Kock, "Promising Approaches to Catechesis," 188, 190.
18. De Kock, "Promising Approaches to Catechesis," 190.
19. De Kock, "Promising Approaches to Catechesis," 192.
20. De Kock, "Being a Church," 230.

meeting between a youngster and a youth minister, "such as living and acting together or discussing and thinking about personal, societal and religious questions together."[21] De Kock even suggests that this way of being together (in the apprenticeship model of religious learning) may be categorized as a sort of tribalism,[22] where the ideal of authenticity centres the encounters of a social group "loosely organized around shared lifestyles, tastes, interests and affinities or the desire to be together."[23] Here youth ministers in the church participate in the communication process of religious learning that is not primarily based on "their positions as leaders, but on their authenticity and charisma."[24] The fundamental core in de Kock's argument is found in how he argues that "religious education for a new generation of Christians requires authorities and communities which are connected in a worldwide pedagogical space with participating youth."[25]

In the previous chapter, we looked at the extent to which it may be meaningful to see the work and vocation of the youth minister as an imitation of Christ. Imitation as a framework for understanding the role of the youth minister also surfaces when scholars try to interpret the youth minister's role in processes of religious learning in youth ministry. Some even argue that the role of the youth minister as a figure of imitation increases in an era where the influence of the institutional church decreases. De Kock (2017) finds that efforts to develop more liquid ways of being church, online or on street level, "prompt a pedagogical focus on the inspirational figure of the youth minister who models the good Christian life in hopes that young people will observe and imitate it." This claim does not only pertain to local youth ministers, but any inspiring figure, like a charismatic Christian leader who create an influential digital presence. Learning here becomes a process of "inspiring and modeling," rather than participation in traditional church practices and acculturation into existing faith communities. Such developments challenge the traditional assumptions of the apprenticeship model of learning, which envisions a social system where the apprentice learns from the expert. De Kock concludes, therefore, that there is a need to re-examine the role

---

21. De Kock, "Being a Church," 231.
22. Cf. Maffesoli, *The Times of the Tribe*.
23. De Kock, "Schools and Religious Communities," 124.
24. De Kock, "Schools and Religious Communities," 124, 129.
25. De Kock, "Schools and Religious Communities," 132.

of practices and relationships within apprenticeship models in youth ministry.[26]

If learning is closely connected with the process of socialization, one cannot escape considering the role of the family. Historically, the question "who is the youth minister?" had a simple answer: the parents, and particularly the father. Ministry to young people, who were not yet married, was still a practice of the domestic domain. With the dawn of a youth ministry taking its cue from post WWII-consumer culture, the youth minister often became a Christianized version of pop cultural youth idols, such as James Dean.

However, as youth ministry negotiated its role as an ecclesial subculture, the role of the parents once again caught the interest of practitioners and researchers in youth ministry. What if parents play a crucial role as "youth ministers"? After all, in most cases young people attend youth ministry because their parents want them to, or at least let them. More importantly, many young people spend lots of time with their parents. It may therefore be argued that parents' potential as youth ministers, or catechists, challenges typical conceptions of instructional learning paradigms in youth ministry. Merging the pedagogical responsibilities of parents and church leaders, both pastors and youth ministers, could be a way to reshape the church as a learning community with four foundational notions of learning faith: (1) learning in life, (2) learning in relation, (3) intergenerational learning and (4) emancipatory learning.[27]

11.4 The Youth Minister as Dialogue Partner

Helen Blier and Graham Stanton argue, with the help of educational philosopher Maxine Greene, that youth ministry should be a place of "dialogue and mutual care," where a key task for the youth minister is to "honour free exploration of meaning at the same time as affirming the conviction of meaning that is offered in the gospel by being willing to pursue the martyr's gift."[28] In other words, the role of the youth minister is to become an active dialogue partner to ensure that youth ministry becomes a place of dialogue and mutual care. Stanton and Blier frame this as youth leaders pursuing "wide-awakeness with young people."

26. De Kock, "Challenges to Apprenticeship Learning," 238.
27. De Kock et al., "The Comeback of Parents," 169.
28. Blier and Stanton, "Wide-Awakeness in the World," 18.

Stanton later elaborates more broadly on the theme, arguing that the purpose of youth ministry is to "move young people to wide-awakeness through developing dialogical spaces of mutual concern that enable young people to take up their responsibility and capacity for meaning in their lived experience."[29] Three core practices emerge from this aim, critical judgement, imaginative projection, and decisive action. To be wide awake is to establish intersubjective dialogical spaces from which imaginative awareness might grow. Similarly, drawing on Charles Taylor's assessment of expressive individualism (in a secular age), Stanton also highlights three themes in expressive individualism that he finds to be "reflective of Christian moral values," namely, "responsibility for personal choices, the alignment of inner beliefs with outward confession and practice, and individual particularity."[30]

Similarly, German theologian Tobias Faix draws on John Travis' much used model of contextualization: C1 to C6, as a spectrum used to interpret how Muslims follow Jesus in different ways, where C1 denotes a high percentage of adaption to a Christian culture and C5 denotes Muslims who follow Jesus within the Islamic ritual community. Faix uses the same model to distinguish how different kinds of youth ministry relate to the digital and to young people's use of the digital, and how the youth minister may be a dialogue partner in the digital. Faix finds that "adolescents have a need to talk about their faith and that it is methodologically possible to give them opportunities to do so." However, "the central prerequisite is that faith is approached in an open manner," as such an "inductive approach gives them the assurance that their understanding of faith is taken seriously and appreciated."[31]

Rito Baring argues that dialogue is essential in catechesis in a highly pluralized society, as religious education is a practice at the crossroads.[32] It is essential in advancing dialogue, Baring finds, to emphasize collaboration, integration, and quest for peace. If done well, even notions of human suffering "can be a platform for youth dialogue and education."[33] Newcomers, or outsiders to youth ministry, are also key in developing faith formation and catechesis in a secular, and pluralized society. The

---

29. Stanton, "Wide-Awake in God's World," 31.
30. Stanton, "Wide-Awake in God's World," 119.
31. Faix, "Hybrid Identity," 83.
32. Baring, "Analyzing Empirical Notions of Suffering," 169.
33. Baring, "Analyzing Empirical Notions of Suffering," 171.

role of youth minister may therefore be understood as initiating a "cruciform catechesis." Such a cruciform catechesis insists that newcomers to youth ministry and the congregation at large are indispensable participants of the *ecclesia crucis*, holding on to "both the newcomer's questioning presence and the congregation's promising context."[34]

Unsurprisingly, one may say, a larger study on Young Life outreach styles in both the US and in Europe found that different styles reach different kids. The study used the so-called "big five" personality traits model as an analytic tool. Studying camps in New York and Bulgaria, they found:

> In the case of the New York sample, teens that scored high on extraversion and emotional instability ("neuroticism") were more likely to make a decision at the end of the camp week (controlling for the influence of other statistically significant factors). Likewise, in the Bulgaria sample not every camper was equally likely to make a commitment to God. Rather, those that scored low on extraversion—that is, introverted teens—and those high on intellectual curiosity ("openness") were more likely to report a new commitment by the end of the week.[35]

The researchers conclude that "rather than standardizing outreach camping so that every camp looks like every other camp, ministries such as Young Life might consider how to marry demonstratively effective Gospel presentation methods with different settings to attract and reach different types of teens."[36] Perhaps these findings may be taken as an incitement to develop a more complex and comprehensive catechetic practice in youth ministry. At least, research on young adults suggests that "the use of ambiguous images is a good way to make young people inquisitive and provoke a response."[37]

11.5 The Youth Minister as Spiritual Director

Spiritual direction is an ancient ministry of the church. In an article from 1986, Gary Davis pointed out that doing spiritual direction with adolescents must take on its own form, "a form which takes into account

---

34. Ducksworth, *Wide Welcome*, 5.
35. Barrett et al., "Different Styles Reach Different Kids," 22.
36. Barrett et al., "Different Styles Reach Different Kids," 25.
37. Savage et al., *Making Sense of Generation Y*, 117.

the special needs, struggles, crises, and capabilities of adolescents."[38] If the youth minister takes on the role of a spiritual director it is critical to embody a compassionate, concerned presence in the life of young people, because *through* that very presence, the youth minister may "provide the model of what it might mean to find a practical, living relationship with the God of one's faith."[39]

What sort of role, then, should the youth minister pursue on the intersection between youth catechesis and art of tending to youth and their spiritual quest? In his 2015 article, Samuel E. Baker presents seven years of collected data from a study, which compares *"spiritual type* similarities and differences of late adolescent students at a private Christian university in the United States."[40] A major finding of the study is the strong influence catechetical models have on faith development during later adolescence. Baker points to Urban Holmes's models of different types of spirituality.[41] Holmes's spirituality model, *Circle of Sensibility*, has four spirituality types, Kataphatic Mind (KM), Kataphatic Heart (KH), Apophatic Mind (AM), Apophatic Heart (AH). In his article, Samuel E. Baker makes an important observation on the "economy" of fostering apophatic and kataphatic models of catechesis in youth ministry:

> Thus, in both catechetical models of youth ministry and Christian higher education's pedagogy, the divine objective allows a student to encounter the "opposite," in order to engage with potentialities for continuing spiritual growth. In this way, kataphatic engagements set forth what can be said and should be learned and confessed by Christians propositionally, while apophatic engagements invite adolescents to fellowship with God in ways that transcend human capacities.[42]

Perhaps the youth minister, in addressing youth spirituality, could take a cue from research on the use of Godly Play, an approach to Religious Education in early childhood, devised by Jerome W. Berryman. In this research, Brendan Hyde points out that four characteristics of children's spirituality stands out as particularly essential—the felt sense, integrating awareness, weaving the threads of meaning, and spiritual

---

38. Davis, "Spiritual Direction," 268.
39. Davis, "Spiritual Direction," 273.
40. Baker, "Raised a Teenage Kataphatic," 47.
41. Holmes, *A History of Christian Spirituality*.
42. Baker, "Raised a Teenage Kataphatic," 68.

questing. These four characteristics were all brought to the fore and were nourished as the result of a Godly Play process.[43] At least the focus on the three latter resonates well with much of the research done on youth spirituality.

Carlton Johnstone argues for the important distinction between inherited and owned faith. It is essential for the youth minister to act as a mentor and guide who helps young people to develop and own faith, because "when faith remains inherited rather than owned, the motivational basis of accepting social influence from church or youth group will be that of compliance." Johnstone's research on life stories also found that "when a person's faith is inherited, then the level of influence from another social circle, such as a friendship group outside of church is potentially stronger, most likely at the level of identification as adolescents and young adults want to either establish or maintain satisfying friendships within the group." What needs to be strived for is for the young person to begin to own their faith, "then the motivational basis of accepting social influence from church and Christian friends will be that of identification and eventually internalization, if they continue to grow and mature in their faith."[44]

Drawing on their research of youth at childcare institutions, Astrid Sandsmark and Tone Stangeland Kaufman suggest that youth ministers need to be attentive to "informal situations and spaces and to non-religious artifacts" if they want to respond adequately to the needs of young people. It is not sufficient to focus on traditional teaching sessions, and explicitly on Christian rituals and practices, to develop a holistic spirituality for young people.[45]

11.6 Learning through the Arts

Sometimes the youth minister is portrayed as a sort of artist, or, better, as someone who brings young people into contact with aesthetic learning—learning through the arts as a means of faith formation. Katherine Douglass points out that the strength of art is that it does not replicate. Rather, it communicates. Because of this power to communicate and provide a strong environment for reflective and reflexive thought, she points

---

43. Hyde, "Godly Play," 515.
44. Johnstone, "Faith Crossroads and Social Networks," 57.
45. Kaufman and Sandsmark, "Spaces of Possibilities," 44.

to how John Dewey found that "art and aesthetic experience redefine traditionally abstract notions of knowledge to encompass a richer, fuller quality." Therefore, if we miss paying attention to the aesthetic dimension of experience, "practical reason is always incomplete."[46]

Like Helen Blier and Graham Stanton, Douglass also draws on educational philosopher Maxine Greene who argues that one danger in a highly success-driven culture is that young people may see themselves described merely as "human resources" rather than "as persons who are centers of choice and evaluation."[47] Faced with these challenges, the youth minister does well to pay attention to the aesthetic dimensions of practical reason as a point of orientation in conceptualizing religious learning in youth ministry. In her empirical study of young adults, Douglass found that "young adults described the arts as helping them connect in congregations that do not always have an obvious place for them." She also discovered how the arts "connected young adults with their own historical faith tradition."[48]

11.7 The Youth Minister as Liturgical Coach

Fred P. Edie has suggested that it is possible for the youth minister to develop contextual pedagogies based on the *ordo*, "an ecology of interrelated liturgical practices dating to the church of antiquity," such as Eucharist, baptism, prayer, and hospitality. Edie's claim draws on his experience with the grants from the Lilly Endowment in the beginning of 2000s, which allowed Duke Divinity School (Edie's school) to invite to Duke's campus older high school youth and adults including Divinity School faculty for the purpose of living together in an intentional Christian community over a period of two weeks. The learning community was shaped by attention to the *ordo*, and proved to be a fertile environment for learning and for rethinking the meaning of the church's ministry with young people, Edie claims.[49]

Similarly, Robert K. Martin argues that youth ministers and other educational leaders of a church need to be rooted in the liturgical life of the church, both with their reflections and in their practice. In this,

46. Douglass, "Aesthetic Learning Theory," 456.
47. Douglass, "Aesthetic Learning Theory," 457.
48. Douglass, "Aesthetic Learning Theory," 463.
49. Edie, "Considering the *Ordo*," 267.

educational leaders need both a micro-perspective (the teaching in the moment) and a macro-perspective. Further, youth ministers and other educational leaders should be trained to assess the different stages and movements of people and communities in a learning process. It comes down to discerning the "pedagogical adequacy of the various activities of ecclesial life."[50]

So, what is the role of the youth minister or youth leader in learning processes in youth ministry? Or more specifically, when young people participate in worship, what role does the youth minister take in the explorative learning process? Sonnenberg and Barnard point out, based on an empirical study on youth worship, that although peer perspective always remains important for young people even in so-called "liturgical conversations," it is critical to emphasize that the adult youth leader or youth minister may serve as a sort of coach. The role of the adult coach is essential "in the process of introducing elements from tradition, the Bible and other perspectives." If the adult coach retreats completely or is absent, the liturgical conversation might "lack engagement."[51] Sonnenberg and Barnard have also shown how the adult youth leader plays an important role in negotiating the role of pop cultural elements in youth worship, even by vouching for them theologically.[52] In liturgical conversations and preparations for youth worship, however, the authority is seldom a set thing. Although a professional, like a youth minister, is often formally in charge, the practice of authority is intersubjective and plural.[53]

11.8 Conclusion: Learning as an Individual or Communal Endeavour?

Perhaps the shifting terrain for catechetical training among youth requires a revision of the education of youth ministers, The National Study on Youth and Religion (NSYR) in the US (2005) forced many churches to rethink their catechetical training. In a case-study on an initiative to rethink catechetical training, Jeffrey Kaster concludes that "successful implementation of a multi-faceted curriculum fostering Christian discipleship will demand that youth ministers, high school religion teachers,

50. Martin, "Education and the Liturgical Life," 48, 62.
51. Sonnenberg and Barnard, "Educating Young People," 6–7.
52. Sonnenberg and Barnard, "Youth Worship as Recreation," 160.
53. Sonnenberg et al., "Shaping Youth Worship," 235.

and catechetical leaders gain additional competencies in doctrinal instruction, community building, teaching forms of prayer, service–justice education, and vocational discernment."[54]

A well-known dilemma in youth ministry is how the youth minister should shift between a more communal focus and an approach more centered on the individual. With regard to this question we also refer to chapter 4 on individual and communal aspects of faith development among youth. This pertains both to diaconal, sacramental, and catechetical dimensions of youth ministry. When it comes to teaching, the focus on situated learning and socialization has been a major focus in the last decades of research. Some researchers would however argue that there needs to be more focus on informal learning, even as children and young people learn in the context of a church or a sanctuary. The benefit of this approach is that it is attentive to the needs of each learning person and therefore more able to identify predictors of informal learning. Ulrich Riegel and Katharina Kindermann find that the church's catechetical ministry with children and young people should learn from museum pedagogy, which has a strong stream of research dedicated to informal learning.[55] We will return to this dilemma—how learning spans the gap between a focus on the individual and a more communal take—in more depth in chapter 14. What makes museums attractive, is that they present to us things that are both strange and familiar at the same time. Therefore, it seems essential to reflect on what it implies when the youth minister is set to communicate something which appears "essentially strange" to many young people. Pete Ward argues that "the youth minister will always be caught between the familiarity and the mystery of God."[56] Sally Nash therefore underlines that the youth minister is both a "reflective practitioner" and a "lifelong learner."[57]

---

54. Kaster, "Evaluating Adolescent Catechesis," 79.
55. Riegel and Kindermann, "Tracing Informal Religious Learning," 137.
56. Ward, *God at the Mall*, 42.
57. Nash, "A Reflective Practitioner."

12

The Youth Minister as *Pastor*

"More than ever, today's youth ministers must function first as missionaries, then as social workers, and finally as pastors."[1]

This chapter explores the role of the youth minister as a pastoral role by examining contemporary youth ministry research. First, we look at different models of youth ministry and how they might conceptualize the role of the youth minister as a pastoral role (12.1). In 12.2, the focus shifts to the practice of listening and how the youth minister may embody a role of attentiveness. In the next section, we discuss what it might imply if we understand the youth minister's role as pastoral (12.3). We then move on to examine the pastoral role in a liturgical context, investigating whether the youth minister might be understood as a mystagogue (12.4). Finally, we shortly address the pastoral role of safeguarding the practice of welcome in youth ministry (12.5).

12.1 Pastoral Models for Youth Ministry

Another strand in youth ministry research is proposing and assessing different models for ministry. These models may be empirically based, theory-driven, more intuitively created, or a combination of all the three. The multitude of models for youth ministry—and for what pastoral role the youth minister should take on—may be taken as a witness of the fluid

1. Borgman, *When Kumbaya Is Not Enough*, 6.

and shifting character of youth ministry as ministry in an exemplary transitional stage of life. Or it may be a testimony to the fact that youth ministry—even commercially—is driven by paradigm shifts. Youth ministry authors sell books, and publishers might perhaps encourage authors who claim to be the promoters of a new paradigm that the youth ministry market needs.

An important shift in youth ministry at the start of the twenty-first century has been the turn from a youth ministry geared towards programs and events to a youth ministry focusing on formation, practices, and relationships, where the youth ministry is portrayed as a sort of pastor. Etymologically, pastor means "shepherd," and when in 2006 Mike King advocated a fundamental remake of youth ministry, he appealed for the role of youth minister to be envisioned as that of the shepherd: "The notion of youth workers as entertainers and program directors must give way to youth workers as authentic shepherds, spiritual guides with a holy anointing to lead youth into the presence of God."[2] Whatever way you imagine the youth minister as a shepherd, it also emphasizes the asymmetric character of the relationship: The youth minister is not primarily identified as an agent of youthfulness, offering fancy programs and events, but as an adult supporter and fellow wayfarer, offering attention and care. Other youth ministry scholars therefore argue that an adult youth minister should act as a sort of sponsor.[3] Dean Borgman finds that "young people often long for mentors who possess moral assurance, who will accept and respect them, and who can point them toward purpose and significance."[4]

Conceptualizing the youth minister as a pastor, as a part of this new paradigm shift, often implies introducing new models for youth ministry and for the role of the youth minister. Some models for the (pastoral) role of the youth minister are presented as typologies, others are less generative in scope and content. Arthur David Canales has examined the theology and pastoral integration of eight different models for adolescent ministry. He underlines that the models he presents are not designed to make one model conceptually more appealing than another. Rather, the eight models are meant to portray different ways of understanding the church and characterizing diverse aspects of youth ministry in its

2. King, *Presence-Centered Youth Ministry*, 25.
3. Rahn, "Focusing Youth Ministry," 170.
4. Borgman, *Hear My Story*, 5.

ecclesial relationship with community and adolescents. The differing models therefore reflect different theologies, ecclesiologies, and pastoral relationships between the parish youth ministry or high school campus ministry and the institutional Church. The eight models are: (1) the friendship model; (2) the spiritual awareness model; (3) the servant-leadership model; (4) the liberation model; (5) the biblical-hermeneutic model; (6) the liturgical-initiation model; (7) the social justice model; (8) the Christian discipleship model.[5]

On what grounds, then, should such models be assessed and examined? Which set of criteria are comprehensive and transparent, and not (too) arbitrary to use, and to what purpose should they be put as different models for ministry are presented? In evaluating the eight models he proposes, Canales argues for the use of five criteria:

1. faithfulness to the 1997 document RTV—*Renewing the Vision: A Framework for Catholic Youth Ministry* (1997), which is found to be the definitive standard for Catholic youth ministry, and establishes the criteria and goals for youth ministry;

2. ecumenical sensitivity in theory, as well as in being able to integrate practically into both Catholic and Protestant traditions, with similar harmony and stressfulness depending on the model;

3. compatibility with Christian theology, primarily, and being attuned to the Bible secondarily;

4. supportiveness when it comes to catechetical integration into an ecclesial youth ministry or high school campus ministry; and

5. correspondence to the religious faith experiences of adolescents as a fruitful implementation of the various pastoral strategies.[6]

Later Canales advocates the use of three other (fundamental) criteria, with faithfulness as the leitmotif: "Youth ministry will be only as successful insofar as it is faithful: faithful to its youth, faithful to its mission, and faithful to the Gospel."[7]

In another article a few years later, the same Canales explores four models of leadership with offer positive attributes and implications for youth ministry. Drawing on the lucid field of leadership studies, Canales

---

5. Canales, "Models for Adolescent Ministry," 205.
6. Canales, "Models for Adolescent Ministry," 222.
7. Canales, "Models for Adolescent Ministry," 230.

argues that leadership involves two crucial components: (1) *process* and (2) *influence*, which both help to move a group or individuals toward a common purpose or goal. Canales suggests a paradigm shift, appealing to the Russian word *perestrojka* that means "a restructuring in thinking," and that it is time that Christian youth ministry restructures its thinking regarding leadership. He therefore advocates that Christian leadership should be less concerned with leadership training or personal development of a person, but rather focus more on a broader framework that empowers people to "think, act, and live differently."[8] The aim of presenting the four models is to present a framework for *doing* leadership in youth ministry, not just educating leaders.[9] The four models for Christian leadership proposed by Canales are: (1) servant-leadership, (2) moral leadership, (3) spiritual leadership, and (4) transformational leadership. Canales finds that all four models are found throughout Jesus' life and public ministry.[10]

12.2 The Youth Minister as a Pastoral Listener

If the youth minister is a sort of pastor—or priest, in a sense—youth ministry might take its cue from pastoral care. Then, perhaps the role of the youth minister is best understood as an art of being attentive, practicing a sort of priestly, holy listening? In other words, the defining role of the youth minister is that of the listener. Dori Grinenko Baker, studying the art of interview as a practice in youth ministry, elaborates on the practice of the interview in the following manner:

> The position of the listener in these interviews is similar to that of a youth minister, pastor, or adult volunteer who has accompanied a youth during a life-changing experience, be it an overseas mission trip or the loss of a friend or loved one. A watcher, participant, witness, and guide, the youth minister stands uniquely positioned to create a space for critical reflection on such experiences. Those who walk alongside youth in faith communities might seize particular moments such as these to invite the youth to be "interviewed." The purpose of the interview is not to help a

---

8. Canales, "Models of Christian Leadership," 26–27.
9. Canales, "Models of Christian Leadership," 42.
10. Canales, "Models of Christian Leadership," 29.

needy youth, but to provide space for theological integration of significant life events.[11]

Baker encourages youth ministers to foster an "ethos of holy listening among all who minister to youth."[12] Similarly, Amanda Hontz Drury emphasizes that it is essential for the youth minister to listen to testimonies of young people, because both young and old articulate identity through narrative. Drury's insightful examination of the practice of testimony in youth ministry, serves as an incitement to re-imagine the role of the youth minister as a pastor.[13]

Obviously, when the youth minister considers themselves as being in the role of the listener, learning from pastoral care and communication studies is helpful. It is therefore essential for the minister to reflect on how they uses their "rhetorical wardrobe." Being yourself may seem like a tempting slogan for ministry, but the slogan betrays the communicative challenge to explore what it takes to clothe the minister's character and make it appear credible and persuasive. Youth ministers are different and appear as different. Factors such as a change in phase of life will influence how a minister speaks, the selection of words, use of symbols, body language etc. More importantly, those that encounter the youth minister will expect different things from the different impressions of character that the minister displays. After all, an experienced granny-type of youth minister and a twenty-two-year-old youth minister with tattoos will create different expectations about how they will communicate and interact. Every minister carries a "rhetorical wardrobe" at their disposal. The key thing is to reflect on how to use it—and expand it.[14]

In conversation, it is key that the youth minister "tunes in" to their audience. This is not simply a plea for relational ministry, but rather situational ministry. Sharing or exploring the gospel in context is always a contextual and situational endeavor. Perhaps drawing on research in conversation analysis could be helpful.[15] It is also essential that a youth minister discerns when is the right time to say the "right" things, what

---

11. Baker, "Evoking Testimony through Holy Listening," 59.
12. Baker, "Evoking Testimony through Holy Listening," 61.
13. Drury, *Saying Is Believing*.
14. Norheim and Haga, *The Four Speeches*, 111–13.
15. See, for instance, Have, *Doing Conversation Analysis*; Sidnell, *Conversation Analysis*.

in classical rhetorical theory is known as *kairos*.[16] Kairos concerns the minister's ability to "tune in" to a situation in such a manner that they are able to discern what is at stake in the actual conversation or situation. More than anything, it concerns the minister's capacity to realize when the atmosphere is shifting or when a dialogue is at a critical junction. Discerning when a filled moment of trust occurs is a key capacity for a youth minister to develop. It is also critical for the youth minister to know the "legacy" of the ministry they represent.

12.3 The Youth Minister as a Pastoral Guide

Etymologically, the term pastor means "shepherd." If a youth minister is a pastor—a shepherd—this may imply that some of the characteristics of the shepherd should be pursued and developed, for example, being a guide and a fellow wayfarer with the flock. At the very least, the term pastor emphasizes the peregrinational nature of ministry, that ministry is a pathway. Steve Griffiths has envisioned (Anglican) youth ministry as *orthoyatra*, a term deriving from *orthos* ("right" or "appropriate" in Greek) and *yatra* ("journey" in Sanskrit). Griffiths has further argued that "*Orthoyatra* has "a different nuance from 'discipleship' in that its focus is more about socio-spiritual negotiation and inner growth than followership." To Griffiths, the term also has "a different nuance to 'sanctification' in that it is a psychosocial ideal rather than predominantly theological." The strength of the concept is that it does not degrade to measuring the success(es) of youth ministry, but rather remains open and explorative.[17] It follows from this that the role of the youth minister becomes that of a fellow wayfarer and sometimes travel guide.

Obviously, the art of being with the people who are given to your care is essential in a pastoral and peregrinational ministry. It calls for a ministry of presence. If a ministry of presence is encouraged as the guiding principle for the youth minister, a few things are worth noting: Michael Hrynjuk advocates that the role of the youth minister should not involve drawing on a charismatic personality to develop exciting seeker-sensitive programs, nor be about simply teaching the core curriculum. Rather it comes down to creating space for young people to attend to the

---

16. Cf. Norheim and Haga, *The Four Speeches*, 119.
17. Griffiths, "Negotiating *Orthoyatra*," 27–28.

presence of God.[18] Hrynjuk argues for the importance of three disciplines that foster such a contemplative spirituality in youth ministry, namely the disciplines of attentiveness, discernment, and accompaniment.[19]

As we explored in chapter 5, Mark Yaconelli has made similar claims for contemplative practices to be incorporated into youth ministry.[20] From the perspective of pedagogy, the purpose of "nurturing contemplative consciousness in young people is to help them to name and respond to the power of God's presence within them and around of them in their daily lives." It comes down to attending to God's presence, and youth ministers needs to equip young people, Hrnynjuk finds, to "more fully appropriate the riches of biblical, doctrinal, sacramental, and practical consciousness in the Christian tradition." Altogether, "a contemplative approach does not negate the importance of solid catechesis and times of fun and games together in community, but it seeks to "re-source" these aspects of youth ministry in a larger experience of attentiveness to God, discernment of the Spirit, and genuine accompaniment by faithful adults on the way of Jesus."[21]

12.4 The Youth Minister as a Mystagogue

Steve Emery-Wright found that the role of youth ministers must be reconsidered. Rather than translating adult worship to a youth context, the youth minister should work to facilitate youth engagement in creating worship. Bottom line, he argued that the church must accept that "the goal of integrating the young people into the traditional worship of the church may never happen and may not even be desirable for the young people's spiritual health." Emery-Wright advocates that the practice of translating worship for young people is "imperialistic," and that that the traditional role of a theologically trained preacher in creating and leading worship must be reconsidered with regard to its effectiveness in shaping meaningful worship for young people. Rather, "a new model, possibly an adaptation model that empowers young people to create worship needs

---

18. Hryniuk, "Creating Space for God," 149–50.

19. Hryniuk, "Creating Space for God," 152–54.

20. Yaconelli, *Contemplative Youth Ministry*. See also Yaconelli, "Focusing Youth Ministry."

21. Hryniuk, "Creating Space for God," 147.

to be embraced."[22] Perhaps the role of the children's—and youth—minister in worship practices may then be understood as the role of the *mystagogue*? Being a mystagogue is a directing role, and adult performances in liturgical practice are mystagogic when they initiate children and young people "into the sacraments or into the mystery of God's relationship with people."[23]

With a liturgical configuration of the role of the youth minister, the question of ordination might surface. For those youth ministers who are ordained, particularly in a Catholic setting, in which way might ordination be formative in shaping the role of youth minister? Robert T. O'Gorman argues that "ordination is about leadership and the energy to make judgments and decisions for others." Further, O'Gorman finds that ritual is essential for sacramental imagination, and that the (ordained) youth minister as a leader is a leader by the power of ritual, as "ritual is agreed-upon symbolic actions prescribed by regulations or tradition and set out by the leadership of the community and is observed very carefully."[24]

12.5 The Youth Minister as the One Who Safeguards the Welcome?

The role of the youth minister is in many ways to ensure that the youth ministry keeps one of its most essential qualities, if not the most essential quality, the practice of welcome and the inclusive and welcoming environment. Here, recent empirical studies of vital youth ministries have shown, the youth minister plays a key role in being the one who models the welcome.[25]

Perhaps the youth minister as pastor is best imagined as the one at the door, who strives to meet and share the realities of young people? Andrew Root, at least, argues that *sharing* is fundamental to pastoring, because "sharing of personhood" is fundamental to Christianity:

> "Through the hypostatic union God has acted for us by sending Jesus the Christ, who is one *person*, making personhood

22. Emery-Wright, "A Qualitative Study Construction," 76.
23. Van Leersum-Bekebrede et al., "Setting the Stage," 172.
24. O'Gorman, "Imagination Embodied," 442, 445.
25. Cf. Tveitereid and Norheim, *"Theological Wiggle Room"*; The-Mertens, "Organisational Strategies."

essential to Christianity, in two natures. Jesus' personhood is the linking of divine and human, the human participating in the life of the divine. . . . Sharing, then, becomes the heart of pastoral ministry.[26]

Similarly, Graham Stanton imagines the youth minister as a sort of pastoral and poetic dialogue partner, where youth ministers are called to "problematize and defamiliarize Christian faith for Christian young people in order to move them toward greater personal ownership of their choices and more mature understandings of the faith."[27] Fundamentally, according to contemporary youth ministry scholarship, the practice of welcome in youth ministry, is envisioned as a dialogical practice, where the youth minister is both a pastoral learner and listener.

---

26. Root, *The Relational Pastor*, 215.
27. Stanton, *Wide-Awake in God's World*, 189–90.

13

The Youth Minister as *Prophet*

"Affirmation and challenge are two separate strands that run right through Scripture."[1]

"A newcomer's presence within a congregation reminds the congregation that there are people who do not yet belong."[2]

THIS chapter explores whether it is possible to interpret the role of the youth minister as a prophetic role. The first section looks at how youth ministry may offer the perfect environment for creating ecclesial prophets who are able to change the church from both the inside and the outside (13.1). The next section discusses the extent to which the youth minister may be seen as a prophet in the light of liminal experiences in youth ministry (13.2). In 13.3, we consider the poetic aspects of prophetic imagination in the light of recent youth ministry research. In the following section, we look at the youth minister's potential prophetic engagement with culture (13.4). Finally, we look at how a prophetic conception of the role of the youth minister may also be part of a holistic ministry (13.5).

---

1. Savage et al., *Making Sense of Generation Y*, 94.
2. Ducksworth, *Wide Welcome*, 4.

13.1 Youth Ministry as the Home of the Ecclesial Prophet

As we have already pointed out, in an article from 1997 Bert Roebben advocates that (postmodern) youth ministry should shape a playground for transcendence, and that the adult youth minister is called to facilitate a ministry, which is both "authentic" and "communicative."[3] In general, youth ministry seems to provide a fertile climate for producing ecclesial prophets, (young) people who strive to challenge the boundaries of what it means to be church and who is eager to bring the gospel to the marketplace, sometimes in confrontation with cultural, and ecclesial, trends and axioms. Kenda Creasy Dean has argued that youth ministry may operate as a sort of ecclesial laboratory, as most youth ministries offer a hospitable climate for ecclesial critique and experimentation. Subsequently, many church leaders, including Dietrich Bonhoeffer, Pope John Paul II, Billy Graham, Billy Hybels, have received their most formative training in youth ministry. Therefore, the formation of young people in youth ministry is beneficial and instrumental to the formation of church life in general, Dean finds.[4]

Drawing on Jürgen Moltmann's theology of hope, Dean envisions youth ministry as an ecclesial laboratory, where the church practices a kind of youthfulness that is not confined to a particular age group. Rather, Dean proposes a youth ministry type of church, fostering leadership and doing church in a manner that is youthful and characterized by play, mission, and a relational ministry with an incarnational pedagogy.[5] In Dean's paradigm for youth ministry, the youth minister becomes a hope generator or play facilitator, or perhaps even a missionary.

13.2 The Youth Minister as a Prophet in Liminal Spaces

Youth is an exemplary liminal life stage that covers the transition from childhood to (young) adulthood. In liminal stages and spaces, authority is always up for grabs, and it is a fertile climate for prophetic imagination. In youth ministry, camp and retreat experiences often represent liminal

---

3. Roebben, "Shaping a Playground," 346.
4. Dean, "Reflections on the Future of Youth Ministry," 80–81.
5. Dean, "Reflections on the Future of Youth Ministry," 89.

experiences which may foster prophetic imagination. At a camp or retreat, the youth minister may be a facilitator of and midwife to prophetic imagination. For many young people, the youth minister is simply the (adult) leader at camp. But what sort of role should the youth minister pursue in a camp setting? In which way is a camp part of a larger ecclesiological fabric? Jacob Sorenson has conducted an empirical study of Finnish confirmation camp ministry and found that to most confirmands the idea of regular church life, outside of camp, was almost laughable. However, Sorenson claims that the camp experience, may be a way to transform the "spiritual storehouse," given that the youth minister serves as a wise spiritual director of some sort. Like Bert Roebben, who has argued that youth ministry should be a playground for transcendence, Sorenson finds that a Christian camp environment may work as "a theological playground with tremendous potential for examining the nature and trajectory of the church."[6]

Timothy Nagy draws on Victor Turner's theory of liminality, and argues that the liminal experiences at a retreat, may be "calculated set of cultural forms which lay the foundation for the building of a strong quasi-spontaneous *communitas*." The term *communitas* was a term coined by Turner to describe the community that may arise as people are joined by destiny during transitional experiences of change. If youth ministry, in the form of retreat or a camp, is interpreted as a *communitas*, this also challenges the role of the youth minister. In a liminal setting, and adolescence may be seen as an exemplary liminal stage in human life, the leader must take its cue from how Jesus approaches the disciples on the way to Emmaus.[7]

Similarly, Bård Norheim, in an article from 2006 in *Journal of Youth and Theology*, also draws on Victor Turner's theory on liminality and the Emmaus story—and missiologist Alan J. Roxburgh's adoption of the theory of liminality—to argue that youth ministry should be understood as a sort of *communitas*. Setting the Emmaus story and the *liminal communitas* as the interpretative framework for youth ministry in a secular world, Norheim claims that the role of the youth minister becomes that of exploring what church is—and may be—*with* young people, as young people experience first hand how it is to live through the stages of liminality as part of their developmental process, while the church needs

---

6. Sorenson, "Transforming the Spiritual Storehouse," 189.
7. Nagy, "Lens of Liminality," 58–59.

young people as *poets, prophets,* and *apostles* to find its way in a radically shifting terrain. For a *communitas* to avoid becoming a ghetto, but remain a community of change during difficult transitions, the community needs to be rooted in play, Norheim advocates. The youth minister in the liminal must facilitate youth ministry as "playful *communitas*."[8] The ecclesiology underlying both these two proposals for youth ministry is peregrinational in orientation.

Yet another use of a pilgrim ecclesiology in youth ministry, is found in Mark Scanlan's study of the Urban Saints youth ministry that originated from the Crusaders movement. Scanlan points out that youth ministry has played a transformative role in stretching the space of the church for a long time. He further argues that a pilgrim ecclesiology might be helpful as a framework for a youth ministry which tends to create such ecclesial space. Scanlan portrays the role of the youth minister as someone who explores the boundaries of church in innovative and creative ways, together with young people. He concludes by claiming that the church, and how we continue to understand the church, need the innovative practices of individuals, like creative youth ministers, and organizations, who "step out from the boundaries of church and thus create space onto which ecclesial life can be stretched."[9]

If youth ministry is about creating space, the youth minister should also take note from Leah Marie Wilson's concluding remark based on her study of two youth ministry placements. She finds that "the youth space will be a waste of space without a conscious effort to make memories and distribute youth responsibility instilling a particular sense of rootedness."[10]

However, one may critically ask what makes a pilgrim any different from a tourist. After all, they are both travelling, and travelling with a purpose. While many youth ministry scholars have taken an interest in pilgrim metaphors and pilgrim ecclesiologies, other have warned of the impact of a tourist paradigm in youth ministry. Nick Shepherd, drawing on tourist studies and a case study of the project "Soul in the City" (2004), has argued that the youth minister has to be more than a tourist guide inviting young people into mission as a "package holiday."[11]

---

8. Norheim, "From Ghetto to Communitas," 78–79.
9. Scanlan, "Youth Ministry Creating Ecclesial Space," 22.
10. Wilson, "Waste of Space or Room for Place?," 37.
11. Shepherd, "Soul in the City."

13.3 The Youth Minister as a Prophetic Poet

We saw in the previous section that in a liminal, missional approach to youth ministry, fostering poetic imagination may serve as a pretext for prophetic imagination in a shifting ecclesial context. In other words, the narrative element is essential in fostering prophetic imagination in youth ministry. In a 2016 article in the *Journal of Youth and Theology*, Bård Norheim argues that the Christian story of the body should serve as the ritual plot for youth ministry. How does such a narrative framing of youth ministry influence how we understand the role of the youth minister? If we shape the practice of youth in the light of a *plot*, it seems essential to understand the youth minister as a sort of *poet*. The youth minister then becomes someone who narrates the Christian story in the light of young people's bodily life experiences, as well as someone who serves as a midwife for young people's own narration of their stories in the light of the Christian story of the body. Norheim claims that "Christian youth ministry has to embrace the created body as the home of youth ministry, not just a point of departure."

He also finds that holding to a Christian story of the body as a ritual plot for youth ministry implies acknowledging the world as both created and fallen (finite), as the Christian story of the body is a three-fold story of the body as created, finite, and living under the hope of resurrection. Pursuing the meaning and impact of that story as a narrative framework for youth ministry makes the youth minister into a midwife-poet, releasing all the youth as poets. But more than that, such a youth ministry becomes communally prophetic in character, as the Christian story of body is a corporeal story of one body, and the community of poets and prophets are called to speak out where this corporeality is broken and violated.[12]

The poetic-prophetic imagination that a youth minister may take on, may also include critiquing contemporary conceptualizations of what a youth person is. In other words, if the youth minister can be aligned with being a prophet, taking on a prophetic posture as youth minister may include reconceiving the meaning of what a young person really is, by challenging dominating paradigms of youthfulness.[13]

---

12. Norheim, "The Christian Story," 95, 97, 104.

13. Cf. Andrew Root's critique of the obsession with youthfulness, in Root, *Faith Formation in a Secular Age*.

Wesley Ellis has challenged what he found to be the dominant model of youth ministry in the US, namely the psychological, developmental model, where the youth minister serves as a sort of cultural gatekeeper to ensure spiritual growth, to produce mature Christian adults. Drawing on Andrew Root and Kenda Creasy Dean's call for a theological turn in youth ministry, Ellis argues that youth ministry has accepted the terminological framework of Erik H. Erikson and others too uncritically. Drawing on Jürgen Moltmann's eschatology, Ellis proposes that "the chief posture of the minister, then, is one which seeks out where God is already present."[14]

Ellis advocates that the youth minister should develop an interpretive framework which allows the minister to see young people not as potential adults, human *becomings*, but a human *being*. Simultaneously, the youth minister needs an eschatological praxis which allows for a practice of story-listening, and this in turn might cultivate a space for young people to describe God's ministry in their own life.[15] Similarly, Anthony Reddie, writing from a Black theological perspective, underlines the importance of contextual hermeneutics as a leader in church, like a youth minister, exercises the role of interpreting the Bible. Reddie finds that "constructs of faith and assumptions about human nature affect how we engage with and interpret the Bible."[16]

In yet another way of combining poetic and prophetic imagination, Kieran Scott has argued that the educator in church, such as a youth minister, should exercise and practice two kinds of imagination, namely both prophetic and sacramental imagination. Drawing on Eggemeier's discussion of the two types of imagination, Scott finds that the two are indispensable to each other:

> The sacramental without the prophetic falls into sentimentality. The prophetic without the sacramental slips exclusively into negativity. They are two conflicting but complementary poles of the religious imagination that need to move toward a unity/synthesis in the life of the congregation/parish.[17]

---

14. Ellis, "Human Beings and Human Becomings," 135.
15. Ellis, "Human Beings and Human Becomings," 136.
16. Reddie, "Re-thinking," 187.
17. Scott, "Alternating Currents," 460.

13.4 The Youth Minister as a 'Cultural' Prophet

If the youth minister can take on the role of the prophet, that prophetic role needs to relate to contemporary culture in a communicative fashion. Richard Rymarz has suggested that the youth minister should explore a more evangelistic role, by seeking to proclaim the gospel to young people, still developing a sensitivity to cultural realities. Rymarz underlines that the new focus on evangelization needs to be shaped by a series of initiatives, and an explorative mindset. It is critical to find and develop the "agents who can best minister to young adults." According to Rymarz, these are often young lay people who can serves as effective "peer ministers," who are able to "manifest both a close relationship with Christ and a desire to evangelize others."[18] Fundamentally, Rymarz concludes "the Catholic minister who works with youth or young adults must be in the 'market square' like Paul at the Areopagus."[19]

Julie Anne Lytle argues that when communities of faith start to explore virtual spaces, the communal and institutional understandings of what it means to be church will inevitably change. This may also influence the role of youth minister. Lytle offers the concept of "virtual incarnation" as a term to help navigate "ecclesial boundaries of churches in a virtual environment," trying to interpret Internet-Mediated interaction as a manifestation of the divine and seek an answer to the question: "Is God present?"[20]

In a digital age, perhaps the youth minister could expand the meaning of the role as a youth minister through blogging? Daniela Zsupan-Jerome argues that "by recognizing the use of the public voice on the blog and the role of the blogger as the one who creates, guides, and moderates conversation, Christian ministerial formation can benefit from the experience of this social media platform for educating Christian leaders to communicate Good News."[21] The life and many roles ascribed to a youth minister, particularly in a digital age, may make for a kind of paradoxical and sometimes demanding ministry. Frantisek Štěch has argued that the challenging calling of the youth minister also means that a "complex" education of youth ministers is needed.[22]

18. Rymarz, "Going Beyond the Plateau," 84.
19. Rymarz, "Going Beyond the Plateau," 89.
20. Lytle, "Virtual Incarnations," 411.
21. Zsupan-Jerome, "Fostering the Public Voice," 343.
22. Štěch, "Fluid Religion in Liquid Age?," 74.

The prophetic role of the youth minister implies reflection on how youth ministry is a part of contemporary culture and engages with culture. Here, some youth ministry scholars, such as Pete Ward, advocate a more constructive and creative approach to the engagement with popular culture in youth ministry,[23] whereas others argue for a more critical engagement. David F. White has argued that youth ministers need to develop the prophetic vocation of youth and encourage them to feel anger and ask questions of the church "that provoke careful thinking about social and cultural injustices."[24] Some youth ministry scholars also argue that the "Happy midi-narrative" of youth and young adults has to be challenged, as it is "a midi-narrative trying to fulfil the role of a meta-narrative." As a celebration of self-fulfillment in this world, rather than anticipation of justice and hope in the coming world, the midi-narrative needs to be addressed in prophetic fashion, Sara Savage, Sylvia Collins-Mayo and Bob Mayo have argued.[25]

13.5 A Prophetic, Holistic Youth Ministry?

Is the prophetic ministry monolithic or could it be part of a holistic youth ministry, and what role does the youth minister have in shaping a more holistic ministry? Jerome Vallabaraj has argued that the youth minister needs to take a holistic approach to ministry and to the young people the minister encounters. Departing from such a holistic approach, the youth minister might become "a trusted advisor and counsellor" and act as "the advocate of young people."[26] Harmen van Wijnen has argued for a similar more holistic take on youth ministry. Based on an empirical study of young people being together in youth groups, he finds that the focus in youth ministry should move from supply to support. This also shifts the role of the youth minister from a supplier to a supporter, someone who walks alongside young people. In other words, the youth minister and youth ministry should provide "fewer products, fewer concepts, fewer organized activities and more facilitating and more co-creating."[27]

---

23. Cf. Ward, *God at the Mall*; Ward, *Liquid Church*.
24. White, *Practicing Discernment with Youth*, 149.
25. Savage et al., *Making Sense of Generation Y*, 164.
26. Vallabaraj, "Youth Ministry," 20.
27. Van Wijnen and Barnard, "From Organized Faith to Lived Faith," 21.

In yet another article, van Wijnen and Barnard suggest that the youth minister becomes a sort of chief, a tribal leader, seeing youth ministry and the youth group as a kind of faith tribe. They argue that "youth ministries should 'bless' faith tribes in their fluidity, occasional gatherings and dispersal."[28]

Perhaps taking care of the whole person of the youth minister is one step towards building a more holistic youth ministry. Based on a survey in the US and EU countries, Len Kageler argues that three factors are particularly important in addressing and fighting youth minister burnout—the feeling of isolation or loneliness, conflicts with your pastor or supervisor, and a feeling of "spiritual dryness." These three factors need to be considered when training and educating youth ministers, Kageler finds.[29]

---

28. Van Wijnen and Barnard, "Faith Tribes as Powerful Communities," 429.
29. Kageler, "Burnout among Religious Youth Workers," 20–21.

14

The Role of the Youth Minister in *Community*

"Many young people who are not especially attracted by the ideas and doctrines of Christian faith are moved by the beauty of a community of youth and adults *embodying* faith in Christ."[1]

This chapter closes the part exploring *who* the youth minister is. Drawing on recent youth ministry research, we move to a close by assessing the role of community in shaping the role of the youth minister. The first section deals with the biblical term *koinonia*, and its impact in understanding youth ministry and the role of the youth minister (14.1). In 14.2, we examine the contours of a communal spirituality for youth ministry, and the youth minister's role in it. The next section focuses on learning in youth ministry as a communal enterprise and how such an educational paradigm shapes the role of the youth minister (14.3). In 14.4, we look at research considering the impact of the youth group, even from the perspective of different denominational backgrounds. Finally, we return to theology in 14.5, asking what a theologically committed, communal vision of the role of the youth minister might imply.

---

1. White, *Practicing Discernment with Youth*, 172.

14.1 *Koinonia*: Community First

The role of youth minister derives from the understanding of the community that youth ministry represents. German, Roman Catholic Theologian, Partrick C. Höring has argued that *koinonia* should serve as the all-encompassing aim and purpose of church practice, and also of youth ministry. Youth ministry from a *koinonia*-perspective emphasizes that "the church's essential nature is that of a collected group of diversely gifted people."[2] As a term, *koinonia*, portrays the unity of both horizontal and vertical relationship, and simultaneously the unity of love of God and of neighbor. Church or ministry as communion in this manner is first and foremost constituted by participation in the sacramental life of the Christian church and then by imitating the actions of Jesus, both are means of achieving unity with Jesus Christ himself, Höring argues.

A *koinonia* model for youth ministry puts the community first, and the role of the youth minister derives from the given (self-) understanding of the community as *koinonia*, as a fellowship part-taking in the presence of Christ in the world and for the world. Making *koinonia* the leitmotif for youth ministry configures youth ministry as a ministry of presence where the role of the youth minister is to be present in the midst of people and near people.[3] In conclusion, Höring suggests that "reflections on the term koinonia as the Church's fundamental concept may help to develop it towards a habitat that corresponds to the gospel and to the needs of people."[4]

The focus on youth ministry as community—or more precisely, *koinonia*—resonates with a claim that Chris Hudson made in the very first edition of the *Journal of Youth and Theology* (2002), namely that "ultimately it is Christ who creates community, and it is the responsibility of each particular person to freely commit to the relationships that constitute that community," and that "youth ministry is about helping young people discover who they are in Christ."[5] Similarly, Mark Yaconelli, director of the Youth Ministry and Spirituality Project, argues that a contemplative approach to youth ministry is practiced within a covenant

---

2. Rahn, "Focusing Youth Ministry," 172.
3. Höring, "Koinonia," 55.
4. Höring, "Koinonia," 56.
5. Hudson, "Community, Identity, & Youth Ministry," 31–32.

community, which is grounded in Christian community rooted in the sacred balance of work and rest.[6]

14.2 Communal Spirituality

The importance of community in youth ministry is closely connected with the liminal feature of all youth ministry, as youth is best imagined as an exemplary liminal stage of life, the transition from childhood to adulthood. Leaders in youth ministry therefore need to acknowledge that becoming an adult is a much more fluid concept than a few generations back. Jeffrey Jensen Arnett points out:

> Entering adulthood is no longer as definite and clear-cut as getting married. On the contrary, the road to young adulthood is long and winding, and the end of it usually does not come until the late twenties. They reach adulthood not because of a single event but as a consequence of the gradual process of becoming self-sufficient and learning to stand alone.[7]

If the transition from childhood to adulthood is a fluid concept, it is key that the youth minister configure their role in relation to the family structures that young people find themselves in, as "the single most important social influence of the religious and spiritual lives of adolescents is their parents."[8]

Taking these societal changes and challenges into account, it is interesting to note how Melissa Ann Brandes finds that we need to see religious communities as intergenerational and therefore give "equal weight to the needs, desires, thoughts, feelings, and ideas of non-adults." Furthermore, Brandes, researching camp experiences for young people with regard to establishing faith, asks:

> How are we helping young people to reflect on these experiences in order to make meaning? I believe these five suggestions—practicing reflection; approaching young people with acceptance, respect, and trust; understanding community as intergenerational; allowing young people to participate in dialogue; and providing a balance of challenge and support—will aid ministries and communities in a variety of contexts to create

---

6. Yaconelli, *Growing Souls*, 58–59.
7. Arnett, *Emerging Adulthood*, 227.
8. Smith, *Soul Searching*, 261.

cultures and environments where young people can be nurtured in their spiritual development in meaningful ways.[9]

14.3 Learning in Community

Barbara J. Fleischer describes a turn in how religious education is understood, where the agency for religious education is now placed with the whole community of faith rather than with individuals who develop specific religious education programs to be used in congregational settings.[10] Drawing on a qualitative study of St. Gabriel the Archangel Parish, a predominantly African-American parish in New Orleans, Fleischer advocates a systemic religious education that is centered on transformative and communal praxis, where religious educators, such as youth ministers, should strive for more concerted efforts at developing the "praxis rhythms of learning organizations," to ensure that faith communities may become "transformative contexts of ongoing religious education, conversion, and action."[11]

Perhaps the youth minister embracing diversity—or what one may a call a sort of polyphonic approach to both ministry and faith—fosters increased interest from young people? Theodore Brelsford's research suggests that communities that "intentionally embrace diversity as part of their identity often invite high levels of participation from youth and newcomers as part of their educational curriculum."[12] Brelsford also points out that it is important to take note of the fact that the youth minister is also *situated*. Or, better, the ministry of the youth minister is a situated ministry. It belongs in a particular context, and it may also shape that context. Theodore Brelsford has therefore suggested that "inviting formative participation in a community entails inviting and empowering others to participate in shaping and defining a community's very identity."[13]

---

9. Brandes, "Integrated Spiritual Development," 201.
10. Fleischer, "The Ministering Community," 104.
11. Fleischer, "The Ministering Community," 120-21.
12. Brelsford, "Educating for Formative Participation," 310.
13. Brelsford, "Educating for Formative Participation," 325.

14.4 The Impact of the Youth Group

To many, a youth minister or a youth worker is simply a leader of youth group, but what really is the effect of pursuing such a role as leader of a group? Or, to put in another way, what really is the long-term effect of being in a youth group? Patricia Snell, drawing on data from the National Study of Youth and Religion (NSYR; 2005), finds, despite some paradoxical data, that youth group participation, by and large seem to bear influence. Youth who have participated regularly in youth groups are less likely to find church boring. They are more prone to wish to attend church more frequently. They even plan to continue to attend when they are twenty-five years old. The same youth also tend to believe "that morality is based on God's law, not thinking that morals are relative, and not agreeing that it is ok to break moral rules." It is important to note, however, that these findings do not tell us as much of the actual effect of the youth group leader (the youth minister), rather the effects of being in a youth group (in the US).[14] Similarly, Nick Shepherd in his study of youth groups finds that the youth group is essential in making faith plausible to young people.[15]

Drawing on empirical data from research conducted at a Catholic charismatic youth rally "Lift Jesus Higher," and on previous research by Hoge and Smith (1982), Flatt and Haskell conclude that "denominational background is a significant predictor of the *kinds* of religious experiences that youth have."[16] They therefore advise youth ministers to consider this when planning peak experiences such as a camp, retreat, or a rally. A certain congruence between the ordinary socialization and peak experiences is required to make the peak experience effective. Therefore, youth ministers, who hope to facilitate peak experiences in youth ministry "would do well to use methods that will resonate with the prior spiritual formation of the young people."[17] Some studies from the US also indicate that the denominational background influences which types of youth ministers who are more likely to be hired, with regard to gender, ethnicity, etc., and whether the congregation is likely to have a paid youth minister in the first place.[18]

14. Snell, "What Difference Does Youth Group Make?," 585.
15. Shepherd, *Faith Generation*.
16. Flatt and Haskell, "Participant Experiences," 148.
17. Flatt and Haskell, "Participant Experiences," 150.
18. Snell, "Denominational Differences."

14.5 The Youth Minister as an Ecclesial Agent— Youth Ministry as Ecclesiology

Presenting "The Youth Theological Initiative" at Emory University, David F. White argues that a youth minister needs to be "socially informed" and "theologically committed."[19] Perhaps we may be even more precise and say that it comes down to ecclesiology. Many of the recent contributions in youth ministry scholarship focus on ecclesiology, such as Mark Scanlan's work on *An Interweaving Ecclesiology* (2021), where he focuses on the dialogical nature of the church to reimagine the relationship between the church, mission, and young people, arguing that these three things belong together as one thing.[20]

A very influential typology categorizing different ways of doing youth ministry as an ecclesial and communal practice is found in the book *Four Views of Youth Ministry and the Church* (2001). Here youth ministry scholars Malan Nel, Wesley Black, Chap Clark, Mark Senter III elaborate on four different models of youth ministry—the inclusive congregational model (Nel), the preparatory model (Black), the missional model (Clark), and the strategic model (Senter III). The typology is developed around four quarters of a grid emerging from four different approaches to youth ministry and the church, with two axes. The first, horizontal axis distinguishes between tendencies either to emphasize training young people (come) or send young people on a mission (go). The second, vertical axis distinguishes between those who see youth ministry as the church of the future (later) or church of the present (now).

The Inclusive Congregational approach (come now—fellowship now), left upper corner of the Johari window, focuses on integrating youth into congregational life, seeing young people as full partners in ministry and congregational life.

The Missional approach (go now—mission now) portrays youth ministry as a missional enterprise. Young people are missionaries, called to communicate the gospel with their own generation.

The Preparatory approach (come later—fellowship later) envisions a more specialized ministry to youth, preparing them to participate in existing church life as (future) leaders. Youth ministry is a viewed as a sort of laboratory for growth.

---

19. White, "The Youth Theological Initiative."
20. Scanlan, *An Interweaving Ecclesiology.*

The *Strategic approach* (go later—mission later) enables the youth group to develop into a new congregation, in other words a church plant. The youth leader here becomes the pastor, as a new church or congregation is formed with the blessing of a mother congregation.[21]

Obviously, the different models for youth ministry as a communal practice require different kinds of leadership, but the authors of the book emphasize that "mature leadership must not be sacrificed for the sake of including youths in leadership positions, so the church may need to find new ways of establishing a succession of godly leaders in the church."[22]

What sort of role is assigned to the youth minister, then, if youth ministry is conceptualized as an ecclesial community? The review of current youth ministry scholarship on the subject reveals a complex and comprehensive picture. The ecclesial role of the (communal) youth minister is on one hand *diaconal*: Writing on the challenges facing young people who have experienced (parental) divorce, Andrew Root argues that "the community of the church cannot eliminate the deep ontological fractures that occur when divorce strikes, but it can, in its communal life, stand with and for these children, bearing their brokenness."[23]

At the same time, the youth minister is pastor, poet, and prophet for anything that contributes to a good life. In rethinking the fundamentals of youth ministry, Andrew Root later (2020) argues that joy (and the good life) is a point of orientation for a transformation of youth ministry, away from making the youth minister a custodian or guardian. Joy, in Root's conception, is "the communal experience of life coming out of death, which produces union with God and neighbor."[24] In the same book, Root re-imagines the role of the youth minister as a sort of communal poet, helping young people to make their life into a story. Instead of competing with other spare-time activities, "things" in Root's terminology, "youth ministry should forget about competing in the battle of *things* and instead profoundly concern ourselves with *stories*."[25] Focusing on narrative in youth ministry, Root emphasizes that youth ministry becomes a community of friends. "This community tells stories and seeks the Good

---

21. Senter et al., *Four Views of Youth Ministry*, xv–xvi.
22. Senter et al., *Four Views of Youth Ministry*, 158.
23. Root, *The Children of Divorce*, 122.
24. Root, *The End of Youth Ministry*, 146.
25. Root, *The End of Youth Ministry*, 165.

life by conforming to the cross through silence, gratitude, humility, and ultimately friendship."[26]

If the youth minister is a sort of communal poet, the minister becomes a resource person, someone striving to bridge young people's experience with the Christian tradition. Pete Ward finds that the role of the youth minister is first and foremost to "act as someone who "translates" biblical stories or insights from church history and theology into the present day context" of a group of young people.[27] Similarly, Kenda Creasy Dean imagines the communal poet=youth minister as a sort of exhorting coach practicing the art of "being there" with young people: "When young people practice their faith in the company of others, Jesus is revealed in those who will "be there" for them in Christian community, and who therefore serve as icons of divine fidelity."[28]

14.6 Conclusion

With the return to ecclesiology as the lens through which the role of the youth minister is conceptualized, it becomes obvious that by assessing the complexity of roles a youth minister may take on, we do more than simply examine roles: The whole understanding of youth ministry is put at the stand. We identify an integral relationship between the role of the youth minister (part 4), the purpose of the youth ministry (part 3), the implicit and explicit theology (part 2), and the conceptions of youth (part 1). As we embark on the final part of the handbook, trying to develop a research framework for research on youth ministry, this interrelated dynamic is an important element of a situated research philosophy.

---

26. Root, *The End of Youth Ministry*, 224.
27. Ward, *God at the Mall*, 71.
28. Dean, *Practicing Passion*, 195.

Part 5

HOW TO RESEARCH PRACTICES IN YOUTH MINISTRY?

How to Research Practices in Youth Ministry?

Introduction to Part 5

THE fifth and final part of the handbook focuses on the question: *How to research practices in youth ministry?* The following chapters deal with research methodology: different methodological approaches in youth ministry research are presented (chapter 15) and a particular practical theological research framework is proposed (chapter 16). This part concludes with chapter 17 and directions for designing a youth ministry research project. Chapter 15 discusses the context of different research methodologies in youth ministry research. It highlights themes such as epistemology as well as offering research paradigms. The chapter pays particular attention to the importance of doing justice to the voice of young people in youth ministry research. The chapter also sheds light on two particular research methodologies that recur in youth ministry research: ethnography and (participatory) action research.

Chapter 16 proposes a practical theological research framework that is directed towards the use of empirical data in the research on, and enhancement of, youth ministry practices. We have reasons for proposing this particular practical theological framework. The first is that empirical research is at the heart of youth ministry research today, and has been for some time,. The second reason has to do with doing justice to the voice and practices of young people in youth ministry research. The latter argument is directly related to a constructivist epistemology which is a core topic in both chapter 16 and chapter 17. With such an epistemology in the background, chapter 16 discusses how to take the empirical as a source for theological reflection and sheds light on the importance of empirical hermeneutical skills. Special attention is given to normativity in the research project.

Chapter 17 then concludes with a couple of directions for designing a youth ministry research project based on the insights contained in previous chapters. We hope this chapter helps the reader to think through, step by step, the research process from the first research idea to the presentation of findings. Where part 5 of the handbook, in particular, supports the more technical part of this research process, the sum of all parts of the handbook supports the reader with the necessary overview of the literature in which the research project can be embedded.

15

Research Methodologies

"The focus in this study is on what occurs in a worship gathering and what meanings adolescents attribute to their participation in this worship. It is a qualitative study using cultural-anthropological tools of empirical investigation. Moreover, it is a qualitative study using theological perspectives in the choice of the domain, and in the concepts chosen."[1]

THE quote above is taken from the introductory chapter of the doctoral dissertation of Ronelle Sonnenberg published in 2015, "Youth Worship in Protestant Contexts: A Practical Theological Theory of Participation of Adolescents." The statement offers a very condensed presentation of the main research methodology choices in a study on youth worship. It is an example of a research paradigm typically chosen in empirical youth ministry research: a qualitative study. The quotation mentions the use of empirical research instruments coming from the field of cultural anthropology. Furthermore, it indicates how the concepts are chosen in presenting the findings that it is, at the same time, a theological study. This chapter will discuss more elaborately what kind of choices can be made in terms of research paradigms and the consequences they have.

The chapter starts by providing some context to different research methodologies in youth ministry research by reviewing some themes raised in the introduction (15.1). Next, we will explain some research methodological concepts that will help in understanding different

---

1. Sonnenberg, "Youth Worship in Protestant Contexts," 21.

research methodologies in youth ministry research (15.2): concepts like epistemology and research paradigms. In section 15.3, we will focus particularly on the importance of doing justice to the voice of young people in youth ministry research. After that, we will describe two particular research methodologies that recur in youth ministry research: ethnography and (participatory) action research (15.4).

15.1 Towards a Reflection on Research Methodology

We start this chapter by re-examining a couple of themes provided in the short historical overview of youth ministry research given in the introduction. In the early days, youth ministry as an academic discipline was characterized and shaped by a theoretical and methodological framework from psychology and social sciences. But in 2003, in the article "Why Theology? It Is Only Youth Ministry," South African practical theologian Malan Nel advocated a (practical) theological approach to youth ministry. He claims that in "practical theology we try to explain how the reality out there is responding to how we communicate what God said and how we can improve ministry in service of the communication of the gospel."[2] Although clearly reformed in its background, this methodological perspective on youth ministry also bears similarity to the practical theological project of US theologian Don Browning.[3]

Another proof that youth ministry mainly operates methodologically through Browning's "practice-theory-practice" model is found in the youth ministry standard, *Starting Right Thinking Theologically about Youth Ministry*, where, in the introduction, Kenda Creasy Dean defines youth ministry as practical theological reflection: "Reflection that connects what we believe about God with how we live as disciples of Jesus Christ—is the first task of ministry with young people."[4] She draws a four-step methodological model: *understand (I), reflect (II), detect and evaluate (III) and project (IV)*[5] mainly based on Browning's model of practical theology, or as Dave Rahn puts it in the epilogue: "We all need

2. Nel, "Why Theology?," 13.
3. See his major book: Browning, *A Fundamental Practical Theology*.
4. Dean et al., *Starting Right*, 17. This notion is developed further on p. 19: "Because Christian action unapologetically invites God to use us to transform the world in Jesus' name, practical theology is intimately connected to the practices of ministry—which is no to say it is limited to the practices of professional church ministers."
5. Dean et al., *Starting Right*, 20.

to be subdued by the reality that what we do in the practice of youth ministry is powerfully shaped by how deeply and faithfully we think about those practices"[6]

At the beginning of the twenty-first century, Kenda Creasy Dean is one of the scholars pleading for theology to be a leading discipline within youth ministry practices and the study of youth ministry practices. At the same time, whether youth ministry as an academic discipline should be focused on theology, on practical theology in particular, or should be multi- or interdisciplinary has been a debate in itself within the circles of youth ministry scholars from the very beginning. In 2012, Bert Roebben reviewed the international developments in the emerging field of youth ministry research since the beginning of the twenty-first century.[7] Roebben detects four different contexts in which youth ministry research was situated at that time: (a) large-scale Western world data sets on youth and religion, religiosity, and spirituality; (b) ecclesiological and ministry studies; (c) youth ministry and young adult ministry studies, largely related to the context of the school campus; (d) the body of research on children's and youth spirituality, and theologizing with children and youth.

Against the background of these diverse contexts of youth ministry research, the question arises as to what kind of research methodology or methodologies should serve youth ministry research. An early attempt to develop a methodology of youth ministry is found in an article written by Australian youth ministry theologians Clive Pearson and Christine Grapes, "A Kick in the Theological Shins: Constructing a Theology for Youth Ministry" where they aim at developing youth ministry as an art of contextual theology or applied theology. They relate this to Pete Ward's definition of youth ministry in *Youthwork and the Mission of God*. "A theology of youth ministry seeks to demonstrate how our understanding of God shapes and influences the practice of youth ministry."[8] By this they want to do justice to the experience of young people, and therefore they want to start a conversation between experience and Christian tradition. Dean Borgman advocates some of the same contextual approach to youth ministry. He mixes it with elements of liberation theology. In both *When Kumbayah Is Not Enough* and *Hear My Story*, he advocates both that

---

6. Dean et al., *Starting Right*, 389.
7. Roebben, "International Developments."
8. Ward, *Youthwork and the Mission of God*, 25.

"ministry precedes systematic theology,"[9] and that youth ministry must perform a holistic exegesis: an exegesis of Scripture, (youth) culture, and of self and community.[10]

In today's discourses in academic research on youth ministry, we observe an explicit reflection on research methodology, in particular related to doing empirical research on youth and faith. The remainder of this chapter will describe different research methodologies in youth ministry research and their backgrounds. These studies that are presented as examples are most often embedded in a practical theological research tradition. At the same time, there is an ongoing conversation of and within practical theological accounts alongside biblical and systematic theology. In chapter 16, we will reflect on this combination of practical, biblical, and systematic dimensions in a practical theological research framework that we will propose.

15.2 Research Concepts

This section explains a number of research concepts that will help with understanding different research methodologies in youth ministry research. In an article in which she explains the backgrounds of participatory action research in religious education, Mary Hess rightly points at the distinction between epistemology, methodology, and method[11]—a distinction that will help to see how in youth ministry research, too, different approaches to conducting research develop. *Epistemology* is about theory of knowledge, including questions such as what can be considered as knowledge, what can be known, and who is the knower. Hess describes *methodology* as a broad theoretically informed framework that informs a particular approach to research. Instead of methodology, we might call this a research paradigm.[12] A methodology or research paradigm refers to both a set of epistemological beliefs and a prototypical research design. *Method* refers to concrete techniques or interventions chosen within a particular research design, like interviews or surveys.

---

9. Borgman, *When Kumbaya Is Not Enough*, xv.
10. Borgman, *When Kumbaya Is Not Enough*, xvii.
11. Hess, "Collaborating with People."
12. Court, *Qualitative Research*.

Epistemology

Deborah Court explains two epistemologies often noticed in research: a positivist epistemology, and a constructivist epistemology.[13] Court explains that a positive epistemology holds the view that all knowledge is provable through observation and testing. A constructivist epistemology "holds that individuals construct their knowledge through experience, and that much personal and cultural knowledge is tacit, intimately tied to context, not easily expressed, and not suitable to the notion of proof."[14] A constructivist epistemology is often described in different terms such as interpretive (the subjective truth of research participants is perceived and understood through the personal framework of the researcher), naturalistic (participants are studied in their natural environments), and hermeneutic (knowing is about searching for meaning, more than for objective facts). Epistemology or epistemological beliefs will not only inform methodologies or research paradigms, but also inform how research problems and research questions are stated (see chapter 16).

Of particular interest in theological empirical research, as many studies in youth ministry research are conducted in this way, is what Richard Osmer calls a meta-theoretical decision or position, that might include the weighing up of the traditional sources of theological truth—Scripture, tradition, reason, and experience.[15] How the researcher perceives the research project as an "experience" is also part of this meta-theoretical basis for research: for example, does the researcher believe they also experience a transcendental dimension while carrying out the research and what does that mean for the research process and outcomes? A good illustration of this issue can be found in an article by Margaret Ann Crain who describes an ethnographic (research) approach in religious education.[16] With regard to asking questions of research participants, she explains: "Just asking a question in this very relational, complicated, multilayered research methodology that is called ethnography creates new obligations and new possibilities to experience the grace of God. We must not take it lightly."[17]

---

13. Court, *Qualitative Research*.
14. Court, *Qualitative Research*, 4.
15. Osmer, "Practical Theology."
16. Crain, "Looking at People."
17. Crain, "Looking at People," 390.

Methodology/Research Paradigm

Epistemological considerations are the basis of methodologies or research paradigms. "A research paradigm is a framework of epistemological beliefs and methods."[18] In this regard, Court sees quantitative research and qualitative research as two broad categories of research paradigms. According to Court, the quantitative research paradigm is informed by positivist or post-positive[19] epistemological beliefs, whereas a qualitative research paradigm is informed by constructivist epistemological beliefs. Quantitative research is a search for general regularities and predictions, often following a deductive pathway from theories and concepts towards the counting of large-scale measurements. Qualitative research is a search for particular meanings, often following an inductive pathway from rich descriptions of particular practices towards "grounded theories."

A good example of giving words to a qualitative research paradigm that follows a constructivist epistemology is Steve Kang, with regard to his research on themes of self-construction and self-integration in the narratives of second generation Korean American young adults.[20] This study was centered on ethnographic interviews and participant observation and Kang describes the philosophical perspective of this research as "a constructive paradigm that understands reality as consisting of the meanings people imbue into their experiences according to their particular sociocultural contexts."[21] Kang argues that an ultimate consequence of this paradigm is that findings are literally created in the course of the study because researcher and participants are inseparably linked and the process of research itself impacts the reality under study.

A particular example of a qualitative research paradigm following a constructivist epistemology has already been discussed in chapter 2, namely the movement of child's theology as discussed by Karl Ernst Nipkov.[22] This theology of the child departs from a New Testament perspective, and a systematic theological perspective, where the latter has to do with self-reflection by children on faith and while doing so produces

---

18. Court, *Qualitative Research*, 4.

19. According to post-positivists total neutrality of the researcher is not possible and it is not always possible to separate the knower from the known (see Court, *Qualitative Research*, 5).

20. Kang, "Reflections upon Methodology."

21. Kang, "Reflections upon Methodology," 408.

22. Nipkow, "Theologie des Kindes und Kindertheologie."

theology. The theology of the child is complementary to the children's theology movement: "Diese fordert die Theologie heraus, sich der komplexen Welt der Kinder in der vollen Pluralität unserer Zeit auszusetzen und mit Kindern zu lernen."[23]

Ronelle Sonnenberg, Elsbeth Visser-Vogel, and Harmen van Wijnen in 2016 strongly plead for an empirical qualitative research paradigm in research on the faith of adolescents.[24] The authors observe a quantitative approach being dominant in studies on adolescents and faith or religious identity, mostly measuring "adolescents' (faith) identity, formal relationship with churches, behavior in specific practices (e.g. attendance at activities) and opinions of some faith doctrines regarding, for instance, images of God, heaven and hell."[25] The authors, however, conceive faith as something which cannot be captured by written surveys and, instead, argue for faith to be considered as a narrative. The study of faith narratives, or in the words of the authors, "the reconstruction of faith narratives," is a complex process and requires a qualitative approach placing importance on the emic perspective.

Research paradigms, whether quantitative or qualitative, "spring from different epistemologies, ask different kinds of questions, are designed and conducted differently, and generate different kinds of knowledge."[26] Apart from choosing either a qualitative or quantitative approach, one might choose to have both: a so-called mixed methods approach. Tobias Faix argues for the use of a mixed methods approach in youth ministry research; in chapter 4 we described the results of his research on what and how young people believe in the context of the Protestant Church of Westphalia in Germany, a study which is actually based on such a mixed methods approach.[27] Besides quantitative and qualitative research paradigms informed by positivist, post-positivist (quantitative research), and constructivist epistemologies (qualitative research), Court mentions two other research paradigms: critical theory (that challenges the status quo) and participatory research (directed towards a democratic and inclusive process of knowledge-building relevant for priorities in the researched community). Although particular epistemological beliefs are

23. Nipkow, "Theologie des Kindes und Kindertheologie," 442.
24. Sonnenberg et al., "Reconstructing Faith Narratives."
25. Sonnenberg et al., "Reconstructing Faith Narratives," 25.
26. Court, *Qualitative Research*, 4–5.
27. Faix, "How Theology Takes Shape"; Faix, "Semantics of Faith."

at the basis of research paradigms, a choice for the one or other research paradigm is not always *because of* the epistemological beliefs underlying it. The choice for a qualitative research paradigm can be informed, for example, by being confronted with situations where very little research has been done yet, or by being confronted with research outcomes from quantitative studies which cannot easily be explained.

Each methodology or research paradigm holds typical approaches to research methods (or, in other words, prototypical *research designs*). Court explains that a quantitative research paradigm can have an experimental approach, a quasi-experimental approach, a causal-comparative, a correlational, or a survey approach. A qualitative research paradigm could hold different approaches: "ethnography, narrative, case study, phenomology, action research."[28]

Method

As has been said, on the most concrete level, each methodological approach can result in different methods being used: interviews, observations, document analysis, surveys, etcetera.

15.3 Doing Justice to the Voice of Young People

This section focusses particularly on the importance of doing justice to the voice of young people in youth ministry research. One of the main arguments for this (see also the introduction) is youth ministry being not only conceived as a practice in which theological concepts are applied, but, the other way around, also conceived as a practice from which (new) theological concepts and understanding originate. This has a direct relationship with a constructivist epistemology which has become dominant in youth ministry research (see the introduction to this chapter and section 15.1). According to Bert Roebben, for youth ministry research to have the potential for constructing theology, it needs to be involved in the lives of young people: "initially, by noticing and respecting their voices, secondly through crafting space within our theorising for young people's insight to shape theological understanding and thirdly by embracing the lives of young people as a site for connection with God and

---

28. Court, *Qualitative Research*, 6.

the construction of theology."[29] According to Cheryl Magrini, it is even a "holy responsibility": "the representation of research participants, particularly children, is an ethical and justice issue for the ethnographer. It is a holy responsibility to represent the research site and research participants in all their complexity."[30]

Doing justice to the voices of young people does not mean that other voices (those of adults, the researcher, history, etcetera) are not relevant in youth ministry research or that the voice of young people should outweigh other voices. In this regard, in her research on children's interpretations of biblical meal stories, Cheryl Magrini also explains the "ethical responsibility" of the researcher to make explicit the sources of thick description that form the basis for data analysis and drawing conclusions. This process is called by the author "intertextual voicing." In her ethnographic research, she points at different voices in her data and data analysis, among which are the individual narratives of children, the artwork of these children, the ethnographer as participant-observer, but also as a photographer, the "group voice," and the literature. The author concludes: "Identifying the layers and interrelated strands of ethnographic intertextual voicing, naming intertextuality broadly beyond a written text, is necessary to validate the theoretical, theological, and practice of ministry conclusions of the study."[31]

As said, Ronelle Sonnenberg, Elsbeth Visser-Vogel, and Harmen van Wijnen plead for an empirical qualitative research paradigm to reconstruct the faith narratives of adolescents. In their article "Reconstructing Faith Narratives: Doing Research on the Faith of Adolescents," the authors explore the set of qualitative methods that can access the faith of adolescents in a way that leads to a sufficient representation and understanding of the lived faith of adolescents. In general, these qualitative methods go through three steps: "1) *accessing* the faith dimensions of adolescents; 2) *disclosing* their faith narratives; and 3) *verifying* their faith narratives."[32] Sonnenberg et al. offer a couple of practical recommendations for each step to reduce the risk of non-access and of misunderstanding the voices of young people (see also section 15.3).

---

29. Roebben, "Light of Day," 23.
30. Magrini, "Children's Interpretations of Biblical Meal Stories," 79.
31. Magrini, "Children's Interpretations of Biblical Meal Stories," 80.
32. Sonnenberg et al., "Reconstructing Faith Narratives," 38.

15.4 Particular Methodologies/Research Paradigms: Ethnography and (Participatory) Action Research

From section 15.2 we can conclude that each methodology or research paradigm is, on the one hand, related to a set of epistemological beliefs and, on the other, holds typical approaches to research methods, or in other words, prototypical research designs. In this section we will discuss two particular methodologies that often recur in youth ministry research: ethnography and (participatory) action research. A red thread in these methodologies is, in the words of Michael Domsgen, a systemic and biographical approach which strives for adequate understanding of how young people construct their faith.[33] This approach, with its attention to both individual narratives and the communal context of young people, is a direct implication of the striving to do justice to the voices of young people in youth ministry research, as explained in section 15.2.

Ethnography: Interviews, Focus Groups, and Participative Observations

As suggested in section 15.2, Sonnenberg et al. plead for an ethnographical approach in studying the faith narratives of young people.[34] This plea does not stand on its own. It reflects a recurrent research paradigm in youth ministry research: the research paradigm of ethnography. The authors see three general steps in research designs based on this paradigm (1) accessing, (2) disclosing, and (3) verifying the faith narratives of youth. For each step in the research design following an ethnographical paradigm, the authors give particular recommendations. For the first, accessing, step, an attentive and relational approach towards youth is important. In the second, disclosing, step, it is important to be creative and to be open: creative by using methods including for example songs and movies to disclose the area of faith and open by not sticking to a semi-structured interview protocol while also being open to unexpected turns. In addition, the step of disclosing is also helped by using concepts that are open to both a cultural-social dimension and a theological dimension. In the third step of verifying, peer debriefing and returning the results to them is recommended.

33. Domsgen, "Plädoyer."
34. Sonnenberg et al., "Reconstructing Faith Narratives," 38.

In the article by Sonnenberg et al., applying interviews with youth is discussed in particular as an often-used method in research designs that follow an ethnographical approach. In interviews, young people can retrospectively discuss their faith development, for example, or they can reflect on current life experiences in relationship to faith. The already mentioned study of Steve Kang on themes of self-construction and self-integration in the narrative of second generation Korean American young adults is an example of applying the method of interviewing.[35] The interviews conducted in this study aimed to describe and explore the construction of the self by second generation Korean American youth. This particular study also shows an often-found combination of interviewing and participative observation. Kang's article provides a description of and reflection on the experiences during the course of this combined strategy of interviewing and participative observation. The study by Van Leersum et al. is another good example of this combined strategy.[36] The article by Margaret Ann Crain that was already mentioned provides an example of combining individual interviews with focus groups.[37] Crain's article provides a description of and reflection on this particular combination of methods.

For further reading on ethnography in youth ministry research we recommend reading two recent dissertations. First, the dissertation of Lydia van Leersum-Bekebrede entitled "Worship with Children: Agentive Participation in Dutch Protestant Contexts." The central question that guided this research project was how liturgical rituals with children are performed in Dutch Protestant contexts, how they contribute to children's agentive participation, and what the theological significance of these practices is. To answer this research question, the researcher used the methods of participant observations and interviewing. Second, the dissertation from Anne-Marije De Bruin-Wassinkmaat entitled "Finding One's Own Way: Exploring the Religious Identity Development of Emerging Adults Raised in Strictly Reformed Contexts in the Netherlands." The central question that guided this research project was how the religious identity development of emerging adults who grew up in strictly Reformed contexts in the Netherlands can be described and interpreted. For answering this research question, participants' narrative accounts of

35. Kang, "Reflections upon Methodology."
36. Van Leersum-Bekebrede et al., "Setting the Stage."
37. Crain, "Looking at People."

essential processes in religious identity development were investigated: current commitments, past explorations, and contextual influences.

(Participatory) Action Research

Participatory action research is a research paradigm which is about professional researchers working together with participants in a practice or community under study in all stages of the research process: from defining the research questions through to drawing practical implications from the outcomes of the study. A good example of what this type of research mean in practice is given by Mary Hess in 2001.[38] In the article in *Religious Education*, Hess argues why and how she applied Participatory action research in her study about how religious educators could and should interact with popular culture. After having explained how she conducted workshops with religious educators on the main theme of interacting with popular culture, Hess detects three sites for the construction of the knowledge she is aiming at in participatory action research:

> The educational workshop itself, which reflects most directly a practice dimension; post-workshop interviews, which reflect upon that practice dimension; and my own attempts to situate the research amidst the larger conversations taking place within academe. All of these sites are intimately and integrally linked to each other, and the synthesis I achieve, if it is achieved at all, will be because I can make that interdependence clear. The "re" "search" process, then, includes all of the ways in which we (the research participants, myself, and my academic colleagues) separately and together, try to enrich and extend our understanding, our knowledge, through returning to our experiences again and again.[39]

Besides participatory action research, action research can also be chosen as a research paradigm. The difference with participatory action research is research participants not having a direct role in co-directing (together with the professional researcher) the different stages of the research process. Although the author does not label it as such, the research of Cheryl Magrini, already referred to in section 15.2, is a good

---

38. Hess, "Collaborating with People."
39. Hess, "Collaborating with People," 283–84.

example of action research.[40] In her research on children's interpretations of biblical meal stories, Cheryl Magrini opts for an ethnographical approach that she actually applies in a teaching-learning environment based on a so called "hospitable pedagogy approach" that she herself created in three congregations. The article by Magrini in *Religious Education* provides an elaborated discussion of the background, experiences, and outcomes of this research paradigm, including the particular methods applied. The common feature of both participatory action research and action research is that conducting the research is purposefully impacting the practice under study. The research design does not merely result in knowledge leaving the practice under study unchanged, but instead it generates knowledge as knowledge-in-action that at the same time transforms the practice under study.

In this section, we have described two particular research methodologies that recur in youth ministry research: ethnography and (participatory) action research. These are examples of so called "collaborative approaches" in research. To learn more about (participatory) action research and many other examples of collaborative research practices, we recommend the book *Collaborative Practical Theology: Engaging Practitioners in Research on Christian Practices* by Henk de Roest. Although the book focuses on the discipline of Practical Theology, much of what is presented can be applied to empirical youth ministry research.

---

40. Magrini, "Children's Interpretations of Biblical Meal Stories."

16

A Practical Theological Research Framework

"Trying to bring this practical theological perspective back to the core, I would say that a practical theologian continuously says to oneself: 'Wait a minute: set aside the quick-fix analysis, be open and receptive in encountering the other and the otherness, to what you see and hear.'"[1]

WHAT does it mean to be open and receptive as a practical theological researcher? In the following chapter we propose a practical theological research framework which is directed towards the use of empirical data in the research on and enhancement of youth ministry practices. By choosing a practical theological research framework we place ourselves in line with Malan Nel who, at the very outset of youth ministry as an academic discipline (see introduction) envisions practical theology as the mother science of youth ministry.[2] Youth ministry as an academic practical theological discipline focuses on communicative actions serving the gospel, "in order to direct and to improve the intentional actions directed at the youth, in collaboration with the youth and by the youth in our modern society."[3] In addition, we believe that empirical research is at the very heart of this practical theological approach. We are aware

---

1. De Kock, *Wait a Minute in Stressful Times*, 15.
2. Nel, "Youth Ministry as Practical Theology."
3. Nel, "Youth Ministry as Practical Theology," 73.

A Practical Theological Research Framework

of other perspectives and fully agree with David White (2017)[4] that there are many other relevant perspectives, such as biblical theological or systematic accounts, but in the following we will argue for the importance of a particular practical theological research framework.

The first reason is that empirical research is at the heart of youth ministry research (see introduction and chapter 15). Therefore, we would like to serve this major field of contributions within youth ministry research with a framework that matches the interests in empirical research designs. The second reason has to do with what we already described as an ethical tendency: doing justice to the voices and practices of young people in youth ministry research. We indeed believe that youth ministry should not only be conceived as a practice in which theological concepts are applied, but, the other way around, also conceived as a practice from which (new) theological concepts and understanding originate. This argument is directly related to a constructivist epistemology (see chapter 15), which we will elaborate rather more in section 16.1. Our conviction is that studying the empirical in youth ministry practices can be the starting point to "gain insight into both the descriptions and interpretations of the religious self-understandings or faith constructs of young people and to be able to build theology and design practices in which these insights are taken seriously."[5]

This chapter is organized as follows. In section 16.1, we will clarify the epistemological basis for our practical theological framework. Sections 16.2, 16.3, and 16.4 will elaborate on different aspects of the methodology or research paradigm of the framework: taking the empirical as a source for theological reflection (16.2), using a threefold set of empirical hermeneutical skills (16.3), and be sensitive for four layers of normativity in the research project (16.4). Finally, in section 16.5, we will reflect on some consequences for research methods.

For writing this chapter we partly used and partly reworked or extended existing texts from the inaugural address of Jos de Kock in 2019, *Wait a Minute in Stressful Times: A Practical Theological Account of Learning in Encounter*.

---

4. White, "The Fire and Light."
5. White, "The Fire and Light," 71.

16.1 Epistemological Basis

As stated in the introduction to this chapter, our framework is directly related to a constructivist epistemology (see chapter 15). A constructivist epistemology "holds that individuals construct their knowledge through experience, and that much personal and cultural knowledge is tacit, intimately tied to context, not easily expressed, and not suitable to the notion of proof."[6] The knowledge construction that is at hand in youth ministry research is related to the study of youth ministry practices from which (new) theological concepts and understanding originate. Furthermore, taking the empirical reality of the here and now of youth ministry practices as a main source for developing theological reflection is based on the assumption, or the theological belief, that God reveals himself in Scripture, tradition, reason, and also in human experience.[7]

> Meta-theoretically, our theological rationale or theological conviction is that God reveals Himself in Scripture, and through tradition and with the help of reason. But reading Scripture, studying the tradition, and examining reason also open the possibility that God may reveal Himself in the empirical world, even in the particular experiences of young people. This means that the empirical world and, therefore, young people's experiences are important sources for constructing theology in the field of youth ministry. We should be open to the possibility of revelation in the empirical world. This is an important, vital, meta-theoretical consideration for practical theological work in youth ministry.[8]

At the same time, empirical research in youth ministry should be conceived as a continuous hermeneutical struggle rooted in the belief that experiences in faith practices, whether by practitioners or scholars, do not necessarily fully coincide with "how God is" and "how God reveals Godself":[9] "The link between the human communication, the interpretation of messengers, and the God-human communication is theologically anchored in the freedom of God, in his initiative and his being *semper maior*, as well as in the fragmented and particular knowledge and acting

---

6. Court, *Qualitative Research*, 4.
7. See De Kock and Norheim, "Youth Ministry Research," 80.
8. De Kock and Norheim, "Youth Ministry Research," 78–79.
9. De Kock and Norheim, "Youth Ministry Research," 80.; Sonnenberg, "God in Youth Worship"; De Kock, "Theologiseren met kinderen."

of people."[10] In other words, the understanding, and what might be called the theologies, including theologies functioning as understanding frameworks within the realms of practical theology in general and in youth ministry in particular, are always under construction.[11]

This epistemological basis for our framework can be captured under the umbrella of critical realism, as explained by Robert Martin with an eye to teaching and learning in Christian congregations.[12] The author summarizes the main features of critical realism in terms of four theses:

> 1. At the heart of knowledge is faith, fundamentally a faith that a particular reality has an objective existence independent of our consciousness of it. . . . 2. To know is to know something. Thus, knowing is a relationship of the knower to something she seeks to know. . . . The knower will be rightly related to reality as she remains open to the self-disclosure of objects in their own ontic reality. . . . 3. Truthful knowledge depends upon an intrinsic correspondence between the person of the knower and the structures of the universe. . . . A correspondence between persons and the deeper structures of the universe is not automatically achieved; it is developed in a relation of intensifying participation. . . . 4. Although grounded in a contact with the object of knowledge, human knowing is inherently limited and fallible. We can be committed to our knowledge while holding it provisionally.[13]

16.2 The Empirical as a Source for Theological Reflection

The study object of practical theology is religious praxis,[14] and its strategic goal is the description, interpretation, and ultimately, the enhancement of religious praxis.[15] Taking on a practical theological perspective in the study of (theological) phenomena is then, more precisely, taking the empirical reality of the here and now as a main source for developing

---

10. Sonnenberg, "God in Youth Worship," 241.
11. De Kock, "Theologiseren met kinderen"; De Kock and Norheim, "Youth Ministry Research."
12. Martin, "Having Faith in our Faith in God."
13. Martin, "Having Faith in our Faith in God," 251–53.
14. Ganzevoort and Roeland, "Lived Religion."
15. Heimbrock, "Practical Theology as Empirical Theology."

theological reflection.[16] For the academic study of youth ministry, Jos de Kock and Bard Norheim discussed how studying the empirical can be the starting point of gaining "insight into both the descriptions and interpretations of religious self-understanding or faith constructs of young people and to be able to build theology and design practices in which these insights are taken seriously."[17] After taking it as a main source for theological reflection, an important task for the scholar taking on a practical theological perspective is to then search for interactions between the empirical data and the theological and nontheological interpretative and normative frameworks.[18]

By presenting the practical theological perspective in this way, we see reflected in it the four tasks of a practical theologian as identified by Osmer (2008): (a) the descriptive–empirical task, (b) the interpretive task, (c) the normative task, and (d) the pragmatic task.[19] We believe that two particular concerns related to tasks (a) and (c) ask for greater than average levels of attention. The first concern is what skills and attitude are needed for an adequate description of religious praxis as an empirical phenomenon. The second concern is how to adequately incorporate a (theological) reflection on the normativity that is at work at different levels in an empirical research project on religious practices.

What we propose in this chapter as constituting a practical theological perspective is actually addressing these two concerns. To adopt a practical theological perspective in the academic reflection on religious praxis means that the youth ministry scholar (a) takes the empirical reality of the here and now as a main source for developing theological reflection, (b) applies a threefold set of empirical hermeneutical skills in the empirical investigation of religious praxis, and (c) thoroughly reflects on the four layers of normativity in empirical research on religious praxis.

Taking the empirical reality of the here and now as a main source for developing theological reflection is based on the assumption, or the theological belief, that God reveals himself in Scripture, tradition, reason, and also in human experience.[20] A practical theological perspective gives particular weight to current-day experiences as a "source of

---

16. De Kock and Norheim, "Youth Ministry Research."
17. De Kock and Norheim, "Youth Ministry Research," 71.
18. De Kock and Norheim, "Youth Ministry Research."
19. Osmer, *Practical Theology*.
20. See De Kock and Norheim, "Youth Ministry Research," 80.

justification" in the theological reflection on religious phenomena.[21] A practical theological perspective asks for the researcher to encounter the empirical, which results in learning theologically. In terms of research design, the encounter with the empirical can take different forms, varying from a somewhat distanced encounter as an observer of religious practices to an engaged encounter where the researcher is part of and a participant in the religious practice under study.

16.3 A Threefold Set of Empirical Hermeneutical Skills

In encountering the empirical, the youth ministry scholar uses a threefold set of empirical hermeneutical skills: observing as reception, listening as reception, and learning language.[22]

The skill of *observation as reception* means that the youth ministry scholar is fundamentally involved in observing people's faith practices, continuously balancing an apophatic mode (being silent and hesitant being unable to describe the One beyond sensation) and cataphatic mode (trying to describe traces of God and God's attributes). The second skill of *listening as reception* means that the youth ministry scholar is fundamentally involved in the skill of listening to people's voices, balancing an apophatic and cataphatic mode, "which makes listening not mere registration of words and expressions but a hermeneutical struggle in itself."[23] Both observation and listening are done in a mode of reception, a mode of "being with the other" and "being with the faith practice," thus being open to what comes to the researcher and being attentive to what comes from within the researcher oneself. When it comes to the third skill of *learning language*, De Kock and Norheim explain: "The youth ministry scholar and practitioner is continuously learning language with which revelations of God and experiences of faith can be described and theologically reflected on, in a way which is appropriate for the flesh and blood experiences of young people."[24] In terms of the broader scope of the practical theological framework we propose here, learning language is the challenge to communicate what can be learned theologically from the encounter with the empirical in a way that is simultaneously appropriate

---

21. See Osmer, "Practical Theology."
22. De Kock and Norheim, "Youth Ministry Research."
23. De Kock and Norheim, "Youth Ministry Research," 81.
24. De Kock and Norheim, "Youth Ministry Research," 81.

for the practice under study and constructive for theological reflection in a broader academic discourse.

In terms of research design, the youth ministry scholar positions themselves, in the words of Richard Osmer, as an artist in his studio.[25]

> "In the artist's studio of the youth ministry scholar, insights deriving from empirical experiences should enter the debate with other sources of justification, such as biblical-theological and systematic theological arguments and interpretive frameworks from other disciplines than theology. The principal starting point for this debate, however, is the youth ministry scholar observing the praxis of young people in faith practices as a basis for construing youth ministry theories."[26]

16.4 Four Layers of Normativity

We agree with Richard Osmer who argues that normativity is a central issue in practical theological research.[27] Therefore, the issue of normativity is a central theme in the research framework as proposed here. A prominent expression of normativity can be found in what can be called "confessionality." Bard Norheim in 2011 argued that different understandings of youth ministry, including the underscoring of biblical-theological concepts such as "the cross" or "Christ image" stem from the different confessional backgrounds of faith communities and/or research communities.[28] As already discussed in the introduction, Norheim challenges youth ministry research in two ways: (a) hermeneutically: youth ministry research should articulate "more broadly and openly how confessional traditions and confessional contexts influence youth ministry research";[29] and (b) ecumenically: by displaying differences in terms of confessionality, youth ministry research should enhance the unity of the church.

But there is more than confessionality when addressing normativity in youth ministry research. In encountering the empirical, the youth ministry scholar should reflect on four layers of normativity in empirical research on religious praxis. The distinctions between, and descriptions

---

25. Osmer, *Practical Theology*.
26. De Kock and Norheim, "Youth Ministry Research," 79.
27. Osmer, *Practical Theology*.
28. Norheim, "Confessionality."
29. Norheim, "Confessionality," 62.

of, these four layers of normativity come from the work Jos de Kock, Ronelle Sonnenberg, and Eric Renkema, published with regard to the question of how one could adequately reflect on normativity in youth ministry and religious education research.[30] This question was raised because the authors found out that in research reports it was not uncommon for practical theologians to fail to explicitly reflect on how normativity exists in practices under study, or how normativity has impacted or directed (in both wanted and possibly unwanted ways) the design, execution, and reporting of the empirical study undertaken. Following De Kock, Sonnenberg, and Renkema (2018), we distinguish four layers of normativity: (1) the layer of discourse in religious practice; (2) the layer of professional theory of practice; (3) the layer of academic theory of practice; and (4) the layer of the metatheoretical foundation of the research project.

(1) The layer of discourse in religious practice is about verbal, non-verbal, and text-based discourses that become visible in practices. "These discourses reflect standards and convictions in the tradition of the practice, as well as the current standards and convictions of actors (including the researcher) in the practice."[31] (2) The layer of professional theory of practice is about "standards and convictions situated in operant theories of practice or, in other words, theories of practice at work. This layer has particularly to do with normativity as observed in theories construed on the basis of or directing performances in these religious practices."[32] (3) The layer of academic theory of practice is about "normativity situated in academic theories of practice that can be found in handbooks, academic journal articles, scientific theories, and so on."[33] (4) The layer of the metatheoretical foundation of the research project has to do with "how the researcher, the research group, or the research community considers the particular empirical research study in terms of how the empirical, the theoretical concepts, and the personal convictions and experiences of the researcher are related to one another."[34]

In terms of the research design, De Kock, Sonnenberg, and Renkema provide some directions for the design, execution, and reporting

30. De Kock et al., "Normativity."
31. De Kock et al., "Normativity," 86.
32. De Kock et al., "Normativity," 87.
33. De Kock et al., "Normativity," 88.
34. De Kock et al., "Normativity," 88.

of practical theological youth ministry research in terms of reflection on normativity. With regard to the design of a research project the researcher should ask himself a couple of questions, such as "for whom is the research problem a problem and why?" and "what is the rationale behind formulating the main and the subquestions of in a research study?" These kinds of questions help the researcher to detect what standards or convictions lie beyond the basis of a research. Furthermore, the authors suggest that the main question to be asked in the design phase of a research project on the meta-theoretical level is as follows: "how do I weigh empirical data in relationship to theological claims? or how do I conceive the relationship between the phenomena under study, on the one hand, and my own perception of these phenomena as a researcher, on the other?"[35]

With regard to the execution phase of a research project, the authors suggests that the researcher be continuously aware of their own normativity and systematically record their own reflections in this regard in field notes or in a logbook. The awareness this raises will help the researcher to take a step back from their own convictions and be open to observing the religious practice under study. At the same time, this makes it possible to report afterwards on the role one's own normativity had during the course of the research project. With regard to the reporting phase, the authors suggest including a reflection or report on (the role of) normativity, both in the research design section and in the discussion section.

16.5 Consequences for Methods

We believe that this practical theological framework requests youth ministry research to follow qualitative research designs, and to use good interviewing techniques and ethnographical methods through which data can be gathered by observing carefully and listening attentively, and then subsequently analyzed in such a way that appropriate language is found to communicate the results of the research. This resembles the approach of a hermeneutic-phenomenological methodology for theology that Robyn Horner proposed in the International Journal of Practical Theology.[36] This hermeneutic-phenomenological methodology encourages practical theologians to refrain "from making judgements in

---

35. De Kock et al., "Normativity," 100.
36. Horner, "Towards a Hermeneutic-Phenomenological Methodology."

advance about the kinds of phenomena it is possible to encounter."[37] It asks the practical theologian to open oneself to "what gives itself and use phenomenological, hermeneutical, and possibly, also, theological tools to uncover its meaning."[38] Horner argues, for example, that "in evaluating what research participants describe of their experience in relation to God, we may well be looking for events, which we can . . . define as descriptions of *happenings that are of such significance that they radically transform the world of the participant*. Such transformation will not prove the divine origin of events but will enable us to interpret experiences in light of this possibility."[39]

In order to learn this methodological approach in practical theology, we find Deborah Court's excellent book *Qualitative Research and Intercultural Understanding: Conducting Qualitative Research in Multicultural Settings* to be extremely helpful. The book is helpful precisely because it positions qualitative research as a personal encounter of the researcher with the other and with otherness: "In qualitative research the researcher is a research participant no less than those whom s/he is studying. Qualitative researchers collect and analyze data through the lens of who they are. Their research journey involves both utilizing and seeing beyond their experiences, knowledge bases and values in order to arrive at understanding of the lives of the research participants."[40] This book can help youth ministry scholars to critically engage in the strengths and weaknesses of research designs and the instruments used in actual research projects and to critically engage with ideas for research designs and instruments that are to be developed.[41]

For additional reading in relation to the practical theological research framework as presented in this chapter, we recommend Andrew Root's article "Regulating the Empirical in Practical Theology," and *The Wiley Blackwell Companion to Theology and Qualitative Research*, edited by Pete Ward and Knut Tveitereid.

---

37. Horner, "Towards a Hermeneutic-Phenomenological Methodology,"153.
38. Horner, "Towards a Hermeneutic-Phenomenological Methodology," 160.
39. Horner, "Towards a Hermeneutic-Phenomenological Methodology," 172.
40. Court, *Qualitative Research*, x.
41. For example, what is proposed with regard to interviewing techniques in practical theology in Campbell-Reed and Scharen, "Ethnography on Holy Ground."

17

Designing a Youth Ministry Research Project

"Youth ministry brings a distinctive lens to the practical theological conversation, emerging from theological reflection on practices of discipleship formation and issues of Christian identity in young people."[1]

YOUTH ministry, if well studied as a research practice, makes a unique contribution to practical theology. Rooted in this conviction, we want to end this handbook with a section on how to research youth ministry practices, paying special attention to a practical theological approach. In this last chapter, we finally sum up a couple of directions for designing a youth ministry research project based on the insights from previous chapters. We hope this chapter helps the reader to think through, step by step, the research process from first research idea to the presentation of findings. We structure the directions in eight steps.

- Step 1: Why? Showing the rationale for the research project. (section 17.1)
- Step 2: What is the problem? Defining what we do not know yet. (section 17.2)
- Step 3: What do you ask for? Posing research questions. (section 17.3)

---

1. Dean, "Reflections on the Future of Youth Ministry," 91.

- Step 4: What is it contributing to? Showing theoretical and practical relevance. (section 17.4)

- Step 5: How to construct? Setting up a research design. (section 17.5)

- Step 6. What do you do? Executing the different phases of the research design. (section 17.6)

- Step 7. What do you see? Reporting the findings of the research project. (section 17.7)

- Step 8. What do you learn? Drawing and discussing conclusions. (section 17.8)

17.1 Step 1: Why? Showing the Reason for the Research Project

Every research project has a reason. Why did the researcher start the project? Where did the idea originated from? These questions are of course also important for youth ministry scholars and anyone who as researcher is engaged in youth ministry research. The answer to the why can be embedded in practical experiences, in theoretical considerations or in both.

We underscored that careful observation and good listening in youth ministry practices is key to a practical theological approach to youth ministry research. The reason for setting up a research project can be embedded in what we observe and hear in these practical experiences in youth ministry. Do we see new developments we do not know much about? Do we observe methods and interventions of which we do not know the impact? Do we hear voices of young people that need further theological reflection? Etcetera, etcetera.

The current handbook tries to give an overview of what we know from previous youth ministry research in terms of a couple of key questions. One of the reasons for doing this is to show what youth ministry scholarship has already found out and what are the interesting openings for further research. The reason for setting up a research project can be embedded in what we see as lacking in previous and current youth ministry research: blank spots in the academic research, intriguing questions triggered by theory or empirical data. We hope the different parts in the current handbook help in the discovery of interesting areas for further youth ministry research.

As a first step in designing a youth ministry research project we recommend reflecting on the question of "why." Why would I start a research project at all? What is the reasoning behind this idea of a research project? What we often see is a double reasoning: it has to do with our own particular observations in the field of interest, and at the same time with the observation that the youth ministry literature leaves us with unanswered questions with regard to the main topic of interest. From previous chapters we learned that, already at the stage of this first step, we should pay special attention to normativity (chapter 16): Which layers of normativity do play an important role in the topic of interest? What about my own normativity in my reasoning for setting up a research project on this topic? What consequences does this have for the phases of design, execution, and reporting of my research project?

A careful reflection on the "why" of the youth ministry research project lays a good foundation for step 2 in which the field of interest will be more narrowly focused.

17.2 Step 2: What Is the Problem? Defining What We Do Not Know Yet

Every research project needs a clear focus. How do you arrive at this focus? We recommend taking two steps. The first step has to do with problem definition (current section). The second step is about asking the right questions (section 17.3).

The key question in step 2 is: what is the problem? And of course, here we mean "what is the *research* problem?" An easy way to explain what is at the core of a research problem is to phrase the question this way: What do we want to know? What is actually unknown as yet? As suggested elsewhere, we hope that the current handbook helps the reader by supplying an overview of what we *do* already know from previous youth ministry research but also by indicating where there are gaps in the academic research and where intriguing follow-up questions are triggered by theory or empirical data. There remain areas where we do not have all the information we need when it comes to the practices of youth ministry.

An important area still needing attention, for example, is how to do justice to the voice of young people (see chapter 16). Addressing this means rephrasing the question in a particular way: what do we want to know from young people? As yet, what do we not know from young people? Sometimes, scholarly works are full of statements, conclusions, and implications stemming from the perspective of youth ministers, researchers, and theoretical positions. And these, of course, are worthwhile in the broad context of youth ministry scholarship. But what youth ministry research also needs, besides these voices, is the voices of young people themselves. And this creates a particular type of research problem: where can we hear these voices? How can we hear these voices? And how do these voices enrich the academic understanding of youth ministry practices?

Coming to a clear definition of a problem is often helped by a thorough literature review, and this handbook is an attempt to review the literature from the perspective of certain key questions. But there might be much more to discover if other perspectives or key questions are brought to bear. The particular perspective that is relevant for your research project has to do with your overall reasoning about the specific research project (see step 1). Conducting a thorough literature review starting from this particular reasoning is what we recommend. For the field of youth ministry research, we specially recommend systematic literature reviews using a combination of the following databases of scholarly work:

1. Atla (Religion Database)
2. APA PsycARTICLES (Database of Psychological Literature)
3. Eric (Database Educational Resources Information Centre)
4. Web of Science (Science citation Index Expanded, and Social Sciences Citation Index)

17.3 Step 3: What Do You Ask For? Posing Research Questions

A next step in arriving at focus in your research project is asking the right questions against the backdrop of your research problem. In most cases we cannot fill the entire knowledge gap with one single research project. Each single research project is a modest partial contribution to solving a bigger research problem. One function of the research question or set of research questions in your youth ministry research project is to delineate exactly the contribution that this particular research project will make to the endeavor of closing the bigger knowledge gap. The other function of the research question or set of research questions is of course to direct your research in the precise direction of what you are looking for.

Each chapter in the current handbook may leave the reader with a variety of potential questions for further research. Any potential research question for your research project should fit your area of interest (step 1) and should contribute to answering your main research problem (step 2). In posing research questions, there also needs to be a reflection on layers of normativity (see chapter 16), especially with an eye to the epistemological underpinnings of the research project (see chapter 15).

17.4 Step 4: What Is It Contributing to? Showing Theoretical and Practical Relevance

If the core research question or the set of research questions is set, it is wise to take a step back and reflect on the question from the perspective of an outsider: What is the research contributing to? In other words: what is the relevance of asking these questions and how does it help if we know the answers? In research projects, we see these questions answered under the heading of "theoretical and practical relevance."

This step is helpful in aligning your research question(s) with your original reasoning for the research project (step 1). Theoretical relevance is about how answers to the research question will enrich existing theories and empirical findings on the research topic and harks back to your original examination of previous and current youth ministry literature. What contribution might your research make to the body of literature on the subject? Practical relevance is about how answers to the research question will inform the enhancement of youth ministry practices: what might practitioners in the field (on different levels, varying from youth ministers to policy makers) learn from the research project? The practical relevance harks back to your original observation of the current practices in youth ministry.

When it comes to the definition of theoretical relevance, it is important to show to what particular research tradition your research project is a contribution. Throughout this handbook we have seen different research traditions in which youth ministry research and its methodologies are rooted (see also chapter 15), e.g., large-scale data sets on youth and religion, ecclesiological studies, research in education, and children's and youth spirituality studies. And we could add more research traditions. Reflecting on theoretical relevance also means detecting the particular research tradition in which you would like to converse about the outcomes of your research project.

17.5 Step 5: How to Construct? Setting up a Research Design

Once research questions are set, the next step emerges: how do you construct your youth ministry research project? This step is about the research design of the project. In chapter 15, we learned that there are two broad categories of research paradigms within which different designs can be chosen: a quantitative research paradigm (in which one may opt for an experimental research design, for example, a quasi-experimental research design, a causal-comparative research design, a correlational, or a survey research design); and a qualitative research paradigm (in which, to give examples, one may opt for an ethnography design, a narrative design, a case study design or an action research design).

In making the choice of a particular design there are two concerns. First of all, which design has the reasonably best fit with the research questions addressed (step 3). Second, which design best fits the epistemological underpinnings of the research project (see chapter 15). In this step, it is crucial to reflect critically on the match between epistemology, the research questions, and the research design. Do they fit appropriately? And if not, what consequences does this have for the formulation of research questions (step 3), the research design (current step), or probably for the epistemological considerations at the basis of your research project.

Whatever research design you choose, there are three main themes to be addressed for the design of your choice: (a) how is data gathered (including a discussion of the procedure and the development of research instruments), (b) how is data analyzed (including a discussion on the role of concepts/theory), (c) reflection on the quality of the data in terms of validity, reliability (including generalizability) and/or trustworthiness. With regard to these three categories we again mention the importance of reflecting on layers of normativity (see chapter 16). In particular with regard to (c) we again point at the importance of doing justice to the voice of young people in your research.

The practical theological research framework we proposed in chapter 16 requests that youth ministry research follow qualitative research designs, e.g., using good interviewing techniques or ethnographical methods. By this means, data are gathered through careful observation and attentive listening, and then subsequently analyzed in such a way that appropriate language is found to communicate the results of the research. Below, we list five books that we find quite helpful for work that develops a research design along the lines of what we propose in chapter 16.

For further reading with an eye on qualitative research designs for youth ministry research we recommend the following books:

- Swinton, John, and Harriet Mowatt. *Practical Theology and Qualitative Research*. 2nd ed. London: SCM, 2016.
- Bennett, Zoë, ed. *Invitation to Research in Practical Theology*. London: Routledge, 2018.
- Court, Deborah. *Qualitative Research and Intercultural Understanding: Conducting Qualitative Research in Multicultural Settings*. London: Routledge, 2018.
- Roest, Henk de. *Collaborative Practical Theology: Engaging Practitioners in Research on Christian Practices*. Theology in Practice 8. Leiden: Brill, 2020.
- Ward, Pete, and Knut Tveitereid, eds. *The Wiley Blackwell Companion to Theology and Qualitative Research*. Hoboken, NJ: Wiley-Blackwell, 2022.

17.6 Step 6. What Do You Do? Executing the Different Phases of the Research Design

With step 6 you find yourself in the midst of the research project: you are actually executing the procedure as defined in the research design (step 5). But this step is not merely about executing. It is equally important to critically reflect on what you are doing along the way. How is it working out? There are four critical questions to be asked as part of reflection while the research is being carried out, and they refer back to the first four steps previously taken:

- What observations are particularly important in the light of the theoretical or practical relevance of the research project? Do I detect unexpected perspectives that have consequences for the relevance of the project? (Step 4)

- Do the data I gather give cause to rephrase, reframe, or add to the research questions I pose? Or does (a particular step in) the data analysis give cause for that? (Step 3)

- In what ways does my research really contribute a partial solution to the original research problem and in what ways does it enlarge or alter the original research problem? (Step 2)

- Does the research still connect with the original reason for setting up the research project or does the research shed light on other motivations and concerns? (Step 1)

The aim in addressing these critical questions along the way is to remain open to the possibility of adjusting the research design accordingly or reframing or re-embedding the research project in different or alternative ways. Thus, the answer to the question in step 6 ("what do you do?") is not merely *executing*, it is *executing and critically reflecting*. In this regard we again point at the importance of doing justice to the voices of young people. Doing justice to the voice of youth in executing the research design is important because youth ministry should not only be conceived as a practice in which theological concepts are applied, but, the other way around, also be conceived as a practice where (new) theological concepts and understanding originate.

17.7 Step 7. What Do You See? Reporting the Findings of the Research Project

How do you tell a friend about the movie you watched yesterday evening? How do you tell your partner how your day at work went? And how do you tell others about what you observe in your research project? Communicating about what you saw, what you experienced, what you learnt in everyday life situations is a complex thing. It is about choosing, selecting, and it is about narration, not merely about dry facts. It is also about individual perspectives and emotions. The same kind of complexity is involved when reporting on research findings. Actually, this reporting or communication phase, is part of the research project itself. Reporting is not something happening outside the research project but is something inherently part of it. In chapter 16 we called this "learning language."

This learning language actually comes together with doing justice to the voices of young people: "The youth ministry scholar and practitioner is continuously learning language with which revelations of God and experiences of faith can be described and theologically reflected on, in a way which is appropriate for the flesh and blood experiences of young people."[2] Whether writing a research journal article, a research report for policy makers or presenting your findings at a conference, the challenge in the reporting phase of the research project is to communicate your findings, i.e., your answers to the research questions, in such a way that it is simultaneously appropriate for the practice under study (including the voices of young people) and constructive for further academic reflection in the broader academic (youth ministry) discourse. And with the latter we are at the doorstep of step 8, our final step.

17.8 Step 8. What Do You Learn? Drawing and Discussing Conclusions

The final step in the research process is about drawing conclusions and discussing these conclusions. What do you learn from the research project with an eye to further academic reflection in the broader academic youth ministry discourse? The question "what do you learn?" should be put in the broad sense. It is not only about answers to research questions, but it is about the whole research process.

- Of course, the main findings of the research project and the answers to the research questions are an important part of the conclusion and discussion phase of the research project (step 7). But there is more.
- What can be learnt from the execution of the research design which was chosen? What worked well, what did not work and why? What consequences are there for follow-up research or for comparable research projects conducted by others? (steps 5 and 6)
- What can be learnt in terms of theory and practice(s)? What are the main contributions of the research project in terms of new theory or adjustment of theory? What are the main contributions when it

---

2. De Kock and Norheim, "Youth Ministry Research," 81.

comes to recommendations for youth ministry practices? (steps 1 and 4)

- What can be learnt in terms of research questions? Are all research questions fully answered, partially answered, or even not answered? What does that mean for re-addressing questions, probably in other contexts, reformulating questions or addressing different questions? (step 3)

- What can be learnt about the research problem? Is it partially solved? What parts of the research problem should have attention in follow-up research? Did you discover related research problems that also need to be addressed? (step 2)

Also, in step 8 we find it important to have regard to layers of normativity. We hope that the content of the current handbook, in general, is helpful in reflecting on the questions in step 8.

Bibliography

Adelson, Joseph. *Handbook of Adolescent Psychology.* Hoboken, NJ: Wiley, 2004.
Alexander, Ellen. "'Tattooed Collage'—A Perspective of Youth Culture." *Journal of Youth and Theology* 3 (2004) 37–48.
Anderson, K. R., and R. D. Reese. *Spiritual Mentoring: A Guide for Seeking and Giving Direction.* Downers Grove, IL: InterVarsity, 1999.
Anderson, Lorin W., and David R. Krathwohl, eds. *A Taxonomy for Learning, Teaching, and Assessing: A Revision of Bloom's Taxonomy of Educational Objectives.* Complete ed. New York: Longman, 2001.
Arnett, Jeffrey Jensen. *Emerging Adulthood: The Winding Road from the Late Teens through the Twenties.* Oxford: Oxford University Press, 2004.
Astley, Jeff. "The Role of Worship in Christian Learning." *Religious Education* 79 (1984) 243–51.
Bailey, David. "Enacted Faith, Youth Ministry, and Theological Shorthand." *Journal of Youth and Theology* 13 (2014) 25–39.
———. "Living amongst the Fragments of a Coherent Theology." *Journal of Youth and Theology* 15 (2016) 173–95.
Baker, Dori Grinenko. "Evoking Testimony through Holy Listening: The Art of Interview as a Practice in Youth Ministry." *Journal of Youth and Theology* 4 (2005) 53–68.
Baker, Jonny. "Ritual as Strategic Practice." In *The Rite Stuff: Ritual in Contemporary Christian Worship and Mission*, edited by Pete Ward, 85–95. Oxford: Bible Reading Fellowship, 2004.
Baker, Samuel E. "Raised a Teenage Kataphatic." *Journal of Youth and Theology* 14 (2015) 45–71.
Baring, Rito V. "Analyzing Empirical Notions of Suffering: Advancing Youth Dialogue and Education." *Religious Education* 105 (2010) 157–74.
Barrett, Justin L., et al. "Different Styles Reach Different Kids: An Empirical Enquiry into Young Life Camping Outreach Programs in the USA and Europe." *Journal of Youth and Theology* 8 (2009) 10–27.
Bass, Dorothy C., and Don C. Richter. *Way to Live: Christian Practices for Teens.* Nashville: Upper Room, 2002.
Bebbington, David. *Evangelicalism in Modern Britain: A History from the 1730s to the 1980s.* London: Unwin Hyman, 1989.
Becker, Ron. "Beyond a Godless Understanding of Youth: Why Exegesis Matters to Youth Ministry." *Journal of Youth and Theology* 5 (2006) 10–30.

Bennett, Zoë, ed. *Invitation to Research in Practical Theology*. London: Routledge, 2018.
Benzaquèn, Adriana S. "Thought and Utopia in the Writings of Adorno, Horkheimer, and Benjamin." *Utopian Studies* 9 (1998) 149–61.
Blier, Helen, and Graham Stanton. "Wide-Awakeness in the World." *Journal of Youth and Theology* 17 (2018) 3–20.
Bloom, Benjamin Samuel. *Taxonomy of Educational Objectives: The Classification of Educational Goals Handbook I*. New York: McKay, 1956.
Blount, Reginald. "Toward Whole-Making: The Power of Voice in the Faith Formation of Black Youth." *Journal of Youth and Theology* 10 (2011) 35–47.
Borgman, Dean. *Foundations for Youth Ministry: Theological Engagement with Teen Life and Culture*. 2nd ed. Grand Rapids: Baker Academic, 2013.
———. *Hear My Story: Understanding the Cries of Troubled Youth*. Peabody, MA: Hendrickson, 2003.
———. *When Kumbaya Is Not Enough: A Practical Theology for Youth Ministry*. Peabody, MA: Hendrickson, 1997.
Boschki, Reinhold. "Re-reading Martin Buber and Janusz Korczak: Fresh Impulses toward a Relational Approach to Religious Education." *Religious Education* 100 (2005) 114–26.
Brandes, Melissa Ann. "Integrated Spiritual Development: A New Approach to Nurturing Adolescent Spirituality and Faith." *Religious Education* 113 (2018) 191–202.
Brelsford, Theodore. "Educating for Formative Participation in Communities of Faith." *Religious Education* 96 (2001) 310–25.
Bronfenbrenner, Urie. *The Ecology of Human Development*. Cambridge: Harvard University Press, 1979.
Bronfenbrenner, Urie., and P. Morris. "The Ecology of Developmental Process." In *Handbook of Child Psychology*, edited by W. Damon, and R. M. Lerner, 1:993–1028. New York: Wiley & Sons, 1998.
Browning, Don S. *A Fundamental Practical Theology: Descriptive and Strategic Proposals*. Minneapolis: Fortress, 1991.
Brueggemann, Walter. *The Prophetic Imagination*. Minneapolis: Fortress, 2001.
Buschmann, Gerd. "Jugendkultur 'Techno' – Säkularisierte Religiosität in der Postmoderne?!" *International Journal of Practical Theology* 5 (2001) 184–204.
Campbell-Reed, Eileen R., and Christian Scharen. "Ethnography on Holy Ground: How Qualitative Interviewing Is Practical Theological Work." *International Journal of Practical Theology* 17 (2013) 232–59.
Canales, Arthur David. "Models for Adolescent Ministry: Exploring Eight Ecumenical Examples." *Religious Education* 101 (2006) 204–32.
———. "Models of Christian Leadership in Youth Ministry." *Religious Education* 109 (2014) 24–44.
Cannister, Mark W. "Moratorium Matters: Creating a Fertile Environment for Faith Formation." *Journal of Youth and Theology* 12 (2013) 23–44.
———. "Youth Ministry's Historical Context: The Education and Evangelism of Young People." In *Starting Right: Thinking Theologically about Youth Ministry*, edited by Kenda Creasy Dean et al., 94–110. Grand Rapids: Youth Specialities, 2001.
Capes, David B. "Imitatio Christi and the Gospel Genre." *Bulletin for Biblical Research* 13 (2003) 1–19.

Carroll, Colleen. *The New Faithful: Why Young Adults Are Embracing Christian Orthodoxy*. Chicago: Loyola, 2002.

Chiroma, Nathan Hussaini. "The Role of Mentoring in Adolescents' Spiritual Formation." *Journal of Youth and Theology* 14 (2015) 72–90.

Clark, Chap, ed. *Youth Ministry in the 21st Century: Five Views*. Youth, Family, and Culture. Grand Rapids: Baker Academic, 2015.

Cloete, Anita. "Spiritual Formation as Focus of Youth Ministry." *Nederduitse Gereformeerde Teologiese Tydskrif* 53 (2013) 70–77.

Cohen-Malayev, Maya, et al. "Religious Exploration in a Modern World: The Case of Modern-Orthodox Jews in Israel." *Identity* 9 (2009) 233–51.

Counted, Victor. "The Psychology of Youth Faith Formation." *Journal of Youth and Theology* 15 (2016) 146–72.

Court, Deborah. *Qualitative Research and Intercultural Understanding: Conducting Qualitative Research in Multicultural Settings*. Londen: Routledge, 2018.

Crain, Margaret Ann. "Looking at People and Asking 'Why?': An Ethnographic Approach to Religious Education." *Religious Education* 96 (2001) 386–94.

Cray, Graham. *Postmodern Culture and Youth Discipleship: Commitment or Looking Cool?* Cambridge: Grove, 1998.

Davie, Grace. *Europe, the Exceptional Case: Parameters of Faith in the Modern World*. Sarum Theological Lectures. London: Darton, Longman & Todd, 2002.

Davis, Gary L. "Spiritual Direction: A Model for Adolescent Catechesis." *Religious Education* 81 (1986) 267–79.

De Bruin-Wassinkmaat, Anne-Marije. "Finding One's Own Way: Exploring the Religious Identity Development of Emerging Adults Raised in Strictly Reformed Contexts in the Netherlands." PhD diss., Protestant Theological University, 2021.

De Bruin-Wassinkmaat, Anne-Marije, et al. "Being Young and Strictly Religious: A Review of the Literature on the Religious Identity Development of Strictly Religious Adolescents." *Identity* 19 (2019) 62–79.

De Kock, Jos. "Being a Church through Religious Learning at the Street Level." *Ecclesial Practices* 2 (2015) 217–34.

———. "Catechists' Conceptions of Their Catechetical Learning Environments." *International Journal for the Study of the Christian Church* 14 (2014) 3–21.

———. "Challenges to Apprenticeship Learning in Religious Education: Narrow Use of the Apprenticeship Model and Current Developments in Youth Ministry." *Religious Education* 112 (2017) 232–41.

———. "Promising Approaches to Catechesis in Church Communities: Towards a Research Framework." *International Journal of Practical Theology* 16 (2012) 176–96.

———. "Schools and Religious Communities' Contributions to the Religious Formation of Christian Youth." *International Journal of Christianity and Education* 19 (2015) 121–34.

———. "Theologiseren met Kinderen als Construerende Theologie." *Handelingen* 42 (2015) 59–66.

———. "A Typology of Catechetical Learning Environments." *International Journal of Practical Theology* 18 (2014) 264–86.

———. *Wait a Minute in Stressful Times. A Practical Theological Account of Learning in Encounter*. Leuven: ETF, 2019.

———. "What about Learning in Practical Theological Studies? Toward More Conceptual Clarity." *SAGE Open* 5 (2015) 1–12.

De Kock, Jos, and Bård E. Hallesby Norheim. "Youth Ministry Research and the Empirical." *International Journal of Practical Theology* 22 (2018) 69–83.

De Kock, Jos, and Ronelle Sonnenberg. "Embodiment: Reflections on Religious Learning in Youth Ministry." *Journal of Youth and Theology* 11 (2012) 7–22.

De Kock, Jos, et al. "Beyond Individualisation: Neo-Evangelical Lessons for Religious Socialisation." *Journal of Beliefs & Values* 32 (2011) 329–42.

De Kock, Jos, et al. "The Comeback of Parents in Catechesis Practices." *Journal of Youth and Theology* 14 (2015) 155–71.

De Kock, Jos, et al. "Normativity in Empirical Youth Ministry Research." *Journal of Youth and Theology* 17 (2018) 81–103.

De Lange, Erlinde, and Bert Roebben. "Seven Propositions on Sacramental Youth Catechesis in the Roman-Catholic Church." *Journal of Youth and Theology* 1 (2002) 47–63.

De Roest, Henk. *Collaborative Practical Theology: Engaging Practitioners in Research on Christian Practices*. Theology in Practice 8. Leiden: Brill, 2020.

De Roos, Simone A. "Young Children's God Concepts: Influences of Attachment and Religious Socialization in a Family and School Context." *Religious Education* 101 (2006) 84–103.

Dean, Kenda Creasy. *Almost Christian: What the Faith of Our Teenagers Is Telling the American Church*. Oxford: Oxford University Press, 2010.

———. "The New Rhetoric of Youth Ministry." *Journal of Youth and Theology* 2 (2003) 8–19.

———, ed. *OMG: A Youth Ministry Handbook*. Nashville: Abingdon, 2010.

———. *Practicing Passion: Youth and the Quest for a Passionate Church*. Grand Rapids: Eerdmans, 2004.

———. "Proclaiming Salvation: Youth Ministry for the Twenty-First Century Church." *Theology Today* 56 (2000) 524–39.

———. "Reflections on the Future of Youth Ministry: Practicing Youthfulness: Youth Ministry as an Ecclesial Laboratory." *Journal of Youth and Theology* 10 (2011) 79–92.

Dean, Kenda Creasy, and Ron Foster. *The Godbearing Life: The Art of Soul Tending for Youth Ministry*. Nashville: Upper Room, 1998.

Dean, Kenda Creasy, et al., eds. *Starting Right: Thinking Theologically about Youth Ministry*. Grand Rapids: Youth Specialties, 2001.

DePaola, Tomie. *The Clown of God*. New York: Simon Schuster, 2018.

Domsgen, Michael. "Plädoyer für eine systemische Religionspädagogik." *International Journal of Practical Theology* 11 (2007) 1–18.

Douglass, Katherine M. "Aesthetic Learning Theory and the Faith Formation of Young Adults." *Religious Education* 108 (2013) 449–66.

Drury, Amanda Hontz. *Saying Is Believing: The Necessity of Testimony in Adolescent Spiritual Development*. Downers Grove, IL: IVP Academic, 2015.

Ducksworth, Jessicah Krey. *Wide Welcome: How the Unsettling Presence of Newcomers Can Save the Church*. Minneapolis: Fortress, 2013.

Edie, Fred P. "Considering the *Ordo* as Pedagogical Context for Religious Education with Christian High School Youth." *Religious Education* 100 (2005) 266–79.

Ellis, Wesley W. "Human Beings and Human Becomings." *Journal of Youth and Theology* 14 (2015) 119–37.
Emery-Wright, Steve. "A Qualitative Study Construction of How 14–16 Year Olds Understand Worship." *Journal of Youth and Theology* 2 (2003) 64–77.
Emery-Wright, Steven. *Now That Was Worship: Hearing the Voices of Young People*. 2nd ed. Calver: Cliff College, 2012.
Emery-Wright, Steven, and Ed Mackenzie. *Networks for Faith Formation: Relational Bonds and the Spiritual Growth of Youth*. Eugene, OR: Wipf & Stock, 2017.
Engebretson, Kathleen. "Young People, Culture, and Spirituality: Some Implications for Ministry." *Religious Education* 98 (2003) 5–24.
Erikson, Erik H. *Identity, Youth, and Crisis*. New York: Norton, 1968.
Estep, James Riley, Jr. "Spiritual Formation as Social: Toward a Vygotskyan Developmental Perspective." *Religious Education* 97 (2002) 141–64.
Faix, Tobias. *Gottesvorstellungen Bei Jugendlichen: Eine Qualitative Erhebung Aus Der Sicht Empirischer Missionswissenschaft*. Empirische Theologie 16. Berlin: Lit, 2007.
———. "How Theology Takes Shape in the Faith of Young People: An Introduction to Youth Theology Based on the Example of an Empirical-Theological Study among Young People." *Journal of Youth and Theology* 13 (2014) 6–24.
———. "Hybrid Identity: Youth in Digital Networks." *Journal of Youth and Theology* 15 (2016) 65–87.
———. "Semantics of Faith: Methodology and Results regarding Young People's Ability to Speak about Their Beliefs." *Journal of Empirical Theology* 27 (2014) 36–56.
Fields, Doug. *Purpose-Driven Youth Ministry*. Grand Rapids: Zondervan, 1998.
Fisherman, Shraga. "Development of Religious Identity through Doubts among Religious Adolescents in Israel: An Empirical Perspective and Educational Ramifications." *Religious Education* 111 (2016) 119–36.
———. "Ego Identity and Spiritual Identity in Religious Observant Adolescents in Israel." *Religious Education* 99 (2004) 371–84.
Flatt, Kevin N., and D. Millard Haskell. "Participant Experiences at a Charismatic Catholic Youth Rally: What Happens When Participant Socialization and Organizer Intentions Do Not Match?" *Religious Education* 111 (2016) 137–52.
Fleischer, Barbara J. "The Ministering Community as Context for Religious Education: A Case Study of St. Gabriel's Catholic Parish." *Religious Education* 101 (2006) 104–22.
Fortosis, Stephen. "Theological Foundations for a Stage Model of Spiritual Formation." *Religious Education* 96 (2001) 49–63.
Fortosis, Steve. "A Developmental Model for Stages of Growth in Christian Formation." *Religious Education* 87 (1992) 283–98.
Fowler, James W. *Becoming Adult, Becoming Christian: Adult Development and Christian Faith*. San Francisco: Harper & Row, 1984.
———. *Stages of Faith: The Psychology of Human Development and the Quest for Meaning*. San Francisco: Harper & Row, 1981.
Frambach, Nathan. "Seen & Heard: A Theology of Childhood." *Journal of Youth and Theology* 4 (2005) 33–50.
Francis, Leslie J. "Christianity and Dogmatism Revisited: A Study among Fifteen and Sixteen Year Olds in the United Kingdom." *Religious Education* 96 (2001) 211–26.
———. "The Relationship between Bible Reading and Attitude toward Substance Use among 13–15 Year Olds." *Religious Education* 97 (2002) 44–60.

Friedeburg, Ludwig von, ed. *Jugend in der modernen Gesellschaft*. Neue wissenschaftliche Bibliothek Soziologie 5. 8th ed. Köln: Kiepenheuer & Witsch, 1976.

Ganzevoort, R. Ruard, and Johan Roeland. "Lived Religion: The Praxis of Practical Theology." *International Journal of Practical Theology* 18 (2014) 91–101.

Gärtner, Claudia, and Karin Kempfer. "Jugendverbände in die Schule? Empirische Erkundungen in einem Kooperationsprojekt von Ganztagsschule und katholischer Jugendverbandsarbeit." *International Journal of Practical Theology* 20 (2016) 26–50.

Gärtner, Stefan. "Education through and to Love—Sexuality as a Source of Conflict in German Pastoral Care of Youth and the Possibilities of Practice in Sex Education." *Journal of Youth and Theology* 2 (2003) 93–103.

Gennerich, Carsten, and Andreas Feige. "Jugend und Religion in neuer Perspektive: Empirisch valide Forschungsergebnisse durch eine theoretisch angemessene Fundierung." *International Journal of Practical Theology* 13 (2009) 22–45.

Girard, Renè. *The Scapegoat*. Baltimore: Johns Hopkins University Press, 1986.

———. *Violence and the Sacred*. Baltimore: Johns Hopkins University Press, 1972.

Goodliff, Andy. "Can the Christian Gospel Speak to the Experience of Young People Today?" *Journal of Youth and Theology* 3 (2004) 41–54.

Griffiths, Steve. *A Christlike Ministry*. Haverhill: YTC, 2008.

———. *Models for Youth Ministry: Learning from the Life of Christ*. London: SPCK, 2013.

———. "'Negotiating *Orthoyatra*': A Rationale for Anglican Youth Ministry." *Journal of Youth and Theology* 9 (2010) 24–36.

Haga, Joar, and Bård Eirik Hallesby Norheim. "The Four Speeches Every Youth Leader Has to Know: The Preaching of Jesus as Model for a Public Rhetoric for Youth Ministry." *Journal of Youth and Theology* 18 (2019) 164–84.

Haitch, Russell. "Free as a Bird in the Path of the Plane: Youthful Liberty amid Global Forces." *Journal of Youth and Theology* 10 (2011) 4–22.

Hankiss, Elemér. *Fears and Symbols: An Introduction to the Study of Western Civilization*. Budapest: CEU, 2001.

Hart, Peter. "Professional Boundaries in the Practice of Youth Ministry: An Ethnographic Study of the Limits of Relationships." *Journal of Youth and Theology* 13 (2014) 24–41.

Have, Paul ten. *Doing Conversation Analysis*. Los Angeles: SAGE, 2007.

Heifetz, Ronald A. *Leadership without Easy Answers*. Cambridge: Belknap, 1994.

Heifetz, Ronald, et al. *The Practice of Adaptive Leadership*. Boston: Harvard Business Press, 2009.

Heimbrock, Hans-Günter. "Practical Theology as Empirical Theology." *International Journal of Practical Theology* 14 (2011) 153–70.

Hess, Mary E. "Collaborating with People to Study 'the Popular': Implementing Participatory Action Research Strategies in Religious Education." *Religious Education* 96 (2001) 271–93.

Hindman, David M. "From Splintered Lives to Whole Persons: Facilitating Spiritual Development in College Students." *Religious Education* 97 (2002) 165–82.

Holmes, Urban T. *A History of Christian Spirituality: An Analytical Introduction*. Harrisburg, PA: Morehouse, 2002.

Höring, Patrik C. "Koinonia: A Roman Catholic Perspective on a Theological Pattern for Youth Ministry in Church as a Community." *Journal of Youth and Theology* 12 (2013) 46–57.

Horner, Robyn. "Towards a Hermeneutic-Phenomenological Methodology for Theology." *International Journal of Practical Theology* 22 (2018) 153–73.

Hryniuk, Michael. "Creating Space for God: Toward a Spirituality of Youth Ministry." *Religious Education* 100 (2005) 139–56.

Hudson, Chris. "Community, Identity, & Youth Ministry." *Journal of Youth and Theology* 1 (2002) 22–33.

Hütter, Reinhard. *Suffering Divine Things: Theology as Church Practice*. Grand Rapids: Eerdmans, 2000.

Hyde, Brendan. "Godly Play Nourishing Children's Spirituality: A Case Study." *Religious Education* 105 (2010) 504–18.

Hyde, Kenneth E. *Religion in Childhood and Adolescence: A Comprehensive Review of the Research*. Birmingham: Religious Education, 1990.

International Association for the Student of Youth Ministry. "About IASYM." https://www.iasym.net/.

Jaeger, Werner. *Paideia: The Ideals of Greek Culture*. Vol. 1, *Archaic Greece, the Mind of Athens*. Oxford: Oxford University Press, 1967.

James, Richard. "Discovering Jesus as a Postmodern Young Person." *Journal of Youth and Theology* 3 (2004) 55–74.

Jenson, Robert W. "Hermeneutics and the Life of the Church." In *Reclaiming the Bible for the Church*, edited by Carl E. Braaten and Robert W. Jenson, 89–106. Grand Rapids: Eerdmans, 1995.

———. *Systematic Theology*. Vol. 1, *The Triune God*. Oxford: Oxford University Press, 1997.

Johnstone, Carlton. "Faith Crossroads and Social Networks: The Transition from Inherited Faith to Owned Faith." *Journal of Youth and Theology* 8 (2009) 43–59.

Jones, Timothy Paul. "The Basis of James W. Fowler's Understanding of Faith in the Research of Wilfred Cantwell Smith: An Examination from an Evangelical Perspective." *Religious Education* 99 (2004) 345–57.

Jones, Tony. *Soul Shaper*. Grand Rapids: Zondervan, 2003.

Kaethler, Andrew. "Towards an Adolescent Hermeneutic." *Journal of Youth and Theology* 5 (2006) 31–50.

Kageler, Len. "Burnout among Religious Youth Workers: A Cross National Analysis." *Journal of Youth and Theology* (2010) 8–23.

———. "Youth and Youth Ministry in Non-Christian Religious Traditions." *Journal of Youth and Theology* 2 (2003) 29–38.

———. *Youth Ministry in a Multifaith Society: Forming Christian Identity among Skeptics, Syncretists, & Sincere Believers of Other Faiths*. Downers Grove, IL: IVP Books, 2014.

Kang, S. Steve. "Reflections upon Methodology: Research on Themes of Self Construction and Self Integration in the Narrative of Second Generation Korean American Young Adults." *Religious Education* 96 (2001) 408–15.

———. "The Socioculturally Constructed Multivoiced Self as a Framework for Christian Education of Second-Generation Korean American Young Adults." *Religious Education* 97 (2002) 81–96.

Kaster, Jeffrey. "Evaluating Adolescent Catechesis." *Religious Education* 106 (2011) 63–81.

Kaufman, Tone Strangeland. "A New Old Spirituality for Youth Ministry? Christian Discipleship and Practice in the Norwegian CrossRoad Movement." *Journal of Youth and Theology* 11 (2012) 40–58.

Kaufman, Tone Stangeland, and Astrid Sandsmark. "Spaces of Possibilities: The Role of Artifacts in Religious Learning Processes for Vulnerable Youth." *Journal of Youth and Theology* 14 (2015) 138–54.

Kelman, Rabbi Stuart. "The Rabbinic Leader and the Volunteer Leader." *Religious Education* (2002) 322–34.

King, Mike. *Presence-Centered Youth Ministry: Guiding Students into Spiritual Formation.* Downers Grove, IL: IVP, 2006.

Kirgiss, Crystal. *In Search of Adolescence: A New Look at an Old Idea.* San Diego: Youth Cartel, 2015.

Kolb, Robert, and Timothy J. Wengert, eds. *The Book of Concord: The Confessions of the Evangelical Lutheran Church.* Minneapolis: Fortress, 2000.

Kotter, John. *Leading Change.* Boston: Harvard Business Review, 1996.

Lathrop, Gordon, and Timothy J. Wengert. *Christian Assembly: Marks of the Church in a Pluralistic Age.* Minneapolis: Fortress, 2004.

Lewis, Jennifer. "Girl Power Gone Right in Exodus 1–2: Miriam as Model for Contemporary Youth." *Journal of Youth and Theology* 18 (2019) 3–18.

Linhart, Terry. *The Self-Aware Leader: Discovering Your Blindspots to Reach Your Ministry Potential.* Downers Grove, IL: IVP Books, 2017.

Luther, Martin. *Luther Works.* Vol 31, *Career of the Reformer I.* Edited by Helmut T. Lehmann. Philadelphia: Fortress, 1957.

———. *Luther Works.* Vol 37, *Word and Sacrament III.* Edited by Robert H. Fischer and Helmut T. Lehmann. Philadelphia: Fortress, 2004.

———. *Martin Luther Studienausgabe.* Edited by Hans-Ulrich Delius. 5 vols. Berlin: Evangelische Verlagsanstalt, 1979–92.

Lytle, Julie A. "Virtual Incarnations: An Exploration of Internet-Mediated Interaction as Manifestation of the Divine." *Religious Education* 105 (2010) 395–412.

Maffesoli, Michel. *The Times of the Tribe: The Decline of Individualism in Mass Society.* London: SAGE, 1996.

Magrini, Cheryl T. "Children's Interpretations of Biblical Meal Stories: Ethnographic Intertextual Voicing as the Practice of Hospitable Pedagogy." *Religious Education* 101 (2006) 60–83.

Maiko, Saneto. "A Psycho-Theological Synopsis of Youth Culture and Faith in Africa." *Journal of Youth and Theology* 3 (2004) 28–36.

Mannheim, K. "Das Problem der Generationen (1928/29)." In *Jugend in der modernen Gesellschaft*, edited by Ludwig von Friedeburg, 23–48. Neue wissenschaftliche Bibliothek Soziologie 5. 8th ed. Köln: Kiepenheuer & Witsch, 1976.

Manning, Patrick R. "Engaging Our Symbols, Sharing Our World: Forming Young People around Symbols for Participation in the Public Sphere." *Religious Education* 109 (2014) 440–54.

Marcia, James E. "Development and Validation of Ego-Identity Status." *Journal of Personality and Social Psychology* 3 (1966) 551–58.

Martin, Robert K. "Education and the Liturgical Life of the Church." *Religious Education* 98 (2003) 43–64.

———. "Having Faith in our Faith in God: Toward a Critical Realist Epistemology for Christian Education." *Religious Education* 96 (2001) 245–61.

Mattes, Mark C. "The Thomistic Turn in Evangelical Catholic Ethics." *Lutheran Quarterly* 16 (2002) 65–100.

Matthaei, Sondra Higgins. "Rethinking Faith Formation." *Religious Education* 99 (2004) 56–70.

McAdams, Dan. P. "Personal Narratives and the Life Story." In *Handbook of Personality: Theory and Research*, edited by Oliver P. John et al., 241–61. 3rd ed. New York: Guilford, 2008.

McCarty, Robert J., and Laurie Delgatto, eds. *The Vision of Catholic Youth Ministry: Fundamentals, Theory, and Practice*. Winona, MN: Saint Mary's, 2005.

McGrath, Alister E. "The Cultivation of Theological Vision: Theological Attentiveness and the Practice of Ministry." In *Perspectives on Ecclesiology and Ethnography*, edited by Pete Ward, 107–23. Grand Rapids: Eerdmans, 2012.

McGuire, Meredith B. *Religion: The Social Context*. Long Grove, IL: Waveland, 2002.

McQuillan, Paul. "Youth Ministry in a World of Diversity: A Review of the International Research Project on Youth Spirituality." *Journal of Youth and Theology* 6 (2007) 70–91.

———. "Youth Spirituality—A Reality in Search of Expression." *Journal of Youth and Theology* 3 (2004) 8–25.

Mercer, Joyce Ann. *Welcoming Children: A Practical Theology of Childhood*. St. Louis: Chalice, 2005.

Moltmann, Jürgen. *The Way of Jesus Christ: Christology in Messianic Dimensions*. Minneapolis: Fortress, 1993.

Moore, Mary Elizabeth, and Joseph Kyser. "Youth Finding and Claiming Religious Voice: Coming Out Religiously in an Interreligious Multivalent World." *Religious Education* 109 (2014) 455–70.

Muchová, Ludmila, and František Štěch. "Sustainable Youth Ministry—Between Human and Divine." *Journal of Youth and Theology* 11 (2012) 59–72.

Myers, Jeremy. "Adolescent Experiences of Christ's Presence and Activity in the Evangelical Lutheran Church in America." *Journal of Youth and Theology* 7 (2008) 27–43.

Myers, William R. "Youth Ministry after Christendom." *Religious Education* 111 (2016) 170–81.

Nagle, James Michael. "Learning to Leave: Expanding Shared Praxis to Understand the Religious Life and Learning of Young Catholics Beyond the Church." *Religious Education* 114 (2019) 528–43.

Nagy, Timothy. "Lens of Liminality: A Reflection on Faith Sharing in Young Adult Retreat Ministry." *Journal of Youth and Theology* 17 (2018) 40–60.

Nash, Sally. "A Reflective Practitioner and Lifelong Learner." In *Christian Youth Work in Theory and Practice*, edited by Sally Nash and Jo Whitehead, 16–29. London: SCM, 2014.

Nel, Malan. "Methodological: What We Do Is Practical Theology." In *Youth Ministry: An Inclusive Missional Approach*, 3–18. HTS Religion & Society Series 1. Cape Town: AOSIS, 2018.

———. "Why Theology? It Is Only Youth Ministry." *Journal of Youth and Theology* 4 (2005) 9–22.

———. "Youth Ministry as Practical Theology: Making a Case for Youth Ministry as an Academic Discipline." *Journal of Youth and Theology* 2 (2003) 68–83.
Nipkow, Karl Ernst. "Theologie des Kindes und Kindertheologie." *Zeitschrift für Theologie und Kirche* 103 (2006) 422–42.
Norheim, Bård Eirik Hallesby. "The Christian Story of the Body as the Ritual Plot for Youth Ministry." *Journal of Youth and Theology* 15 (2016) 88–106.
———. "'Confessionality' in Youth Ministry." *Journal of Youth and Theology* 10 (2011) 48–64.
———. "Cultivating a Vision of the Unseen: The Apophatic Mode in Ecclesiological Research." *Ecclesial Practices* 2 (2015) 40–56.
———. "From Ghetto to Communitas: Post-Soviet Youth Ministry and Leadership on a Pilgrimage to Emmaus." *Journal of Youth and Theology* 5 (2006) 67–84.
———. "The Global Youth Culture: Targeting and Involving Youth in Global Mission." In *The Church Going Glocal: Mission and Globalisation*, edited by Tormod Engelsviken et al., 168–75. Oxford: Regnum, 2011.
———. "Naming Glocal Fear in Local Youth Ministry—And the Migrating Presence of Christ." *European Journal of Theology* 26 (2017) 162–72.
———. "Den norske kyrkjas retoriske sjølvforståing i valfridomens tidsalder: Å leva med frykta for å bli avvist." *Luthersk Kirketidende* 18 (2018) 408–11.
———. *Practicing Baptism: Christian Practices and the Presence of Christ*. Eugene, OR: Pickwick, 2014.
———. "Practicing Baptism: The Church as Communio and Congregatio *Sanctorum*. Rethinking Ecclesiology in the Context of Nordic Youth Ministry." *Journal of Youth and Theology* 9 (2010) 37–55.
———. "The Presence of Christ in Qualitative Research: Four Models and an Epilogue." In *The Wiley Blackwell Companion to Theology and Qualitative Research*, edited by Pete Ward and Knut Tveitereid, 514–24. Hoboken, NJ: Wiley-Blackwell, 2022.
Norheim, Bård, and Joar Haga. *The Four Speeches Every Leader Has to Know*. London: Palgrave Macmillan, 2020.
Norheim, Bård Eirik Hallesby, and Knut Tveitereid. "'Stemning har ikke noe med selve kirkerommet å gjøre': Unges utforming av gudstjenesterommet." In *Skjønnhet og tilbedelse*, edited by Svein Rise and Knut-Willy Sæther, 229–45. Oslo: Akademika forlag, 2013.
Noval, Christian. "Wired for Holiness: A Theological Anthropology of Youth Based on David Kelsey's 'Eccentric Existence.'" PhD diss., Rheinische Friedrich-Wilhelms-Universität, 2018.
———. "Youth and Creation: A Biblical Theology of Growth & Development." *Journal of Youth and Theology* 12 (2013) 35–45.
O'Gorman, Robert T. "Imagination Embodied: The Sacraments Reappropriated." *Religious Education* 111 (2016) 430–46.
Ojala, Eveliina. "Finnish Confirmands' Social Media Use and Experience of the Sense of Community – How They Are Reflected in Confirmands' Community Perceptions about Their Parish." *Journal of Youth and Theology* 17 (2018) 150–77.
Osmer, Richard R. "Practical Theology: A Current International Perspective." *HTS Teologiese Studies / Theological Studies* 67 (2011) 1–7.
———. *Practical Theology. An Introduction*. Grand Rapids: Eerdmans, 2008.

Osmer, Richard R., and Kenda Creasy Dean, eds. *Youth, Religion, and Globalization: New Research in Practical Theology*. International Practical Theology 3. Berlin: Lit, 2006.
Ospino, Hosffman. "Theological Horizons for a Pedagogy of Accompaniment." *Religious Education* 105 (2010) 413–29.
Parmach, Robert J. "Christian Families, Educative Lenses, and Incarnational Roots 1." *Religious Education* 103 (2008) 62–83.
Pearson, Clive, and Christine Gapes. "A Kick in the Theological Shins: Constructing a Theology for Youth Ministry." *Journal of Youth and Theology* 1 (2002) 9–21.
Peek, Lori. "Becoming Muslim: The Development of a Religious Identity." *Sociology of Religion* 66 (2005) 215–42.
Penn, David S. "Against the Generation Gap: Thinking 'Otherwise' about Adolescence." *Religious Education* 113 (2018) 61–72.
Prins, Rian. "Values to Be Caught and Taught: The Response of the Church to the Teenage Moral Dilemma." *Journal of Youth and Theology* 1 (2002) 23–35.
Rahn, Dave. "Focusing Youth Ministry through Student Leadership." In *Starting Right: Thinking Theologically about Youth Ministry*, edited by Kenda Creasy Dean et al., 199–216. Grand Rapids: Zondervan, 2001.
Reddie, Anthony. "Re-thinking Biblical and Theological Perspectives: Christian Nurture of Children." *International Journal of Practical Theology* 14 (2011) 171–88.
Riegel, Ulrich, and Katharina Kindermann. "Tracing Informal Religious Learning." *International Journal of Practical Theology* 19 (2015) 122–37.
Rodkey, Christopher Demuth. "The Practice of Music in Youth Ministry and the Mystery of the Divine." *Journal of Youth and Theology* 5 (2006) 47–62.
Roebben, Bert. "International Developments in Youth Ministry Research: A Comparative Review." *Religious Education* 107 (2012) 192–206.
———. "Light of Day Scaffolding a Theology of Youth Ministry." *Journal of Youth and Theology* 4 (2005) 23–32.
———. *Seeking Sense in the City: European Perspectives on Religious Education*. Berlin: LIT, 2009.
———. "Shaping a Playground for Transcendence: Postmodern Youth Ministry as a Radical Challenge." *Religious Education* 92 (1997) 332–47.
Roehlkepartain, Eugene C., ed. *The Handbook of Spiritual Development in Childhood and Adolescence*. The Sage Program on Applied Developmental Science. Thousand Oaks, CA: SAGE, 2006.
Root, Andrew. *The Children of Divorce: The Loss of Family as the Loss of Being*. Grand Rapids: Baker Academic, 2010.
———. *Christopraxis: A Practical Theology of the Cross*. Minneapolis: Fortress, 2014.
———. *The End of Youth Ministry: Why Parents Don't Really Care about Youth Groups and What Youth Workers Should Do About It*. Grand Rapids: Baker Academic, 2020.
———. *Faith Formation in a Secular Age: Responding to the Church's Obsession with Youthfulness*. Grand Rapids: Baker Academic, 2017.
———. "God's Hiddenness, Absence, and Doubt: The Theology of the Cross as Theological Direction for Youth Ministry." *Journal of Youth and Theology* 8 (2009) 60–76.
———. *The Pastor in a Secular Age: Ministry to People Who No Longer Need a God*. Grand Rapids: Baker Academic, 2019.

———. "Regulating the Empirical in Practical Theology." *Journal of Youth and Theology* 15 (2016) 44–64.
———. *The Relational Pastor*. Downers Grove, IL: InterVarsity, 2013.
———. "Relationality as the Objective of Incarnational Ministry: A Reexamination of the Theological Foundations of Adolescent Ministry." *Journal of Youth and Theology* 3 (2004) 97–113.
———. *Relationships Unfiltered: Help for Youth Workers, Volunteers, and Parents on Creating Authentic Relationships*. Grand Rapids: Zondervan, 2009.
———. *Revisiting Relational Youth Ministry: From a Strategy of Influence to a Theology of Incarnation*. Downers Grove, IL: IVP Books, 2007.
———. *Taking Theology to Youth Ministry*. Grand Rapids: Youth Specialties, 2012.
———. "Youth Ministry as Discerning Christopraxis: A Hermeneutical Model." *Journal of Youth and Theology* 6 (2007) 9–30.
Root, Andrew, and Kenda Creasy Dean. *The Theological Turn in Youth Ministry*. Downers Grove, IL: IVP Books, 2011.
Rosa, Hartmut. *Resonance: A Sociology of Our Relationship to the World*. Cambridge: Polity, 2019.
Rymarz, Richard. "Catechesis and Religious Education in Canadian Catholic Schools." *Religious Education* 106 (2011) 537–49.
———. "Going Beyond the Plateau: Ministry to Young Catholic Adults in the Third Millennium." *Journal of Youth and Theology* 9 (2010) 78–93.
———. "Reaching the Plateau: A Follow Up Study on Active Adolescent Catholics." *Journal of Youth and Theology* 6 (2007) 9–23.
Savage, Sara, et al. *Making Sense of Generation Y: The World View of 15–25 Year Olds*. London: Church House, 2006.
Scanlan, Mark. *An Interweaving Ecclesiology: The Church, Mission, and Young People*. London: SCM, 2021.
———. "Youth Ministry Creating Ecclesial Space: The Work and History of 'Urban Saints' and the Development of Ecclesiological Thinking within Youth Ministry." *Journal of Youth and Theology* 14 (2015) 7–24.
Schachter, Elli P., and Jonathan J. Ventura. "Identity Agents: Parents as Active and Reflective Participants in Their Children's Identity Formation." *Journal of Research on Adolescence* 18 (2008) 449–76.
Scharmer, Otto, and Katrin Kaufer. *Leading from the Emerging Future: From Ego-System to Eco-System Economics*. Oakland: Berett-Koehler, 2013.
Schlink, Edmund. *Theology of the Lutheran Confessions*. St. Louis: Augsburg Fortress, 1961.
Schoon Tanis, Gretchen. *Making Jesus Attractive: The Ministry and Message of Young Life*. Eugene, OR: Wipf & Stock, 2016.
Schwab, Ulrich. "'. . . try and find the thread . . .' The Relationship between Generations in Youth Ministry—Covering Also the Issue of Family and Faith." *Journal of Youth and Theology* 7 (2008) 10–23.
Schweitzer, Friedrich. "Adolescents as Theologians: A New Approach in Christian Education and Youth Ministry." *Religious Education* 109 (2014) 184–200.
Scott, Kieran. "Alternating Currents: Sacramental and Prophetic Imagining and Church Education." *Religious Education* 111 (2016) 447–61.
———. "Inviting Young Adults to Come Out Religiously, Institutionally, and Traditionally." *Religious Education* 109 (2014) 471–84.

Senter, Mark H., III, et al. *Four Views of Youth Ministry and the Church*. Grand Rapids: Youth Specialities, 2001.
Shelton, Charles M. *Adolescent Spirituality: Pastoral Ministry for High School and College Youth*. Chicago: Loyola University Press, 1983.
Shepherd, Nicholas M. "Soul in the City—Mission as Package Holiday: The Potential Implications of a 'Tourist' Paradigm in Youth Mission." *Journal of Youth and Theology* 5 (2006) 63–83.
Shepherd, Nick. "Being a Christian Youth Worker: Finding Ourselves by Losing Ourselves." In *Christian Youth Work in Theory and Practice: A Handbook*, edited by Sally Nash and Jo Whitehead, 1–12. London: SCM, 2014.
———. *Faith Generation: Retaining Young People and Growing the Church*. London: SPCK, 2016.
Sidnell, Jack. *Conversation Analysis: An Introduction*. Malden, MA: Blackwell, 2010.
Smith, Christian. *Soul Searching: The Religious and Spiritual Lives of American Teenagers*. Oxford: Oxford University Press, 2005.
Snell, Patricia. "Denominational Differences in Congregation Youth Ministry Programs and Evidence of Systemic Non-Response Biases." *Review of Religious Research* 51 (2009) 21–38.
———. "What Difference Does Youth Group Make? A Longitudinal Analysis of Religious Youth Group Participation Outcomes." *Journal for the Scientific Study of Religion* 48 (2009) 572–87.
Sonnenberg, Ronelle. "God in Youth Worship." *Jaarboek voor Liturgie-onderzoek* 30 (2014) 223–41.
———. "Youth Worship in Protestant Contexts: A Practical Theological Theory of Participation of Adolescents." PhD diss., Protestantse Theologische Universiteit, 2015.
Sonnenberg, Ronelle, and Marcel Barnard. "Educating Young People through Christian Youth Worship: Reclaiming Space for Learning in Liturgical Contexts." *HTS Teologiese Studies / Theological Studies* 68 (2012) 1–8.
———. "Youth Worship as Recreation." *International Journal of Practical Theology* 19 (2015) 138–63.
Sonnenberg, Ronelle, et al. "Being Together in Youth Worship: An Empirical Study in Protestant Dutch Contexts." *HTS Teologiese Studies / Theological Studies* 71 (2015) 1–10.
———. "Shaping Youth Worship: Modes of Active Participation." *Questions Liturgiques/ Studies in Liturgy* 95 (2014) 216–36.
Sonnenberg, Ronelle, et al. "Reconstructing Faith Narratives: Doing Research on the Faith of Adolescents." *Journal of Youth and Theology* 15 (2016) 23–43.
Sorenson, Jacob. "Transforming the Spiritual Storehouse." *Journal of Youth and Theology* 14 (2015) 172–90.
Stanton, Graham D. *Wide-Awake in God's Word: Bible Engagement for Teenage Spiritual Formation in a Culture of Expressive Individualism*. Eugene, OR: Wipf & Stock, 2020.
Štěch, František. "Fluid Religion in Liquid Age? De/Traditionalization and Its Implications for Youth Ministry in the Czech Republic." *Journal of Youth and Theology* 9 (2010) 61–77.
———. "Who Are Youth in Theological Perspective?" *Journal of Youth and Theology* 15 (2016) 124–45.

Stirrup, Andy. "Growing Faith with the Help of Extended Family and Friends." *Journal of Youth and Theology* 13 (2014) 63–75.

———. "Is Jesus My Superhero?" *Journal of Youth and Theology* 7 (2008) 64–76.

Stortz, Martha Ellen. "Practicing Christians: Prayer as Formation." In *The Promise of Lutheran Ethics*, edited by Karen L. Bloomquist and John R. Stumme, 55–73. Minneapolis: Fortress, 1998.

Streib, Heinz. "Extending Our Vision of Developmental Growth and Engaging in Empirical Scrutiny: Proposals for the Future of Faith Development Theory." *Religious Education* 99 (2004) 427–34.

Strommen, Merton P., and Dick Hardel. *Passing on the Faith: A Radical New Model for Youth and Family Ministry*. Winona, MN: St. Mary's, 2000.

Swartz, Sharlene. "The State of Youth Research in South Africa." *Journal of Youth and Theology* 3 (2004) 75–92.

Swinton, John, and Harriet Mowatt. *Practical Theology and Qualitative Research*. 2nd ed. London: SCM, 2016.

Tanner, Kathryn. "Theological Reflection and Christian Practices." In *Practicing Theology: Beliefs and Practices in Christian Life*, edited by Miroslav Volf and Doroth C. Bass, 228–42. Grand Rapids: Eerdmans, 2001.

Taylor, Charles. *The Ethics of Authenticity*. Cambridge: Harvard University Press, 1991.

———. *A Secular Age*. Cambridge: Belknap, 2007.

Ter Avest, Ina, et al. "Gendered Subjective Theologies: Dutch Teenage Girls and Boys on the Role of Religion in Their Life." *Religious Education* 105 (2010) 374–94.

The-Mertens, Stephie. "Organisational Strategies to Bridge the Theological Language Gap." *Journal of Youth and Theology* 16 (2017) 3–24.

Thesnaar, Christo. "Facilitating Healing and Reconciliation with Young People Living in the Aftermath of Political and Cultural Conflict. The Challenge to the Church and Its Youth Ministry." *Journal of Youth and Theology* 2 (2003) 8–28.

Thomas á Kempis. *The Imitation of Christ*. Peabody, MA: Hendrickson, 2004.

Thompson, Naomi, and James Ballantyne. "'Being Church': The Social and Spiritual Purposes and Impacts of Christian Detached Youth Work." *Journal of Youth and Theology* 16 (2017) 89–116.

Thurman, Howard. *Disciplines of the Spirit*. Richmond, IN: Friends United, 2003.

———. *The Search for Common Ground: An Inquiry into the Basis of Man's Experience of Community*. Richmond, IN: Friends United, 1986.

Trigg, Jonathan D. *Baptism in the Theology of Martin Luther*. Studies in the History of Christian Thought 56. Leiden: Brill, 1994.

Tveitereid, Knut, and Bård Eirik Hallesby Norheim. "Theological Wiggle Room as a Resource in Ordinary Theology Significance for Ecclesiology, Leadership, and Personal Development." *International Journal of Practical Theology* 25 (2021) 206–23.

Tzuriel, David. "The Development of Ego Identity at Adolescence among Israeli Jews and Arabs." *Journal of Youth and Adolescence* 21 (1992) 551–71.

Vallabaraj, Jerome. "Youth Ministry Called 'To Behold' the Young." *Journal of Youth and Theology* 3 (2004) 8–27.

———. "Youth Ministry: Beyond 'Inside-Out' and 'Outside-In.'" *Journal of Youth and Theology* 2 (2003) 39–56.

Van Dijk-Groeneboer, Monique C. H. "Youth Ministry: About Youth?" *Journal of Youth and Theology* 14 (2015) 25–44.

Van Leersum-Bekebrede, Lydia. "Worship with Children: Agentive Participation in Dutch Protestant Contexts." PhD diss., Protestant Theological University, 2021.
Van Leersum-Bekebrede, Lydia, et al. "Deconstructing Ideals of Worship with Children." *Studia Liturgica* 49 (2019) 71–88.
———. "Setting the Stage for Children's Participation in Worship Practices." *International Journal of Children's Spirituality* 24 (2019) 166–82.
Van Wijnen, Harmen. "Faith in Small Groups of Adolescents: Being Together as a Basic Given." PhD diss., Protestant Theological University, 2016.
Van Wijnen, Harmen, and Marcel Barnard. "Faith Tribes as Powerful Communities of Adolescents in Highly Differentiated Societies." *Religious Education* 112 (2017) 418–30.
———. "From Organized Faith to Lived Faith: The Need for De-Laboratoryzing and De-Conceptualizing Youth Ministry." *Journal of Youth and Theology* 13 (2014) 6–23.
Van Wyngaard, Cobus. "Post-Apartheid Whiteness and the Challenge of Youth Ministry in the Dutch Reformed Church." *Journal of Youth and Theology* 10 (2011) 23–34.
Vestøl, Jon Magne. "Textbook Religion and Lived Religion: A Comparison of the Christian Faith as Expressed in Textbooks and by Young Church Members." *Religious Education* 111 (2016) 95–110.
Visser-Vogel, Elsbeth, et al. "Developing a Framework for Research on Religious Identity Development of Highly Committed Adolescents." *Religious Education* 107 (2012) 108–21.
Visser-Vogel, Elsbeth, et al. "Sources for Religious Identity Development of Orthoprax Muslim Adolescents in the Netherlands." *Journal of Muslims in Europe* 4 (2015) 90–112.
Volf, Miroslav. *Exclusion and Embrace: A Theological Exploration of Identity, Otherness, and Reconciliation*. Nashville: Abingdon, 1996.
Volf, Miroslav, and Ryan McAnnaly-Linz. *Public Faith in Action: How to Think Carefully, Engage Wisely, and Vote with Integrity*. Grand Rapids: Brazos, 2016.
Ward, Pete. "Christian Relational Care." In *Relational Youthwork*, edited by Pete Ward, 13–40. Oxford: Lynx Communications, 1995.
———. *God at the Mall: Youth Ministry that Meets Kids Where They're At*. Peabody, MA: Hendrickson, 1999.
———. *Growing Up Evangelical: Youthwork and the Making of a Subculture*. London: SPCK, 1996.
———. *Liquid Church*. Peabody, MA: Hendrickson, 2002.
———. *Participation and Mediation: A Practical Theology for the Liquid Church*. London: SCM, 2008.
———. *Youthwork and the Mission of God: Frameworks for Relational Outreach*. London: SPCK, 1997.
Ward, Pete, and Knut Tveitereid, eds. *The Wiley Blackwell Companion to Theology and Qualitative Research*. Hoboken, NJ: Wiley-Blackwell, 2022.
Ward, Peter, and Heidi Campbell. "Ordinary Theology as Narratives: An Empirical Study of Young People's Charismatic Worship in Scotland." *International Journal of Practical Theology* 15 (2011) 226–42.
Webber, Ruth, et al. "Models of Youth Ministry in Action: The Dynamics of Christian Youth Ministry in an Australian City." *Religious Education* 105 (2010) 204–15.

Webb-Mitchell, Brett. "Leaving Development Behind and Beginning Pilgrimage." *Religious Education* 96 (2001) 136–51.

Wenh-In Ng, Greer Anne. "Beyond Bible Stories: The Role of Culture-Specific Myths/Stories in the Identity Formation of Nondominant Immigrant Children." *Religious Education* 99 (2004) 125–36.

White, David F. "Adolescence: Social Construct or Eternal Verity?" *Journal of Youth and Theology* 15 (2016) 115–23.

———. "The Fire and Light at the Heart of Youth Ministry." *Journal of Youth and Theology* 16 (2017) 46–59.

———. *Practicing Discernment with Youth*. Cleveland: Pilgrim, 2005.

———. "Profiles in Vocation: A Study in the Conceptual Resources of Youth." *Journal of Youth and Theology* 4 (2005) 10–31.

———. "The Youth Theological Initiative: An Experiment in the Pedagogy of Communion." *Journal of Youth and Theology* 3 (2004) 77–96.

Wilson, Leah Marie. "Waste of Space or Room for Place? A Critical Reflection on the Theology of Place Exhibited in Two Youth Ministry Placements." *Journal of Youth and Theology* 18 (2019) 19–48.

Wimberly, Anne Streaty, et al. *Youth Ministry in the Black Church: Centered in Hope*. Valley Forge, PA: Judson, 2013.

Wright, Andrew. *Christianity and Critical Realism: Ambiguity, Truth, and Theological Literacy*. London: Routledge, 2013.

Yaconelli, Mark. *Contemplative Youth Ministry: Practicing the Presence of Jesus*. Grand Rapids: Zondervan, 2006.

———. "Focusing Youth Ministry through Christian Practices." In *Starting Right: Thinking Theologically about Youth Ministry*, edited by Kenda Creasy Dean et al., 184–98. Grand Rapids: Zondervan, 2001.

———. *Growing Souls: Experiments in Contemplative Youth Ministry*. London: SPCK, 2007.

Yaconelli, Mike. *The CORE Realities of Youth Ministry: Nine Biblical Principles That Mark Healthy Youth Ministries*. Grand Rapids: Youth Specialties, 2003.

Yukl, Gary. *Leadership in Organizations*. New York: Pearson, 2010.

Zsupan-Jerome, Daniella. "Fostering the Public Voice: Blogging as a Pedagogical Practice in Ministerial Education." *Religious Education* 109 (2014) 331–45.

Index

Absence (of God), 85, 86
Accompaniment, 98, 149, 150, 204
Action research, 227, 230, 232, 236, 238, 240–41
Adaptive change, 169
Adolescence, 17, 35, 37, 38, 42, 45, 51, 61, 145, 147, 181, 193, 209
Adolescent hermeneutic, 54, 55
Agora – market square, 163, 164, 165–66, 167, 213
Anthropology, 39, 128, 229
Apocalyptic, 152
Aporia, 115
Apprenticeship model of learning, 189
Appropriation, 73, 74, 137
Asymmetry, 168
Attachment theory, 83, 84
Attentiveness, 198, 204
Authenticity, 88, 169, 179, 183, 184–85, 189
Authority, 53, 73, 74, 130, 169, 170, 183, 184–85, 188, 196, 208
Autonomy, 35, 183, 184–85

Baptism, baptismal theology, 148, 161, 173, 180, 195
Behavioral model of learning, 139, 141, 187, 188
Biblicism, 105
Blog, blogging 213
Body, 23, 24, 40, 53, 100, 101, 102, 130, 211
Bricolage, 73, 74

Camp (experience/ministry), 128, 192, 208, 209, 218, 220
Case study, 58, 94, 148, 155, 156, 196, 210, 236, 257
Cataphatic theology, 80, 107, 115
Catechesis, 84, 131, 133, 139–42, 147, 149, 150, 155, 156, 185, 191, 192, 193, 216
Charismatic, 72, 189, 203, 220
Childcare, 194
Christian Education, 6, 7, 126, 155
Christian practice, 91, 92, 93, 114, 116
Christology, 87, 93, 106, 118, 146
Christopraxis, 86, 115, 178
Cognitive goals, 131, 132
Communication, 166, 167, 184, 189, 230, 244
Communitas, 209, 210
Confessionality, 9, 10, 248
Confirmands, 70, 71, 209
Confirmation, 70, 71, 151, 153, 209
Constructivist epistemology, 227, 233, 234, 236, 243, 244
Consumer culture, 4, 190
Consumerism, 23, 25, 26, 28, 118, 147
Contemplative (practices), 92, 146, 149, 151, 204, 217
Contextual, Contextualization, xii, 24, 52, 104, 109, 163, 166, 191, 195, 202, 212, 231, 240
Conversation analysis, 202
Counter-culture, 22
Creation theology, 83, 107
Creativity, 37, 40, 163
Critical realism, 86, 115, 117, 245

Critical theory, 235

Deconversion, 171
Detached youth work, 129, 179
Deus Semper Major, 116
Developmental model of learning, 140, 141, 187, 188
Developmental psychology, 53, 59, 130
Diaconal, 85, 114, 176, 197, 222
Dialectic, 80, 86, 103, 107, 115, 116, 117
Dialogue, 36, 66, 100, 136, 151, 152, 162, 171, 183, 186, 190–92, 203, 206, 218
Digitalization, 28, 29
Disaffiliation, 171
Discernment, 79, 81, 97–101, 115, 144, 156, 168, 197, 204
Docetism, 88
Doctrine, doctrinal 73, 107, 110, 197, 204, 216, 235

Ecclesia crucis, 192
Ecclesial agoraphobia, 165
Ecclesiology, 117, 148, 210, 221–23, 223
Educational philosophy, 186
Educational, 24, 32, 123, 125, 130, 131, 132, 133, 139, 143, 150, 153, 161, 184, 185, 186, 195, 196, 216, 219, 240
Ego identity, 47, 50, 51
Embodiment, 101, 184
Empirical turn, 107
Encounter, 8, 44, 84–86, 87, 88, 89–90, 90, 91, 93, 97, 98, 107, 108, 111, 115, 129, 135, 136, 149–51, 15, 161, 179, 184, 188, 193, 202, 247, 251
Epistemology, 117, 227, 230, 232, 233, 234, 236, 243, 244–45, 257
Eschatology, 79, 81, 102, 212
Ethnography, ethnographic research, 117, 179, 227, 230, 233, 234, 236, 237, 238–40, 241, 250, 257, 258
Ethos, 118, 202

Evangelization, evangelism, 2, 4, 136, 176, 213
Expert (youth minister as), 167, 187, 188, 189
Expressive individualism, 191

Faith development, 46–59, 60–78
Faith formation, 34, 55–57, 58, 60, 67, 69, 83, 88, 91, 126, 127, 128, 131, 139, 156, 186, 187, 191, 194
Faith narratives, 235, 237, 238
Faith practices, 5, 10, 18, 20, 61, 75, 110, 152, 244, 247, 260
Fear, 85, 101–4, 164
Focus groups, 238–240
Freedom, 22, 23, 31, 40, 97, 100, 132, 147, 244
Friend (youth minister as), 137, 168, 176, 179, 200
Friendship, 64, 110, 137, 168, 176, 179, 194, 200, 223

Ghetto, 210
Globalization, 8, 28, 29
Glocal, 104
Godly Play, 58, 193, 194
Growth in faith, 46, 58
Guide (youth minister as), 167, 180, 194, 199, 201, 203–4, 210

Healing, 88, 134, 135, 144
Heresy, 88
Hermeneutical struggle, 79, 80, 108, 115, 116–18, 244, 247
Hermeneutics, 54, 112, 115, 116, 117, 171, 212
Holistic (youth) ministry, 125, 156, 162, 176, 194, 207, 214–15
Holy listening, 201, 202
Hope, 28, 40, 100, 101, 101–104, 125, 138, 167, 168, 189, 208, 211, 214
Hybrid identity, 49

Identity development, 12, 17, 26, 29, 33, 47, 48, 49–53, 59, 130, 141, 148, 239, 240
Identity formation, 18, 20, 26, 27–29, 33, 38, 50, 135, 136, 140

Index

Identity theory, 37, 47
Imitation, 161, 162, 171, 173, 174, 174–176, 177, 180–81, 182, 183
Immanence, 84
Incarnational ministry, 71, 154
Individualism, 17, 20, 23, 31, 53, 147, 152, 191
Individualization, 26, 31, 32, 187
Institutional church, 32, 43, 97, 189, 200
Interdisciplinary research, 6, 7, 9, 231
Interviewing, 239, 250, 258
Intimacy, 30, 43, 73, 89, 179, 181

Joy, 44, 87, 138, 175, 222

Kairos, 40, 176, 203
Kindertheologie, 41
Koinonia, 31, 95, 162, 216, 217–218

Leadership theory, 163, 168
Learning community, 190, 195
Learning environment, 126, 139, 140, 141, 142, 188, 241
Learning goals, 123, 126, 130–133, 139–42, 188
Learning products, 132
Liberation theology, 103, 168, 231
Lifecycle, 42
Liminal, liminality, 162, 170, 207, 208–10, 211, 218
Listening, 10, 100, 102, 103, 162, 184, 198, 201, 202, 212, 247, 250, 253, 258
Literature review, 1, 52, 140, 255
Liturgy, 73, 91, 132, 138
Lived faith, 49, 57, 127, 237

Martyr, martyrdom, 103, 190
Mediatization, 27, 28, 136
Mentoring, mentorship, 174, 175, 181, 182
Metatheory, metatheoretical foundation, 108, 109, 209
Mimesis, 177
Mission, 118, 135, 155, 156, 174, 177, 181, 200, 208, 210, 221, 222

Missional, missionary, 10, 63, 101, 165, 188, 211, 221
Missionary (youth minister as), 5, 198, 208
Mixed methods, 64, 235
Modernism, modernity, 33, 97
Music, 20, 21, 23, 24, 29, 30–31, 65, 94
Mystagogue (youth minister as), 198, 204–5

Narrative (research) design, 129, 257
Narrative approach, 52, 69
Negotiation, 73, 74, 117, 203
Neo-evangelicalism, 32
New Testament, 41, 53, 95, 130, 234
Normativity, 10, 11, 108, 130, 228, 243, 246, 248–50, 254, 256, 257, 261
Notae ecclesiae, 114

Old Testament, 38, 39
Ordination, 205
Ordo, 195
Orthopraxy, 51
Orthoyatra, 145, 203
Outreach, 192

Parachurch movements/organizations, 2, 3, 4
Paradigm shift, 199, 201
Participation, 70–71, 73, 74, 75, 91, 97, 111, 112, 132, 140, 153, 156, 165, 189, 217, 219, 220, 229, 239, 245
Participatory research, 235
Pastor (youth minister as), 5, 162, 171, 179, 185, 198–206, 222
Pastoral care, 24, 133, 201, 202
Pathos, 100, 169
Peace, 134, 137, 191
Pedagogy, 13, 98, 100, 149, 150, 181, 186, 193, 197, 204, 208, 241
Peregrinational, 180, 203, 210
Perestrojka, 201
Performance, 97, 119, 205, 249
Pilgrim (youth minister as), 167, 180
Pilgrim ecclesiology, 168, 210

Pilgrimage, 53, 95, 97, 98, 99, 130
Poet (youth minister as), 206, 211–12, 222, 223
Positivist epistemology, 233, 234, 235
Postcolonial critique, 135
Postmodern, postmodernism, postmodernity, 17, 20, 23, 24–26, 29, 33, 34, 43, 111, 118, 133, 146, 147, 152, 153, 208
Practicing baptism, 148, 180
Presence of God, 12, 79, 81, 82–83, 83, 84, 85, 86, 87, 89, 90, 91, 92, 93, 94, 95, 96, 98, 99, 100, 106, 107–9, 109–10, 110–16, 116–18, 118, 137, 199, 204
Privatization (of faith/belief), 29, 43
Prophet (youth minister as), 162, 171, 207–15
Prophet(s) (young people as), 38
Public space, 164
Purpose (of youth ministry / youth ministers), 2, 4, 13, 37, 55, 71, 92, 95, 102, 121–57, 168, 179, 191, 195, 199, 200, 201, 204, 210, 217, 223

Qualitative research, 25, 31, 68, 69, 72, 74, 107, 108, 109, 234, 235, 236, 237, 250, 251, 257, 258
Quantitative research, 65, 234, 235, 236, 257

Racism, 50, 128
Reconciliation, 133, 134–35
Recreation, 74, 91, 151
Reformation, 112, 139
Regnocentric youth ministry, 155
Relational youth ministry, 71, 83, 86, 154, 162, 173, 175, 176, 178–80, 202, 208
Relationality, 71, 154
Reliability, 91, 257
Religious education, 1, 32, 36, 53, 54, 58, 63, 130, 131, 136, 150, 189, 191, 219, 232, 233, 249
Research design, 9, 106, 107–9, 112, 116, 232, 236, 238, 239, 241, 243, 247, 248, 249, 250, 251, 253, 257–58, 258–59, 260
Research instruments, 229, 257
Research methodology, 10, 13, 63, 106, 227, 229–41
Research paradigm, 227, 229, 230, 232, 233, 234–36, 237, 238–41, 243, 257
Research question, 233, 239, 240, 252, 255–56, 256, 257, 259, 260, 261
Resonance, 185
Resurrection, 86, 100, 101, 102, 103, 113, 152, 211
Retraditionalization, 44, 45
Retreat, 196, 208, 209, 220
Revelation, 13, 98, 108, 117, 150, 171, 244, 247, 260
Revival, 73
Ritual, 5, 23, 46, 73, 91, 101, 138, 149, 150, 156, 191, 194, 205, 211, 239
Role model, 39, 174, 176, 177

Sacrament, 84, 93, 113, 114, 137, 149, 150, 155, 205
Sacramental, Sacramentality, 84, 93, 111, 112, 147, 149, 150, 197, 204, 205, 212, 217
Salvation, 7, 8, 41, 73, 114, 118, 124, 145, 151–53, 157
Sanctification, 92, 203
Secular, secular age, 23, 30, 52, 88, 91, 161, 163, 164, 165, 180, 184, 185, 191, 209
Secularization, 3, 136, 170
Self-construction, 49, 234, 239
Self-integration, 234, 239
Self-reflexivity, 170
Servant-leadership, 137, 174, 200, 201
Sex, sexuality, 24, 133, 134
Shepherd (youth minister as), 199, 203
Situated learning, 197
Social justice, 30, 43, 137, 200
Social media, 28, 43, 70, 71, 213
Social theory, 185
Social worker (youth minister as), 5, 198

Socialization, 21, 32, 60, 61, 70, 84, 104, 134, 149, 162, 183, 184, 185, 187–90, 197, 220
Sociology, 7, 13
Solidarity, 92, 136, 176
Spiritual direction, 147, 181, 192
Spiritual director (youth minister as), 162, 183, 192–94, 209
Spiritual formation, 30, 47, 49, 57–58, 59, 155, 175, 181, 220
Spiritual type theory, 55, 126, 193
Sponsor, 199
Stage theory (faith development), 54
Subculture, 21, 33, 68, 190
Suffering, 56, 85, 87, 89, 137, 175, 178, 191
Sunday School movement, 2
Symbol, 31, 104, 126, 165, 174, 202
Symmetry, 168
Systematic theology, 9, 232

Teacher (youth minister as), 161, 162, 171, 180, 182, 183–97
Telos, 85, 100, 114, 179
Tentatio, 117
Testimony, 93, 103, 199, 202
Textbooks, 63
Theologia crucis, 117, 178
Theological shorthand, 30, 174
Theological turn, 79, 85, 212
Theology of the child, 41, 234, 235
Theology of the cross, 9, 86, 87
Theology of youth ministry, 42, 81, 82, 92, 231
Theology of youth, 39, 40, 41
Theotokos, 177

Traditional, 5, 24, 26, 32, 64, 94, 97, 104, 133, 151, 152, 153, 164, 165, 188, 189, 194, 204, 233
Transcendence, 30, 167, 208, 209
Transformation, 87, 89, 98, 103, 137, 222, 251
Transformational leadership, 201
Transmission (of faith) 36, 151, 153
Tribalism, 189

Utopia, 101–4

Validity, 257
Virtual reality, 27, 28
Virtual, 27, 28, 49, 89–90, 213
Virtue(s), 38, 99, 165, 177
Volunteer(s), 1, 5, 129, 183, 201

Welcome, 26, 46, 89, 96–97, 162, 170, 198, 205–6
Whole-making, 50, 127–28, 128
Wide-awakeness, 89, 103, 190, 191
Wiggle room, theological wiggle room, 79, 107, 118–19
Witness, 156, 167, 198, 201

Youth group, 18, 61, 69, 70–71, 91, 194, 215, 216, 220, 222
Youth ministry practices, 1, 5, 6, 11, 12, 13, 17, 25, 34, 42, 46, 49, 58, 59, 71, 123, 126, 132, 136, 142, 143, 145, 150, 154, 227, 231, 242, 243, 244, 252, 253, 254, 255, 256, 261
Youth worship, 18, 31, 61, 72–75, 75, 91, 94, 95, 111, 132, 150, 196, 229

www.ingramcontent.com/pod-product-compliance
Lightning Source LLC
Chambersburg PA
CBHW071239230426
43668CB00011B/1499